Poverty and Deprivation in Europe

Poverty and Deprivation in Europe

Brian Nolan and Christopher T. Whelan

OXFORD

UNIVERSITY PRESS

OXFORD

UNIVERSITY PRESS

Great Clarendon Street, Oxford OX2 6DP

Oxford University Press is a department of the University of Oxford.
It furthers the University's objective of excellence in research, scholarship,
and education by publishing worldwide in

Oxford New York

Auckland Cape Town Dar es Salaam Hong Kong Karachi
Kuala Lumpur Madrid Melbourne Mexico City Nairobi
New Delhi Shanghai Taipei Toronto

With offices in

Argentina Austria Brazil Chile Czech Republic France Greece
Guatemala Hungary Italy Japan Poland Portugal Singapore
South Korea Switzerland Thailand Turkey Ukraine Vietnam

Oxford is a registered trade mark of Oxford University Press
in the UK and in certain other countries

Published in the United States
by Oxford University Press Inc., New York

© Brian Nolan and Christopher T. Whelan 2011

British Library Cataloguing in Publication Data

Data available

Library of Congress Cataloging in Publication Data

Data available

Typeset by SPI Publisher Services, Pondicherry, India
Printed in Great Britain
on acid-free paper by
MPG Books Group, Bodmin and King's Lynn

ISBN 978-0-19-958843-5

1 3 5 7 9 10 8 6 4 2

Acknowledgements

We would like to express our gratitude to the many colleagues who have contributed to the development of the research on which this book is based. Close collaboration with Bertrand Maître over a decade has been invaluable, and we are enormously in his debt. We have also benefited greatly from collaboration with Tim Callan, Denis Conniffe, Tony Fahey, Richard Layte, Helen Russell, and James Williams. We are highly appreciative of the unstinting support from our colleagues in the Schools of Applied Social Sciences and Sociology in University College Dublin. Discussion and debate with colleagues in various international research networks and projects have been both illuminating and enjoyable, in particular the EQUALSOC network and GINI project funded by the EU's Framework Programmes and so ably coordinated by Robert Eriksson and Wiemer Salverda, respectively. Tony Atkinson and John Goldthorpe have continued to be both an inspiration and a source of advice and encouragement, as they have for more years than they (or we) care to remember. We are entirely reliant on comparative data coordinated by Eurostat and greatly appreciate the efforts of staff there. Funding from the European Union's Framework Programmes and the Irish Research Council for the Humanities and Social Sciences has helped to support our research and is gratefully acknowledged. Aimee Wright and Sarah Caro of Oxford University Press have been extremely helpful throughout. Finally, our families—spouses Mary and Yvonne and the next generation of Eimear, Claire, and Daniel (Nolan), and Karl and Alan (Whelan)—are to be thanked for their forbearance and continued support.

We would like to thank the copyright holders for allowing us to use work that has appeared in the following journals: Nolan, B. and Whelan, C T. (2010). 'Using Non-Monetary Deprivation Indicators to Analyse Poverty and Social Exclusion in Rich Counties: Lessons from Europe?' *Journal of Policy Analysis and Management*, 29: 305–23; Whelan, C. T. and Maître, B. (2010). 'Welfare Regime and Social Class Variation in Poverty and Economic Vulnerability', *Journal of European Social Policy*, 20 (4, 3): 316–32; Whelan, C. T. and Maître, B. (2010). 'Comparing Poverty Indicators in an Enlarged European Union', *European Sociological Review*, 26: 713–30; Whelan, C. T. and Maître, B. (2009). 'Europeanization of Inequality and European Reference Groups',

Journal of European Social Policy, 19: 117–30; Whelan, C. T. and Maître, B. (2008). 'Social Class and Risk': A Comparative Analysis of the Dynamics of Economic Vulnerability', *The British Journal of Sociology*, 60 (4): 637–59; Whelan, C. T. and Maître, B. (2006). 'Comparing Poverty and Deprivation Dynamics: Issues of Reliability and Validity', *Journal of Economic Inequality*, 4(3): 303–23; and Whelan, C. T., Layte, R., and Maître, B. (2004). 'Understanding the Mismatch Between Income Poverty and Deprivation: A Dynamic Comparative Analysis', *European Sociological Review*, 20 (4): 287–301.

Contents

List of Figures

List of Tables

1
Why Measure Material Deprivation?

1.1 Introduction

Research on poverty in rich countries relies primarily on household income to capture living standards and distinguish those in poverty, and this is also true of official poverty measurement and monitoring for policy-making purposes in those countries. However, awareness has been increasing of the limitations of income and the role that non-monetary measures of deprivation can play in improving our measurement and understanding of poverty, and by doing so contribute to the design of more effective anti-poverty strategies and policies. This is true when one focuses on an individual country, but even more so when the perspective is comparative, notably in learning from comparisons across the countries of the European Union, as the Union and its member states now seek to do. Our aim in this volume is to explore why and how non-monetary indicators of deprivation can play a significant role in complementing (not replacing) income in order to capture the reality of poverty in Europe.

By doing so, we also seek to contribute to the development of multidimensional approaches to measuring and understanding poverty, an important strand in current research and policy debates. The interest in a multidimensional perspective reflects unease with reliance on income to identify the poor, but even more so the desire to capture more fully the variety of circumstances and disadvantages that go to make up poverty and exclusion. While this perspective is rich in potential, the variety of different conceptual starting-points and empirical approaches that come under the broad heading of 'multidimensional' means that it can also be a source of some confusion. Here we show concretely how non-monetary indicators can be used to capture the multidimensionality of poverty across the enlarged European Union in a consistent and harmonized fashion, and in doing so help to bring out the meaning and value of such an approach.

In this opening chapter we set out the rationale and the point of departure of the book, the issues it addresses, and the structure it employs in doing so.

We begin with an introductory discussion of why it is important to go beyond income in capturing poverty and exclusion, developed in more depth later. We then sketch out key features of the European context in which the core questions at issue arise. The aims and distinctive features of the book are then set out, and its structure outlined with a road-map for readers of the voyage on which they are embarking and the intended destination.

1.2 Going Beyond Income in Capturing Poverty

Most research on poverty in Europe takes as point of departure the definition that people are in poverty when 'their resources are so seriously below those commanded by the average individual or family that they are, in effect, excluded from ordinary living patterns, customs and activities'—the influential formulation by the sociologist Peter Townsend (1979: 31). This is echoed in the definition put forward by an influential expert panel in the USA as insufficient resources for basic living needs, defined appropriately for the United States today (Citro and Michael, 1995). Poverty from this starting-point has 2 core elements: it is about inability to participate, and this inability to participate is attributable to inadequate resources. Most quantitative research then employs income to distinguish the poor, with a great deal of research and debate on how best to establish an income cut-off—examples from a very large literature being Atkinson et al. (1995) and the OECD's (2008) comparative study *Growing Unequal*.

In parallel, though, non-monetary indicators of living standards and deprivation have also been developed and investigated for many years. This was first of all from the perspective that low income could be used to identify the poor, but did not tell us all we needed to know about what it was like to be poor, and how people arrived in and coped with that situation. This is exemplified by Townsend's (1979) pioneering work on the use of non-monetary indicators of deprivation in the context of poverty measurement. He used these indicators both to derive and validate an income poverty threshold and to bring out graphically what it meant to be poor in Britain at the time in terms of deprivation of everyday items and activities widely regarded as essential.

As these deprivation indicators started to become more widely available, they were used to underpin a more radical critique of reliance on income: that low income fails in practice to identify those who are unable to participate in their societies due to lack of resources. This argument was put forward most emphatically by Ringen (1987, 1988), who asserted that income was both an indirect and unreliable measure of the underlying concept of poverty. In a similar vein, Mack and Lansley (1985) used deprivation indicators directly to identify those experiencing exclusion in Britain, and subsequent British 'poverty and social exclusion' studies (Gordon et al., 2000; Pantazis et al., 2006) have employed a more extensive sets of indicators. Our own studies for Ireland (Callan et al., 1993; Nolan and Whelan, 1996) identified the 'consistently poor'—those both on low income and reporting deprivation in terms of specific 'basic' items—as meeting both elements of the underlying concept, inability to participate and inadequate financial resources. A similar approach has been applied in some other countries (for example, Förster, 2005), and the UK is also using a combination of low income and material deprivation among the range of indicators being used to monitoring progress in relation to child poverty (DWP, 2003; Child Poverty Act 2010[1]). Other studies have looked at those not only reporting both low income and deprivation but also saying they regard their own financial situation as very difficult—what Bradshaw and Finch (2003) term 'core poverty'. Non-monetary indicators of deprivation have by now been used in various ways in measuring poverty in many European countries and comparatively, as we will describe in Chapter 2.

Rather than (or as well as) the more accurate identification of the poor, a further argument for the use of non-monetary indicators is that they can help to capture the multidimensionality of poverty and social exclusion. It has long been said that poverty is 'not just about money', and the widespread adoption of the terminology of social exclusion/inclusion in Europe reflected *inter alia* the concern that focusing simply on income misses an important part of the picture. Social exclusion may involve not only poverty as low income/financial resources, but also educational disadvantage, poor health, and access to health services inadequate housing, and exclusion in the labour market. This can reflect the view that conceptually social exclusion is distinct from and broader than poverty, or that the underlying notion of poverty that evokes social concern is itself (and always has been) intrinsically multidimensional and about more than money (see for example Burchardt et al., 2002; Nolan and Whelan, 2007). In either case, a variety of non-monetary indicators come into play in seeking to capture such multidimensionality. While a wide range of approaches has been employed empirically, there has been increasing recognition of the desirability of directly measuring and monitoring—and on occasion even targeting—key dimensions of well being and disadvantage (Bradshaw and Finch, 2003; Boarini and D'Ercole, 2006).

So, in sum, the case for going beyond income to use non-monetary indicators is that they can bring out what it means to be poor, help to do a better job than income on its own in identifying the poor, and also directly capture the multifaceted nature of poverty and exclusion. While returning to these

[1] See http://www.parliament.uk/briefingpapers/commons/lib/research/briefings/snsp-05585.pdf

distinct but interlocking rationales later, we now turn to the EU context which will also loom large in our examination of the use of such indicators.

1.3 The EU Context

The definition of poverty formulated by Townsend and widely employed in Europe has also been adopted by politicians and policy-makers in a European Union context. The European Council, the political leaders of the member states of the (then) European Economic Community, adopted the following definition in the mid-1980s:

The poor shall be taken to mean persons, families and groups of persons whose resources (material, cultural and social) are so limited as to exclude them from the minimum acceptable way of life in the Member State in which they live. (European Economic Communities, 1985)

This definition now underpins the EU's Social Inclusion Process, whereby member states work together to tackle poverty and exclusion via what is called the open method of coordination, involving agreed common objectives, national plans to promote social inclusion, and joint reports by the Commission and Council. Like individual European countries, the European Union as a whole has been grappling with how best to learn from research and incorporate a multidimensional perspective into policy design and the monitoring of outcomes. Since 2000 the Social Inclusion Process has at its core a set of indicators designed to monitor progress and support mutual learning (which we will review in some detail in Chapter 3) that is explicitly and designedly multidimensional.

The need for such an approach has become even more salient with the enlargement of the EU from 2004 to cover countries with much lower average living standards, sharpening the challenge of adequately capturing and characterizing exclusion across the Union (Alber et al., 2007; Kogan et al., 2008). The difference from richest to poorest member states in terms of average income per head is now very much wider than before. Widely used income poverty thresholds in the more affluent member states are higher than the average income in the poorest member states, and those below them have higher standards of living than the well-off in the poorest countries. The strikingly different picture produced by these 'at risk of poverty' indicators compared with average GDP per head, and unease with the EU tendency to keep distinct concerns about the divergence in living standards across versus within countries, helps to motivate interest in moving beyond reliance on relative income in identifying those at risk of poverty and exclusion.

Despite widespread interest in a multidimensional perspective, only limited progress has been made in teasing out how best to apply it in practice in the EU. This state of affairs reflects limitations in the information available, but also in the conceptual and empirical underpinnings provided by existing research. Despite this, when the EU took the very important step of including a poverty reduction target among the 5 headline targets it set for 2020 in the high-level strategy adopted in 2010 in the face of the economic crisis, it framed the target population in terms not only of low income but also two other indicators, of material deprivation and household joblessness (as we describe and analyse in detail in our final chapter). So a multidimensional perspective and the role therein of direct measures of material deprivation, on which this book is focused, have come centre stage in the EU's efforts to tackle poverty and exclusion.

1.4 The Content and Structure of this Book

This book thus takes as starting-point that research on poverty and social exclusion has been undergoing a fundamental shift towards a multidimensional approach; that researchers and policy-makers alike have struggled to develop concepts and indicators that do this approach justice; and that this is highly salient not only within individual countries but also for the European Union post-Enlargement. While multidimensional approaches can be rooted in influential concepts such as capabilities or economic and social rights, the linkage from concept through to application has often been weak and implementation rather ad hoc. As Grusky and Weeden (2007) have emphasized, there is a pressing need to develop a methodological platform for analysing the shape and form of poverty and social exclusion.

The central aim of this book is to contribute to the development of the conceptual and empirical underpinnings required, building on what is now a quite substantial literature across a range of disciplines, by bringing out the key role that can be played by non-monetary indicators of deprivation. We combine an explicit focus on multidimensionality and how it is best captured empirically with a comparative approach, exploiting newly available data on all 27 current EU member states. Dynamic as well as cross-sectional perspectives on income, deprivation, and economic vulnerability are included, with a focus on methods that are technically sophisticated but also as transparent as possible in order to maximize their practical value in monitoring progress and designing policy. We highlight and illustrate the ways in which key conceptual and methodological choices made—explicitly or implicitly— shape one's core conclusions about how poverty varies across countries and over time, as well as who is affected and which groups should be targeted in framing anti-poverty strategies. In this context, the value and limitations of national versus EU-level benchmarks and points of reference is critical. In mapping out the current landscape and a way forward, we have sought to appeal to an audience that spans disciplinary perspectives and that, rather than being confined to those whose primary interest is methodological, includes those more focused on policy design and monitoring.

The book is structured in the following way. Chapter 2 describes in detail the background and context from which the volume is departing in terms of the evolution of research using non-monetary indicators of deprivation. In reviewing the research literature the chapter describes the types of indicators employed and their key characteristics, and brings out the various approaches that have been adopted in using them to capture poverty and social exclusion. The specific indicators available in the 2 core comparative datasets providing such information for EU countries, namely the European Community Household Panel (ECHP) and the more recent European Union Statistics on Income and Living Conditions (EU-SILC), are described in some detail. It also discuss the types of conceptual framework into which such analysis can be set, and identifies the key challenges in developing empirical methods that are both more firmly rooted conceptually and succeed in identifying the individuals and households of most interest from a policy-making perspective.

Chapter 3 deals with the development of social inclusion indicators in an EU context. It provides some background on the development of the EU's engagement with social policy, and the development of the Social Inclusion Process from around 2000. It then looks in more depth at the adoption of a set of common indicators to monitor progress, the so-called Laeken indicators, in 2001 and the development of this set of indicators since then. In particular, the development of the indicator of material deprivation incorporated into the agreed set in 2009 is described. Finally, the adoption of a poverty reduction target in 2010 as part of the EU's 2020 Strategy is discussed, focusing on the way the target population is identified and the role of material deprivation in doing so.

Chapter 4 focuses on the limitations of relative income poverty measures in an enlarged Europe and the potential of complementing them with indicators of deprivation. The chapter starts by describing the conventional approach to setting and employing income poverty lines framed in relative terms, with average or median income in the country in question as the point of reference. It presents the patterns of poverty this approach produces for the countries of the EU as seen in the ECHP and EU-SILC, and discusses their interpretation and robustness. It explores the option of continuing to rely on income but applying a threshold that is common (in purchasing power terms) across EU countries, with results on that basis also presented and discussed. It then looks at the alternative perspective provided by deprivation indicators and indices, and describes the overall patterns of deprivation across countries revealed by analysis of the ECHP and EU-SILC. The relationship between low income and deprivation is shown to be much weaker than is commonly assumed, and respondents' subjective assessments of their own circumstances are also shown to be strongly related to measured deprivation. This underpins the case for not only trying to improve the measurement of income and broader financial resources, but also for broadening the information set employed in measuring poverty and exclusion beyond income to include non-monetary indicators of deprivation. In ways illustrated in the rest of the book, these—in combination with rather than instead of income—can help to identify with more confidence the 'truly poor and excluded', provide ways of capturing the multidimensional nature of that poverty and exclusion, and address the limitations of conventional relative income-based measures in an enlarged EU with much greater variation in average living standards across countries.

In using non-monetary indicators a variety of analytical challenges must be faced, especially when one of the core objectives is to be able to draw meaningful conclusions across countries. Chapter 5 explores some core issues in this regard, once again using the deprivation items in the ECHP and EU-SILC. Taking into account previous studies on this topic, the chapter first investigates the most satisfactory dimensional structure for the analysis of material derivation—that is, a grouping of items into different sets that reflect distinct aspects of living standards and deprivation, such as the capacity to afford basic requirements, possession of consumer durables, housing conditions, and quality of neighbourhood environment. The chapter then examines the reliability of the dimensional structure and indices we propose and how they relate to those advanced in other EU-level studies on this topic. It then documents the variation across countries in terms of the deprivation dimensions identified, taking into account alternative ways of assigning importance or weight to different items. The relationship between different dimensions of deprivation, income, and social class is then investigated, and the case advanced that the particular form of deprivation that we label 'consumption deprivation' is the most suitable if one is seeking to capture generalized deprivation. The chapter finally investigates the extent to which different dimensions of deprivation are correlated with each other and how frequently they are to be found together in households experiencing multiple deprivation.

The scale, sources, and implications of the 'mismatch' between poverty measured using low income versus direct measures of deprivation is investigated in depth in a comparative context in Chapter 6. The chapter opens with a discussion of the various reasons why one might expect a priori that a household's current equivalized income would not in fact fully capture its command over financial resources in relation to its needs. It then quantifies the extent of overlap or mismatch between being below a relative income poverty threshold and above a corresponding consumption-related deprivation threshold, and how that varies across EU countries. To help tease out the nature and implications of the mismatch, persons are cross-classified by relative income poverty and deprivation and the chapter then compares the social class profiles of those who are income-poor but not deprived, deprived but not income-poor, both income-poor and deprived, and neither income-poor nor deprived. The levels of subjective economic stress being reported by these four different groups are also compared. Finally, it turns from a static cross-sectional perspective to an analysis of the persistence of income poverty and deprivation over time. Research using panel data has drawn attention to the fact that movements into and out of poverty are a great deal more frequent than had been supposed, so a much greater proportion of the population experience poverty at some point than is revealed by cross-sectional studies, motivating development of income-based indicators that take into account experience of poverty over time, including in the EU's set of social inclusion indicators. Here panel data from the ECHP, which was a fully longitudinal survey by design, are used to analyse the persistence of income poverty and deprivation over time, demonstrating that even when such information about income is available it can still usefully be complemented by direct measures of deprivation.

As well going beyond income to incorporate deprivation, another core question in measuring poverty in Europe relates to the frame of reference to be applied: in assessing whether someone is poor or at risk of poverty, is the relevant comparison with the living standards and resources of others within the same country, or with others in the EU irrespective of country? A major source of concern about the relative income poverty rates widely used as the basis for headline poverty figures in the EU is that they show higher poverty rates in some of the richer countries than in some new member states with much lower average incomes and living standards. Chapter 7 addresses this directly, taking as its point of departure how the relative income poverty measures constructed at national level compare with ones using a proportion of median income across the EU as a whole. It then constructs and analyses a number of 'consistent' poverty measures, combining information on relative income poverty and material deprivation framed vis-à-vis national or EU-wide benchmarks. The variation in patterns these different approaches show across countries categorized by welfare regime is investigated in some depth. This demonstrates how much understanding of the consequences of different welfare regimes arrangements can be enriched by such analysis at both national and European levels and by a comparison of unidimensional and multidimensional approaches.

Implicit in the notion of multidimensional measurement of social exclusion is that there is no one 'true' indicator of the underlying concept. To move beyond the accumulation of a mass of descriptive detail one needs to develop appropriate measurement models, and Chapter 8 sets out one promising approach to investigating the notion of 'vulnerability', conceptualized as insecurity and exposure to risk and shocks. To apply this empirically, the statistical techniques of latent class analysis are applied to indicators of household low income, life-style deprivation, and subjective economic stress, in order to identify underlying groups with distinctive multidimensional profiles. The extent of vulnerability and its patterning are examined at national, welfare regime, and European levels. We then examine how vulnerability, captured this way, is associated with wider patterns of multidimensional deprivation.

In Chapter 9 we extend our analysis of dynamics to this measure of economic vulnerability. Recent studies of poverty dynamics have shown the importance of taking measurement error into account and employing explicit models of poverty dynamics. This chapter applies such approaches to statistical modelling of the dynamics of economic vulnerability. The results show that an economically vulnerable class can be identified across nations and time, and that cross-national differences in persistence of vulnerability are wider than for income poverty and deprivation and less affected by measurement error. Economic vulnerability profiles vary across welfare regimes in a manner consistent with theoretical expectations. The implications are fundamental: the emergence of new forms of social risk and efforts by welfare states to shift responsibility to the individual do not mean that factors such as social class have become less important in determining key socio-economic outcomes.

The impact of objective circumstances depends to a great extent on the reference groups that people adopt, the standards and expectations against which they judge their situation. The reference groups which people look to when orienting themselves are central to the appropriateness (or otherwise) of an EU-wide perspective on the distribution of material deprivation. Chapter 10 starts by distinguishing between 2 versions of an EU frame of reference: the weak form assumes that a common standard relating to an acceptable level of participation in one's own society emerges as a consequence of knowledge of conditions in other societies, while the stronger one requires that people perceive themselves as part of a larger European stratification system, and the perception of being advantaged or disadvantaged within this system plays an important role in individuals' evaluations of their own life circumstances. Data from EU-SILC are then used to empirically assess whether these operate in practice, and the results lead us to reject both versions. Material deprivation, rather than having a uniform effect on self-reported levels of satisfaction, is seen to have an impact that is highly dependent on national context: if a process of convergence is under way it is one that as yet has had limited impact. In circumstances where the Europeanization of inequality is raising issues relating to both national and transnational forms of legitimacy, it is important to understand that there is no necessary relationship between such Europeanization and the Europeanization of reference groups.

Chapter 11, our final chapter, highlights some key implications of the approaches and analyses presented throughout the book for the understanding of poverty and social exclusion in Europe, and for the best ways to monitor progress in combating them. Previous chapters have employed non-monetary indicators to identify distinct dimensions of deprivation and explore how they relate to each other, to capture generalized deprivation and 'consistent' poverty, and to identify those vulnerable to poverty and exclusion; these approaches and the empirical results produced have important lessons for the monitoring of progress and assessment of strategies at national and EU level. This chapter brings out some of these lessons by focusing on the way the EU has chosen to identify the population 'at risk of poverty and social exclusion' in framing its headline target for poverty reduction for 2020. The chapter presents an in-depth analysis and critique of the way that target is formulated, and discusses alternative approaches to combining low income and material deprivation to identify those most in need from a poverty reduction perspective. This serves as to highlight what can be learned from the application to empirical data of such approaches to capturing deprivation, serving to advance the development of this perspective in research and policy development in the future.

2

Non-Monetary Indicators

2.1 Introduction

As noted in Chapter 1, there is by now quite a substantial literature using non-monetary indicators of life-style and deprivation for developed countries, with studies focused on a considerable number of individual countries and a more limited set having a comparative focus. This chapter charts the evolution of this research, describes the types of indicators employed and their key characteristics, including the indicators available in the core comparative datasets providing such information for EU countries, and brings out the various ways such indicators have been used to capture poverty and social exclusion. It then discusses the types of conceptual framework into which these studies can be set, and identifies the key challenges in developing empirical methods which are both more firmly rooted conceptually and more successful in identifying poor individuals and households.

2.2 The Evolution of Poverty Research Using Non-monetary Deprivation Indicators

In everyday use, poverty in rich countries is generally seen in terms of inability to attain a decent or adequate standard of living. In the context of such countries, adequacy is not confined to subsistence: what is considered adequate changes over time as living standards rise; poverty is in that sense relative. The notion that perceptions of what constitutes poverty are framed in relation to the standards familiar to people in a particular time and place was captured over 200 years ago by Adam Smith when he wrote that 'necessaries' included 'what ever the custom of the country renders it indecent for creditable people, even the lowest orders, to be without'. While the reference to 'lowest orders' may jar with current sensibilities, the point being made has as much force now as it had then.

From a European perspective, the most influential formulation of such a definition of poverty has been the one by Peter Townsend already referred to in Chapter 1:

Individuals, families and groups in the population can be said to be in poverty when they lack the resources to obtain the type of diet, participate in the activities and have the living conditions and amenities which are customary, or at least widely encouraged, or approved, in the societies to which they belong. Their resources are so seriously below those commanded by the average individual or family that they are, in effect, excluded from ordinary living patterns, customs and activities. (1979, p. 31)

This has been very widely adopted as a point of reference in academic research not only in Europe but also in, for example, Australia and New Zealand. As Chapter 1 noted, the European Council adopted a similar definition in the mid-1980s, and this underpins the European Union's Social Inclusion Process, as we discuss in detail in Chapter 3.

The situation in the USA is somewhat different. The USA is distinctive in having had an official poverty measure since the 1960s, based on an income threshold, and this threshold has been increased over time only in line with prices rather than general living standards. This reflects, but has also feeds back into, prevailing views about the meaning of poverty in the USA. The relatively modest increases in median income, and even more so in bottom incomes, in the USA since the 1970s have also meant that the price-indexed threshold has lagged behind but has not become as detached from ordinary incomes as it would have done in many other industrialized countries over the period.[1] None the less, the official poverty measure is increasingly questioned, not only because of technical limitations in the measure of income it employs, but also because of its failure to reflect, to at least some degree, changes in general living standards. For example, the expert panel assembled by the National Academy of Sciences put forward the definition of poverty as having insufficient resources for basic living needs, defined appropriately for the United States today (Citro and Michael, 1995). To implement this they proposed that the income poverty threshold be updated regularly in line with expenditures on necessities (defined as food, clothing, and housing). The threshold would not then increase as rapidly as average income—since expenditures on necessities increase more slowly than overall income growth—but would still increase in real terms, representing as Blank (2008) puts it a 'quasi-relative' poverty threshold.

---

[1] Blank (2008) notes that the US official threshold for a family of four has fallen from about 50% of median income at introduction to 28% in 2005; it has not declined relative to the 20th percentile, though, since there has been no real income growth since the mid-1970s in that part of the income distribution.

While the broadly relative nature of poverty is more widely accepted in European research and discourse, this core issue of the reference standard to be used in assessing poverty remains both critical and unresolved. In an EU context in particular it has two dimensions: how the poverty standard should change over time within a given country, but also how it should vary across countries. As in the USA, most quantitative research employs income to distinguish the poor, with a great deal of research and debate on how best to establish a poverty threshold. The most common practice in comparative research is to employ thresholds set as a proportion of mean or median income, for example 50% or 60% of the median; comparative studies using this approach go back to OECD (1976), Smeeding et al. (1988), O'Higgins and Jenkins (1990), and Atkinson, Rainwater, and Smeeding (1995); more recent examples include OECD (2008) and Ward, Lelkes, Sutherland, and Toth (2009). As we shall see in the next chapter, this is also the basis for the headline 'at-risk-of-poverty' measures included in the EU's set of social inclusion indicators.

A variety of other approaches to deriving income poverty thresholds has been employed in comparative or national studies, based on, for example, budget standards specifying and costing necessities, the views of survey respondents about minimum income needs, or prevailing rates of social security payments. These are reviewed in some detail in Nolan and Whelan (1996); for a more recent discussion see, for example, Bradshaw and Mayhew (2011). For present purposes, though, our primary focus is on the limitations of income as the sole basis for distinguishing the poor, and as we shall see these persist irrespective of how the income threshold employed is determined. This is not to suggest that the location of the income threshold does not matter—on the contrary, the choice of threshold makes a great deal of difference to how well it does in identifying those unable to participate due to lack of resources; however, as we shall see, even the income poverty threshold that does best in those terms may not do very well.

As well as how the threshold is set, another key issue in measuring poverty via income is how income itself is measured. Critiques of the US official measure have centred on the fact that, for historical reasons, it is based on pre-tax income and does not take important in-kind benefits such as food stamps and housing assistance into account (Citro and Michael, 1995; Blank, 2008). More generally, though, the need to broaden the measure of financial resources to take into account, for example, housing costs (notably the imputed rent associated with home ownership), free or subsidized services, and wealth has been widely recognized, and each is the subject of significant recent research (see, for example, the discussion on these topics in OECD, 2008, and the output from the AIMAP collaborative research project[2]).

---

[2] See http://www.iser.essex.ac.uk/research/euromod/research-and-policy-analysis-using-euromod/aim-ap/deliverables-publications

Improving the measure of income or financial resources in the harmonized way required for comparative analysis across countries clearly represents a particular challenge, although some progress is being made.

At the same time, though, relying purely on income in seeking to measure and understand poverty has also been increasingly questioned, and it is in this context that the potential uses of non-monetary indicators of deprivation, the central focus of this volume, come to the fore. Scandinavian countries, in particular Sweden, were to the forefront in developing and employing non-monetary indicators, but with the emphasis on capturing 'level of living' more broadly rather than on poverty (see, for example, Erikson and Aberg, 1987). The use of non-monetary indicators in monitoring living conditions or quality of life has a long history, with peaks and slumps over time but a major resurgence in recent years, as exemplified by the OECD's compilations of comparative data on social indicators across its member countries in *Society at a Glance* (e.g. OECD, 2009) as well as the Stiglitz–Fitoussi–Sen commission on the measurement of economic performance and social progress set up by the French government (2009). While the latter dealt with a very wide range of issues to do with the limitations of current measures of GDP and quality of life, here our focus is much narrower, on the use of non-monetary indicators specifically to capture deprivation and poverty.

In that context, Townsend's pioneering British study (1979) provided much of the impetus. He developed a set of 60 indicators designed to capture what was conceived as 11 different types or aspects of deprivation, and used them to validate an income poverty threshold and to bring out what it meant to be poor in Britain at the time. Since then an extensive research literature on measures of material deprivation in OECD countries has grown up, with the valuable review by Boarini and Mira d'Ercole (2006) listing over a hundred studies. Some examples for European countries include Gordon et al. (2000), Vegeris and McKay (2002), Vegeris and Perry (2003), Berthoud, Bryan, and Bardarsi (2004), Pantazis et al. (2006), and Cappellari and Jenkins (2007) for Britain; Muffels and Dirven (1998) with Dutch data; Halleröd (1995) and Halleröd and Larsson (2008) for Sweden; Kangas and Ritakallio (1998) for Finland; Bohnke and Delhey (1999), Pfoertner, Andress, and Janssen (2010), and Busch and Peichl (2010) for Germany; Paugam (1996), Lollivier and Verger (1997), and Verger (2005) for France; Pérez-Mayo (2005), Poggi (2007), and Ayala and Navarro (2008) for Spain; Brasini and Tassinari (2004) for Italy; Tsakloglou and Panopoulou (1998) for Greece; and our own studies for Ireland (including Callan, Nolan, and Whelan, 1993; Nolan and Whelan, 1996; Layte, Nolan, and Whelan, 2000; Layte et al., 2001; Whelan et al., 2003; Maître, Nolan, and Whelan, 2005; Whelan and Maître, 2007a, b). There has also been significant interest in OECD countries outside Europe, such as Bray (2001), Saunders et al. (2007), and Scutella et al. (2009) for Australia, and Jensen et al.

(2002) and Fergusson et al. (2001) for New Zealand. The use of deprivation indicators in a US context has been more limited until recently (though see Mayer and Jencks, 1989; Mayer, 1993; Bauman, 1998, 1999, 2003), leading Blank to conclude that

We should catch up with our European cousins and, like them, work to develop multiple measures of economic deprivation. (2008, p. 252)

A much more limited set of studies employs non-monetary indicators to capture and analyse poverty and exclusion in a comparative perspective. Studies covering a few countries using national data sources include Halleröd et al.'s (2006) analysis of Britain, Finland, and Sweden, Saunders and Adelman (2006) on Australia and Britain, and Mayer's (1993) comparison of the USA with Canada, Sweden, and Germany. Drawing on a variety of sources and studies, Boarini and Mira d'Ercole (2006) present a range of comparative data for different OECD countries on the percentage of households unable to satisfy 'basic needs' and basic leisure activities, lacking various consumer durables, in poor housing conditions, etc. There are also a number of such studies covering most of the countries of the EU, before and after enlargement, and these are particularly relevant here given the centrality of the comparative European perspective for this book. We therefore review these studies in some depth in Section 2.4, but first we seek to clarify why and how such non-monetary indicators can be employed in a national or comparative context.

2.3 Rationales and Approaches to Using Non-Monetary Indicators

The types of non-monetary indicator employed in these studies cover a very wide range, and their development has been rather ad hoc, with different countries learning from each other while having their own preoccupations. National studies have expanded the set of items used and aspects covered, sometimes drawing on the results of in-depth qualitative research on people's everyday consumption and activities and what they regarded as important. Comparative studies, on the other hand, often must rely on a limited set of items, and also face problems of ensuring the relevance and comparability of those items from one country to another. Before looking in detail at the indicators involved, though, it is important to distinguish a number of distinct, though inter-related, motivations for and approaches to using such indicators in the first place. Insufficient recognition of these distinctions contributes to some confusion in research and application, since the appropriate selection and use of indicators will depend on the underlying rationale and point of departure.

One perspective or point of departure on the value of non-monetary indicators is that while conventional poverty measures based on low income provide a satisfactory way of identifying the poor, they do not tell us all we need to know about what it *means* to be poor. Non-monetary deprivation indicators can then play a central role in capturing and conveying the realities of the experience of poverty, bringing out concretely and graphically what it means to be poor in terms of deprivation of everyday items and activities. This was central to Townsend's use of the indicators he developed, and has been important in many subsequent studies and in their dissemination and reception in the media.

A distinct, though certainly in Townsend's case related, rationale is that in using income to identify the poor, non-monetary indicators may help in arriving at the most appropriate income threshold. By relating scores on a deprivation index to resources, he identified an income threshold representing the point below which deprivation scores, it was tentatively suggested, 'escalated disproportionately', and saw that as the appropriate income threshold. The existence and indeed plausibility of such a threshold was hotly debated (see Desai, 1986; Piachaud, 1987), and for the most part this approach to deriving an income poverty threshold has not been adopted more widely (though see Gordon et al., 2000). However, the analysis of the relationship between income and measured deprivation levels continues to be a key aspect of the use of non-monetary indicators.

As deprivation indicators started to become more widely available, they served to fuel a fundamental critique of reliance on low income in measuring poverty: that it fails in practice to identify those unable to participate in their societies due to lack of resources. This argument was put forward most emphatically by Ringen (1988), who asserted that income was both an indirect and unreliable measure of the underlying concept of poverty. If income is taken to be fundamentally unreliable for this purpose, then some other approach must be found, and non-monetary deprivation indicators provide a direct and potentially more reliable measurement tool. Mack and Lansley (1985) thus used deprivation indicators directly to identify those experiencing exclusion in Britain, and a number of subsequent British studies (Gordon et al., 2000, Pantazis et al., 2006) have done so with a more extensive set of indicators.

An alternative measurement approach employed in our own Irish studies (Callan, Nolan, and Whelan, 1993; Nolan and Whelan, 1996) is to identify those both on low income and reporting (certain types of) deprivation as 'consistently poor'. Since some people on low income manage to avoid deprivation for a variety of reasons, while some of those with high levels of deprivation also have reasonably high incomes, then focusing on the 'intersection' between low income and high deprivation counts as poor only those who are manifestly unable to participate *and* for whom this inability is most plausibly attributable to severely limited financial resources. A similar approach has been applied in some other countries (for example, Forster, 2005), and the UK is using both low income and material deprivation in monitoring progress towards its target of eradicating child poverty by 2020. A related approach is to focus on those reporting not only low income and deprivation but also a subjectively bad financial situation—what Bradshaw and Finch (2003) have termed 'core poverty'.

Rather than (or as well as) the more accurate identification of the poor, another argument for the use of non-monetary indicators goes back to the underlying concept, and seeks to move beyond what is seen as a narrow focus on financial poverty. It has long been said that poverty is about 'more than just money', and the widespread adoption of the terminology of social exclusion/inclusion in Europe reflects *inter alia* the concern that focusing simply on income misses an important part of the picture. As well as low income or financial resources, poverty may be associated with educational disadvantage, poor health and access to health services, inadequate housing, and exclusion in the labour market and in social relations. Reacting to such concerns, a multidimensional approach to capturing poverty and exclusion is now being adopted in many countries, as well as at EU level as we shall see. This may reflect the view that conceptually social exclusion is distinct from and broader than poverty. On the other hand, it can be argued with some force that the underlying notion of poverty that evokes social concern itself is (and always has been) intrinsically multidimensional (on which see the discussion in, for example, Nolan and Whelan, 1996, chapter 8; Burchardt, Le Grand, and Piachaud, 2002). Tomlinson, Walker, and Williams, for example, in arguing that poverty is a complex and multidimensional phenomenon, note that:

Following Henry Mayhew (1851) and Charles Booth (1892), Seebohm Rowntree (1901) grappled with the complexity, distinguishing between different categories of poverty and noting the need to take account of social conditions, diet and health as well as income in assessing living standards. (2008, p. 597)

The widespread adoption of the notion of multidimensionality has not meant greater clarity about precisely what that is intended to mean or why it would be preferable to low income as a focus. Some discussions highlight that the *processes* giving rise to poverty are multifaceted and cannot be reduced to low income and its proximate causes: poverty in the highly complex societies of the industrialized world can only be understood by taking a variety of causal factors and channels into account. Others focus more on *outcomes*, emphasizing that low income and its correlates are only one aspect of the variety of exclusions that one would wish to empirically capture, understand, and address. Finally, from a policy perspective it may be argued that focusing on income is, at least in some circumstances, likely to be less effective than directly tackling low education, poor housing, or health inequalities.

Much of this is not new. Swedish welfare research, for example, has for many years employed a multidimensional approach to capture 'level of living', defined in terms of access to resources in the form of money, possessions, knowledge, mental and physical energy, and social relationships, through which an individual can control and consciously direct his or her living conditions. This represents first of all a very substantial broadening beyond purely economic resources to include health, knowledge and skills, etc. However, it also goes beyond resources to include essential conditions. Some conditions, especially good health, are both important resources and ends in themselves, while aspects of living conditions such as quality of the work environment or amenities in the home are important for an individual's well being but can only be regarded as resources in a very remote sense. Finally, the value of a given set of resources depends on the context in which it is used, so the characteristics of the arenas in which resources are used also affect the scope for individuals to direct their own lives. The core notion is that it is not simply *outcomes* that matter—because these can be affected by the different choices people make—but rather the capacity to affect those outcomes in a purposive way.

As Erikson (1993) points out, this position, although independently arrived at, has much in common with the thrust of Sen's more recent, influential concept of 'capabilities' (see, e.g., Sen, 1993). Sen defines *functionings* as the various things a person manages to do or be in leading a life—such as being adequately nourished and in good health, having self-respect, and being socially integrated. The *capability* of a person then reflects the alternative combination of functionings he or she can achieve. If resources are very severely constrained, it may, for example, not be possible to both eat enough to be healthy and have clothing decent enough to maintain one's dignity and self-respect. It is freedom or ability to achieve rather than simply outcomes that we care about:

If our paramount interest is in the lives that people can lead—then it cannot but be a mistake to concentrate exclusively only on one or other of the *means* to such freedom. We must look at impoverished lives and not just depleted wallets. (Sen, 2000, p. 3)

Empirically 'capabilities' has proved to be an elusive concept, and investigators pursuing it have very often fallen back on outcomes when it comes to measurement.[3] Like Scandinavian welfare research, the capability approach

---

[3] Much of the discussion of Sen's approach has revolved around his argument that a capability approach helps to clarify the absolute versus relative poverty debate: 'Poverty is an absolute notion

serves to emphasize the processes linking resources and outcomes, the concern with the manner in which outcomes combine to constitute particular life-styles, and the importance of empowerment, freedom, and expansion of choice. These certainly are critical to understanding and addressing poverty, although this has always been recognized in the best poverty research: Townsend, for example, argued that poverty was not the lack of income necessary to purchase a basket of goods but rather the lack of resources to participate fully in society that resulted, through a process he termed 'structuration', from a variety of resource allocation systems operating in society.

It is also important to clarify that the multidimensionality of the concept may or may not have direct implications for measurement in the sense of identification of the poor. In some circumstances, a single indicator might be perfectly adequate to identify empirically those experiencing poverty or social exclusion in a particular society. To take the example most relevant to actual measurement practice, it could be that household income, accurately measured, is sufficient to identify those who would be generally thought of as poor or socially excluded. They might well be experiencing all sorts of other types of deprivation and exclusion—poverty is in that sense multifaceted—and documenting what being poor entailed would require the use of appropriate indicators across various dimensions. However, the poor could still be accurately identified via their income alone, if income were indeed very strongly associated with those other dimensions of deprivation and exclusion. The need for a multidimensional measurement approach in identifying the poor/excluded is an *empirical* matter, rather than something one can simply read off from the multidimensional nature of the concepts themselves. In a similar vein, identifying the poor is only the first step in understanding the causes of poverty, and the measure employed does not determine the best approach to exploring those causes. A single dimension may well serve to identify the poor, providing a basis for investigation of the disparate causal mechanisms. Focusing finally on policy, the way poverty is measured should not in itself imply a particular set of policy prescriptions to combat it, or a narrow versus broad approach to doing so. Measuring poverty via income does not in itself imply that the only way to tackle poverty is to directly target the incomes of the poor and try to raise them via social transfers. A multi-sectoral anti-poverty strategy involving 'joined up government' can be justified on the basis of the complex and interlocking nature of the underlying causal mechanisms and structures, irrespective of the measurement approach employed.

in the space of capabilities but very often it will take a relative form in the space of commodities or characteristics'. There is substance in Piachaud's criticism that 'Sen's absolute goals, save that of physical survival, are too vague to be of any theoretical or practical use' (Piachaud, 1987, p. 14).

Non-monetary indicators can thus be used in a variety of ways: to bring out what it means to be poor, help to do a better job than income on its own in identifying the poor, and directly capture the multifaceted nature of poverty and exclusion. There is no consensus about how best to employ them for these purposes, and the underlying rationale(s) may often be implicit rather than explicit, but the volume of recent research employing material deprivation indicators and the interest in policy circles illustrates the potential they are seen to have. We now look at the use of such indicators in the specific context of comparative European analysis, our central focus in this book.

2.4 Non-Monetary Indicators and Comparative European Research

In reviewing the use of non-monetary indicators in a European cross-country perspective, we start by describing the types of indicator available from core EU comparative datasets, which are employed in the comparative studies we review as well as in our own analysis in subsequent chapters. These indicators are drawn in the first instance from the European Community Household Panel Survey (ECHP) organized by Eurostat and carried out in most of the (then) EU member states from the mid-1990s to 2001, and more recently from the EU-Statistics on Income and Living Conditions (EU-SILC) data-gathering framework which replaced the ECHP.

The ECHP was a harmonized longitudinal survey coordinated by Eurostat which ran from 1994 to 2001 (2002 in some member states), covering a wide range of topics such as income, employment, household structures, health, education, and housing. In the first wave a sample of some 60,500 households, containing approximately 130,000 adults aged 16 years and over, were interviewed across 12 of the then member states. Austria and Finland joined the ECHP in 1995 and 1996 respectively.[4] In most countries the surveys were carried out using a harmonized questionnaire, harmonized definitions, and sampling requirements, so the high degree of cross-national comparability from a design perspective is distinctive.[5] Some missing data were imputed by Eurostat, which also developed weights to apply to the samples, to reflect initial sample design, response rates, and population structure.[6] The fact that individuals were followed from one year to the next makes it possible to examine how their circumstances changed and, in particular, to measure the

---

[4] Sweden did not participate in the ECHP, but from 1997 provided some cross-sectional data derived from its National Survey on Living Conditions.

[5] See Eurostat (1996) and Peracchi (2002) for descriptions of the survey and methods employed.

[6] Procedures for imputing missing values are described in Eurostat (2001a), while Eurostat (2001b) sets out the development of weights.

persistence of low income and poverty. This can come at a cost: attrition—losing respondents from one survey to the next—is a general problem with longitudinal surveys, and was substantial in some countries over the life of the ECHP. The impact on the composition of the samples generally seems to have been limited, but it remains a consideration in longitudinal analysis.[7] Data from the ECHP have been made available to researchers in the form of a USER Data Base or UDB, as described in Eurostat (2001c, d).

While a wide range of questions included in the ECHP produced information that could potentially serve as non-monetary indicators of life-style or deprivation, we focus primarily on 24 items that have been most intensively used for this purpose, covering a variety of areas and largely drawn from those used in influential national studies such as Townsend (1979). The format of the questions used in the survey to capture the required information varied across these items, and since this is relevant to important issues in the construction and use of such indicators it is worth spelling out in some detail.

For six of these items, the survey first asked whether the household had or availed of the item, and if not whether this was due to inability to afford it:

- A car or van;
- A colour TV;
- A video recorder;
- A microwave oven;
- A dishwasher;
- A telephone.

For another six items, absence and affordability elements were combined into 'There are some things many people cannot afford even if they would like them. Can I just check whether your household can afford these if you want them?':

- Keeping your home adequately warm;
- Paying for a week's annual holiday away from home;
- Replacing any worn-out furniture;
- Buying new, rather than second-hand clothes;
- Eating meat, chicken, or fish every second day, if you wanted to;
- Having friends or family for a drink or meal at least once a month.

For three items the question simply asked whether the household had:

- A bath or shower;
- An indoor flushing toilet;
- Hot running water.

---

[7] See Eurostat (2002); Watson (2003); Behr, Bellgardt, and Rendtel (2005).

For eight items respondents were asked 'Do you have any of the following problems with your accommodation?':

- Shortage of space;
- Noise from neighbours or outside;
- Too dark / not enough light;
- Leaky roof;
- Damp walls, floors, foundation, etc.;
- Rot in window frames or floors;
- Pollution, grime, or other environmental problems caused by traffic or industry;
- Vandalism or crime in the area.

Finally, households were asked separately whether they had been in arrears at any time during the past 12 months on their rent, on mortgage payments, on utility bills, and on hire purchase instalments or other loan repayments. The responses have generally been combined into one indicator of arrears on any of these payments.

Since we will be focusing on this set of indicators throughout much of this volume, for convenience and future reference Table 2.1 lists the individual items once again.

Table 2.1. Selection of Items Included in the European Community Household Panel Survey Used as Indicators of Material Deprivation

Replacing any worn-out furniture
A week's annual holiday away from home
Buying new, not second-hand clothes
Having friends or family for a meal once a month
Keeping home adequately warm
Meat, chicken, or fish every second day
In arrears on rent, utilities, and hire purchase
Microwave oven
Dishwasher
Telephone
Video recorder
Car
Colour TV
Bath or shower
Indoor flushing toilet
Hot running water
Damp walls, floors, foundations, etc.
Rot in window frames or floors
Leaking roof
Noise from neighbours or outside
Pollution, grime, or other environmental problems caused by traffic or industry
Shortage of space
Too dark / Not enough light
Vandalism or crime in the area

The ECHP was discontinued in 2001 (or 2002 in a few countries), and was replaced by the EU-SILC, which is now the EU reference source for the level and composition of poverty and social exclusion.[8] EU-SILC is coordinated by Eurostat and covers all 27 member states of the EU (plus some others such as Iceland, Norway, and Turkey). It was launched in 2003 in six member states, and by 2005 was operating in all of the then EU-25 countries, subsequently extending to Bulgaria and Romania when they joined the EU in 2007. EU-SILC takes a very different approach to the ECHP: rather than a common design and questionnaire, it is based on a common framework for the production of specified statistics on income and living conditions. Member states have considerable autonomy in the areas of sampling design, questionnaire editing, and data compilation, but the 'target' variables required are tightly defined in the framework Regulation, which also sets out common guidelines and procedures, common concepts (such as what constitutes a household and how income components are defined), and classifications aimed at maximizing comparability of the information produced. Both household surveys and administrative registers can be used to produce the data, provided they are 'linkable' at the micro-level; while there is a longitudinal element, it generally involves following an individual only for four years, and the cross-sectional element can be separate from the longitudinal one.[9]

Considerable effort is being invested by Eurostat and national statistics offices into assessing the quality of the data produced by EU-SILC, with each country being obliged to provide a detailed annual quality assessment report, and Eurostat producing an overall assessment of quality each year focused on accuracy, timeliness, and comparability, and covering areas such as sample design, sampling and non-sampling errors, mode of data collection, and imputation procedures (see for example Eurostat, 2010).[10] However, both changes in the income concept used and in the way the data are produced mean that caution is required in linking key poverty indicators directly with those from the ECHP.[11] Here our focus is on patterns and relationships rather than on trends in poverty, but the fact that the data we use for the mid 1990s versus the mid-2000s are from different instruments still needs to be kept in mind.

---

[8] Reasons advanced for doing so were that results from the ECHP were available only after a substantial lag and were seen as out of date, the results it produced on some key indicators for several countries were questioned, and in most countries it was not satisfactorily integrated with the national statistical systems.

[9] For general descriptions of EU-SILC and discussion of its key features, see Clemenceau and Museux (2007); Marlier et al. (2007); Wolff, Montaigne, and Gonzalez (2010).

[10] For valuable discussions of accuracy in EU-SILC, see also Wolff, Montaigne, and Gonzalez (2010) and Verma and Betti (2010).

[11] On which, see Eurostat (2005); Marlier et al. (2007); Atkinson, Marlier, Montaigne, and Reinstadler (2010).

EU-SILC includes a more limited but still substantial set of non-monetary indicators, as exemplified by the following seventeen items (mostly comprising a sub-set of those in the ECHP):[12]

The household cannot afford:

- To pay unexpected required expenses;
- A week's holiday away from home;
- A meal with meat, chicken, fish (or vegetarian) every second day;
- Personal computer;
- Car;
- Telephone (including mobile);
- Colour TV;
- Washing machine.

The household reports:

- No bath or shower in dwelling;
- No indoor toilet in dwelling for sole use of household;
- Being unable to keep their home adequately warm;
- Rooms too dark, not enough light;
- Leaking roof, damp walls/ceilings/floors/foundations, rot in doors, window frames;
- Noise from neighbours or noise from the street;
- Pollution, grime, or other environmental problems in the area;
- Crime, violence, or vandalism in the area.

The household has in the previous 12 months been in arrears relating to:

- Rent or mortgage payments;
- Utility bills;
- Hire purchase.

Once again, since we will be using these indicators intensively the items involved are summarized in Table 2.2.

Since the coverage of EU-SILC is more restricted that the ECHP, a special module included in EU-SILC in 2009 contained a broader set of indicators to inform the selection of additional items for inclusion in EU-SILC in the future; for present purposes, though, the more limited range has to be accepted as a constraint.

While these are the items on which research has been most concentrated, both the ECHP and EU-SILC also include data on other variables that could

---

[12] Since EU-SILC is not a harmonized survey, the precise format of the questions employed may not always be identical across countries.

Table 2.2. Selection of Items Included in EU-SILC Used as Indicators of Material Deprivation

Afford to pay unexpected required expenses
Week's holiday away from home
Meals with meat, chicken, fish (or vegetarian)
Can afford a PC
Arrears relating to mortgage payments, rent, utility bills, hire purchase
Inability to keep home adequately warm
Respondent for household can afford to have a car
Bath or shower in dwelling
Indoor toilet
Can afford a telephone
Can afford a colour TV
Can afford a washing machine
Pollution, grime, or other environmental problems in the area caused by traffic or industry
Noise from neighbours or noise from the street
Crime, violence, or vandalism in the area
Rooms too dark, light problems
Leaking roof, damp walls/ceilings/floors/foundations, rot in doors, window frames

serve as non-monetary indicators of deprivation. In the ECHP these cover for example:

- Social contact—how often respondents talk to neighbours, meet friends, or talk to someone outside the household, and whether they are members of a club or organization;

- Subjective indicators of levels of satisfaction with work or main daily activity, financial situation, housing, and amount of leisure time;

- The respondent's evaluations of how difficult it is to make ends meet, the lowest monthly income the household requires to make ends meet, and whether there normally is some money left after expenses that could be saved;

- The respondent's health status and use of health services.

EU-SILC also includes several of these, as well as the number of rooms in the house and whether housing costs or loan repayments are seen as a major burden.

The availability of these comparative data for the EU, first from the ECHP for most of the pre-Enlargement 15 member states and subsequently via EU-SILC to cover all 27 of the current members, has underpinned an expanding set of research studies, including a significant number carried out in association with Eurostat as the interest in such indicators at EU level has grown. We describe in the next chapter the evolving role these indicators have come to play in the EU's own processes, notably the Social Inclusion Process and most recently the poverty reduction target adopted as part of the Union's high-level 2020 strategy, but at this point our focus is on the underlying research. Without describing individual studies in any great detail, our aim in reviewing them is to convey the main directions taken and issues and challenges faced.

Early comparative studies of poverty and social exclusion in the EU using non-monetary indicators from the ECHP included Eurostat (2000), Whelan, Layte, Maître, and Nolan (2001), Layte, Nolan, and Whelan (2001), Layte, Whelan, Maître, and Nolan (2001), Layte and Whelan (2002), Whelan, Layte and Maître (2002a, b, 2003), Tsakloglou and Papadopoulous (2001, 2002a), Muffels and Fourage (2002, 2004), and Eurostat (2003). The first *European Social Statistics: Income, Poverty and Social Exclusion* produced by Eurostat (2000), based on analysis by Dirven and colleagues, looked at some 40 ECHP indicators intended to comprehensively describe life-style deprivation for the 13 EU countries by then covered by the ECHP. These indicators included 'objective' indicators (such as the availability of basic amenities, car, and housing conditions), 'subjective' indicators (such as responses to questions about satisfaction with different aspects of life, perceived economic hardship or health status, etc.), and indicators on social relations (such as membership of formal networks and access to informal networks). The variation in reported aggregate deprivation levels on this basis across countries and household types was described in tabular form and discussed. Around the same time, Eurostat issued a Statistics in Focus statistical release by Mejer (2000) showing how reported levels of financial difficulty ('making ends meet'), satisfaction with income, and ability to afford a holiday varied between those falling below relative income thresholds versus above those thresholds in each country.

Our own research at this point with colleagues Richard Layte and Bertrand Maître focused on a narrower set of 'objective' deprivation indicators, the way they related to each other, to income, and to subjectively assessed financial pressures, and the dynamics of deprivation versus income over time. Whelan et al. (2001) examined the relationship between income and deprivation at household level in the first wave of the ECHP, and their combined impact on households' perceptions of financial pressures. Five distinct dimensions of deprivation were identified, consistently across individual countries, and the relationship between what was termed 'current life-style deprivation' (which combined two of these dimensions) and income was investigated in some depth. Layte et al. (2001) focused directly on the mismatch between income and deprivation using the first two waves of the ECHP, showing the level of deprivation reported by a household to be related to the persistence of income poverty but also to a range of other resource and need-related factors for the household. Layte, Whelan, Maître, and Nolan (2001) extended this analysis to explore differences in deprivation across countries and the role of differing welfare regimes. Whelan et al. (2002b) examined the relationship between persistent income poverty and deprivation across different dimensions, showing that only a modest proportion of the persistently income poor can be characterized as being exposed to multiple deprivation. Layte and Whelan

(2002) brought out the implication that traditional risk factors for poverty combine in complex ways to put a significant proportion of the population at risk of poverty rather than impacting simply on a multiply disadvantaged minority. Whelan, Layte, and Maître (2002b, 2003) further explore the dynamics of income poverty and deprivation with the first three waves of the ECHP, showing that persistent income poverty over three waves does predict or explain levels of deprivation better than in a single cross-section, but still fails to capture much of the process of accumulation and erosion of resources relative to needs.

Also relying on the first three waves of the ECHP, Muffels and Fouarge (2002) constructed deprivation indices using 21 items covering durables, financial stress, housing, and health, and looked at the percentage persistently below a deprivation threshold over three years. Those both persistently deprived and persistently income-poor were deemed to be socially excluded, and the level and variation in this measure and each of its components across countries and welfare regimes was examined. Muffels and Fouarge (2004) related deprivation measured in this fashion to household characteristics and welfare regimes. Tsakloglou and Papadopoulos (2002a, b) used these waves to investigate cumulative deprivation across deprivation indicators covering living conditions, necessities, and social relations, together with relative income poverty. Those who reported at least two out of these four were counted as excluded, and their characteristics were examined and compared across countries.

Eurostat (2003) presented results based on the first 4 waves of the ECHP[13] using the 24 non-monetary items described earlier. These are combined into a single summary index, and the five dimensions of deprivation proposed by Whelan et al. are also analysed separately. Levels of deprivation and profiles of those affected are reported across countries, and the relationship with income poverty cross-sectionally and over the four years is examined. Much of the analysis is based on using a common deprivation standard across countries and simply comparing the proportions doing without a particular number of items, whereas most of the previous research in effect applied a relative standard that gave greater weight to being deprived of an item or activity that most people in the country have or can do. The report brings out how much difference this makes, concentrating on thirteen items in the 'current life-style deprivation index', which are most strongly related to the risk of income poverty.

Till and Giorgi (2002) also employ the five dimensions of non-monetary deprivation suggested by Whelan et al. and examine the distribution of the

---

[13] This report was produced for Eurostat by a team of researchers led by L. Giorgi (ICCR) and V. J. Verma (Siena), with the results on non-monetary deprivation produced by Verma and one of the present authors (Whelan).

27

latter among the population in 1997 and also by years of poverty from 1994 to 1997. They also pay particular attention to housing-related aspects of deprivation and how these relate to tenure, other aspects of deprivation and low income.

These may be regarded as the first generation of comparative studies of deprivation across the EU, followed by further studies also based on the ECHP such as Dekker (2003), Whelan, Layte, and Maître (2004), Whelan and Maître (2006), Bossert, D'Ambrosio, and Peragine (2007), and Figari (2009). Dekker (2003) uses data from the 1996 to 2000 waves of the ECHP for seven countries, investigating how 37 items cluster into dimensions and how deprivation scores relate to relative income poverty and socio-economic characteristics. Whelan, Layte, and Maître (2004) analyse the mismatch between income poverty and deprivation over time with five waves of the ECHP, and find that while both cross-sectional and longitudinal measures of deprivation are systematically related to persistent income poverty, the scale of mismatch is not reduced by extending the time period covered. Those experiencing both persistent low income and persistent deprivation are clearly differentiated from others in terms of factors affecting household needs and resources. Whelan and Maître (2006) focus on the dynamics of income poverty and deprivation, taking measurement error into account via the modelling approach applied by Breen and Moisio (2004) to income poverty. Measurement error means exits from income poverty and deprivation are over-estimated, so persistence in both is higher than it appears, but each continues to provide valuable and distinct information about the households affected. Bossert, D'Ambrosio, and Peragine (2006) use data from all eight waves of the ECHP from 1994 to 2001 to illustrate new individual and aggregate measures of deprivation and social exclusion that they develop which satisfy a set of appealing axioms; for this purpose they use 11 non-monetary deprivation items covering the domains of financial difficulties, basic necessities, housing conditions, and durables. Bellani and D'Ambrosio (2009) also use longitudinal data from the ECHP to investigate the relationship between self-declared satisfaction with life and an individual's well being as measured by such indices of deprivation. Figari (2009) uses 13 items to construct a deprivation index and study how it varied across countries and over time, showing that changes in income and deprivation do not strictly coincide and that often lagged income has a larger effect than current income.

The third generation of comparative studies, making use of data emerging from EU-SILC from the mid-2000s, includes Guio (2005), Guio and Engsted-Maquet (2007), Guio, Fusco, and Marlier (2009), Ward et al. (2009), Bossert, Chakravarty, and D'Ambrosio (2009), Fusco, Guio, and Marlier (2010), some statistical releases from Eurostat, and our own studies (including Whelan and Maître, 2005a, b, 2007a, 2009a, b, 2010a, b; Nolan and Whelan, 2007, 2010).

The studies by Guio et al. have been carried out in association with Eurostat with a particular eye to the use of deprivation indicators in the EU's Social Inclusion Process: we come back to that context in the next chapter, but here concentrate on the indicators used and how they are analysed. Much of the analysis in Guio (2005) is in fact based on the ECHP, but supplemented by new data from EU-SILC for 6 EU15 member states for 2003 and focusing only on deprivation items available in both sources—which is why we review it now together with other EU-SILC-based studies. Having discussed the selection of appropriate items, the best way of grouping 11 deprivation items into dimensions is investigated, arriving at 3: what is termed 'economic strain', enforced lack of durables, and housing; a combination of the first two dimensions is also analysed. The proportion affected by deprivation in each dimension is set out, as is the proportion over a threshold, and this is compared with relative income poverty risk. The difference made by making the weight accorded to each deprivation item a function of the proportion possessing it in the country is considered, as are risk factors associated with deprivation and the proportion facing both relative income poverty and deprivation ('consistent poverty'). Guio and Maquet (2006) repeat much of this analysis with EU-SILC data for 2004 for 12 EU15 member states, Estonia, and Norway, now with 13 items, arriving at the same grouping in terms of dimensions and presenting results on that basis. Guio (2009) employs data from EU-SILC 2006 for 26 countries to look at similar issues, developing the investigation of alternative approaches to weighting items in particular. Reference is also made to the results of a Eurobarometer survey on the perception carried out in 2007 on the items which citizens in the different member states consider to be necessary for people to have an 'acceptable' standard of living in the country where they live.[14] Guio, Fusco, and Marlier (2009) use data from EU-SILC 2007 together with this Eurobarometer survey to discuss a similar range of issues and compare material deprivation and income-based poverty measures. Fusco, Guio, and Marlier (2010) also investigate in some depth the relationship between income poverty and deprivation in EU-SILC and how each relate to socio-economic characteristics. Marlier, Atkinson, Cantillon, and Nolan (2007) and Marlier, Cantillon, Nolan, Van den Bosch, and Van Rie (2011) look at the cross-country patterns in aggregate indicators of social exclusion, including not only relative income poverty and material deprivation but also other indicators included in the EU's common set to be described in the next chapter.

Guio's studies have been very influential in the development of the use of deprivation indicators in the EU's Social Inclusion Process and will be

---

[14] For detailed analysis of the results of this survey, see Dickes, Fusco, and Marlier (2010).

discussed in more detail at various points in this book, notably in Chapters 3 and 5. Among other studies using such indicators and based on data from EU-SILC, though, Ward's chapter in Ward, Lelkes, Sutherland, and Toth (2009) uses data from 2006 to examine the variation across countries in the percentage unable to afford a telephone, colour TV or washing machine, a car, a meal with meat or fish (or the vegetarian equivalent) at least every other day, and one week's holiday away from home a year, in arrears with utility bills, and unable to cover an unexpected cost from their own resources. The proportion concerned varies with the median level of income per head of countries, but only relatively broadly, and in the new member states many of those affected have incomes above the risk-of-poverty threshold. This, it is argued, suggests a need to supplement the (relative) income-based measures with indicators of material deprivation and financial difficulty. Bossert, Chakravarty, and D'Ambrosio (2009) characterize a class of aggregate measures of multidimensional poverty and material deprivation that allows for the assignment of different weights to different indicators, and illustrate the application of these distribution-sensitive measures using data on 18 non-monetary deprivation indicators from EU-SILC for 2005 and 2006, with weights for the different dimensions based on views about necessities as reflected in the Eurobarometer 2007 survey already mentioned.[15]

We have ourselves published a range of analyses of non-monetary deprivation indicators based on data from EU-SILC (including Nolan and Whelan, 2007, 2010; Whelan and Maître, 2005a, b, 2006, 2007a–c, 2008, 2009a, b, 2010a, b); since we will be drawing on and developing these in the course of this book, we will not review them at this point.

2.5 Key Issues in Using Non-Monetary Deprivation Indicators

This chapter's introduction to the use of non-monetary deprivation indicators and review of the comparative research literature employing them serves to bring out some core issues, which will run through this book but may usefully be highlighted at this point in summary form:

---

[15] While not focused specifically on the use of deprivation indicators, a good deal of attention has been paid of late to the issue of how best to combine information about deprivation or exclusion across dimensions. Tsui (2002) and Bourguignon and Chakravarty (2003) have explored this issue from a welfare-theoretic perspective. Atkinson (2003) contrasts what he terms 'social welfare' versus 'counting' approaches to summarizing multidimensional deprivation, emphasizing that each builds in strong assumptions about the underlying structure and interaction between the dimensions. Alkire and Foster (2007) have developed a counting approach that they have recently applied to a wide range of developing countries in the 2010 Human Development Report from the UNDP (see also Alkire and Santos, 2010).

- What is the relationship between deprivation indicators and household income, how is that to be interpreted, and what conclusions can be drawn?
- What is the best way to analyse and incorporate the clustering of deprivation items into different dimensions?
- What is the best way to weight individual items in constructing deprivation scales—in particular in a comparative European context, are country-specific versus common weights across countries appropriate?
- What is the most satisfactory way to use deprivation indicators to capture poverty and exclusion—in particular, are they best seen as a substitute or complement to income-based measures, and if the latter how can the information content in both be taken into account?
- How can deprivation indicators best be used to capture the multidimensionality of exclusion and disadvantage—how should one aggregate across dimensions?

As we will try to bring out in subsequent chapters, the answers to many of these questions will vary depending on the purpose of the analysis—what precisely one is trying to achieve. For example, if the primary aim is to capture differences in living standards across European countries, that will require a different approach to a study focused on identifying those most excluded within each country. Similarly, a study setting out to distinguish and capture different aspects of deprivation in order to assess the scale of multiple deprivation may not adopt the same measures and methods as one more focused on identifying generalized exclusion. The failure to distinguish clearly between such different objectives, and to make clear how the methods employed are oriented towards the specific objective at hand, has created some confusion in the use of non-monetary indicators that we try to clarify as we proceed through this book.

Before proceeding, though, the other major issue that has pre-occupied this research field needs to be addressed, namely how best to measure deprivation via specific non-monetary indicators in the first place. In particular, it is important that we spell out the basis for the choices we make here in that regard, since that affects all our subsequent analysis and discussion.

To have a basis for deciding what indicators are appropriate, one must start with what deprivation itself means. Deprivation is a widely used term, but usually without definition of the underlying concept and with significant variation across studies in the way it is applied. Townsend (1979) set out to clarify the meaning of deprivation and its relationship with poverty, defining it as a state of observable and demonstrable disadvantage relative to the local community or the wider society or nation to which an individual, family, or group belongs:

People can be said to be deprived if they lack the types of diet, clothing, housing, household facilities and fuel and environmental, educational, working and social conditions, activities and facilities which are customary, or at least widely encouraged or approved, in the societies to which they belong. (pp. 125–6)

He referred *inter alia* to people who lead restricted or stunted social lives, who do not or cannot enter into ordinary forms of family or other social relationships. Deprivation then refers to conditions, which constitute poverty when they are attributable to lack of resources rather than other factors.

However, a central element in the concept of deprivation itself as it is widely understood, which a focus on conditions per se may not capture, is that it refers to being *denied* the opportunity to have or do something.[16] To constitute deprivation, lack of an item or failure to participate in an activity must reflect what most people would regard as *inability* to participate. This inability could be attributable to various different factors, such as lack of resources, ill-health, or discrimination, but not having the item or doing the activity is not simply a matter of choice. Even if there is a societal consensus that something is an 'undesirable circumstance', some people may still choose it freely, and they should not then be considered deprived. Extreme examples such as people who choose to be hermits in the desert make the point, but so more conventionally do those who choose not to have a car or a television, or not to socialize with their families or neighbours. Deprivation we therefore take to mean inability to obtain the types of diet, clothing, housing, household facilities, and environmental, educational, working, and social conditions generally regarded as acceptable in the community in question. It refers to the results of the constraints on people's choices, not simply to outcomes themselves. Since our primary interest is in poverty, we are then most directly interested in capturing types of deprivation that can most readily and reliably be attributed to financial constraints.

However, the empirical reality is that outcomes are much easier to observe than constraints: we can measure whether people lack or fail to do particular things, but face far greater difficulties determining why. One response to the difficulty of assessing opportunity sets rather than outcomes is to employ as deprivation indicators only those items/activities that we could reasonably expect most people to wish to avoid if possible. Thus Erikson (1993) describes the Scandinavian surveys that sought to capture 'levels of living' across a wide range of different areas as measuring 'evil conditions' rather than welfare itself, because it is much easier to order such states in ways that most people would accept. One can then seek to identify problems or 'evil conditions' directly—a leaky roof, damp walls, or crime-filled neighbourhood, for

---

[16] This is also the dictionary definition.

example—that it is safe to assume people would avoid if they could. In the same vein, one can focus on items that, it seems reasonable to assume, most people want and would do without only if they really have to: for example, an indoor toilet, adequate heating, hot and cold running water.

However, this only takes us so far, and to capture the ability to participate across the range of areas and activities generally regarded as important in rich societies, a wider span of items and activities must be probed, where distinguishing the impact of constraints from choices is a central problem. A strategy pioneered by Mack and Lansley (1985) and widely copied subsequently is then to ask the respondent explicitly whether they are doing without an item because they cannot afford it. As we have seen in relation to the items described above from the ECHP and EU-SILC, in some cases the respondent is first asked whether they possess or avail of the item, and if they say they do not then a follow-up question probes whether this was because they could not afford it. In others, absence and affordability elements are incorporated in one question, along the lines of 'There are some things many people cannot afford even if they would like them. Can I just check whether your household can afford these if you want them?'

These subjective evaluations of affordability do seem to help in capturing resource constraints (see, for example, the analysis in Mack and Lansley, 1985; and Nolan and Whelan, 1996), though they cannot be taken as entirely unproblematic since a range of circumstances may affect whether a respondent sees 'doing without' a particular item as attributable to choice or constraints, and how readily they will be willing to admit they cannot afford it. Studies suggest that preferences may 'adapt' to lived experiences, and so life on a low income can depress aspirations, leading some to say that they do not want items that, in other circumstances, they might well desire. There may also be systematic differences between different groups in whether non-ownership of a good is attributed to choice versus inability to afford—older people, for example, may be less likely to say they could not afford an item they lacked (see, for example, McKay, 2004; and Halleröd, 2006). None the less, while being aware of these limitations and biases the use of these subjective evaluations seems helpful.

In the light of these considerations, in seeking to empirically capture deprivation we will be focusing on the non-monetary items from the ECHP and SILC listed in Tables 2.1 and 2.2 and described in detail above. These refer to conditions of life and, in terms of the way they are framed in the surveys, they:

- Are explicitly framed as problems that people would avoid if they could;
- Refer to items that most people in the society in question would do without only if they really have to; or

- Refer to being unable to afford an item, where that is incorporated into the question.

Unlike some of the studies reviewed, we do not include items relating to frequency of social contact as deprivation indicators, although these are available in the ECHP. This is because limited social contact, while associated with poorer subjective well being and health outcomes, is not self-evidently something that people would avoid if they could, it is difficult to control for the role of choice, and the question format did not probe it. These factors are reflected in significant variations across countries that bear no simple relationship to levels of deprivation relating to other dimensions of deprivation. (This does not preclude us from studying the relationship between social contact and low income or poverty using these items, as we do and will report.) Furthermore, in focusing on conditions we concentrate on more 'objective' measures (albeit sometimes with a subjective element), and do not include purely subjective evaluations available in the data of, for example, levels of satisfaction with financial situation or housing, or of how difficult it is to make ends meet. These contain valuable information, and the responses on how difficult it is to make ends meet will play an important role in our analysis, but we do not use them as direct indicators of deprivation because they may be heavily influenced by previous experiences and the frames of reference they create. Finally, while measures of health status and the presence of chronic or limiting illness are available in the data and have been included on occasion in other studies as deprivation indicators, we regard them as more suitably employed as explanatory variables, helping to understand patterns of limited participation or non-participation in other domains.

It is also worth pointing to some indicators that we include in our analysis that some other studies exclude. In particular, we retain items relating to problems in the local area such as noise from neighbours, pollution, grime or other environmental problems, and crime, violence or vandalism, which are excluded from, for example, the studies by Guio et al. reviewed earlier. Their rationale for exclusion is that there seems to be no systematic relationship between these items and poverty: 'such problems can reflect urban social problems that can affect the whole society rather than just the poorest groups' (Guio and Engsted-Maquet, 2007, p. 201). We would argue that for our purposes these clearly constitute problems that people would avoid if they could, and that they represent an important aspect of daily living that one would like to capture. Including them in the analysis, distinguishing them, and seeking to understand their complex relationship with financial and other constraints is therefore the strategy we adopt.

Finally, it is worth noting that the deprivation indicators we employ are not chosen on the basis of a strictly 'consensual' approach, as pioneered in Mack and Lansley's (1985) British research and employed subsequently in some national and comparative studies (notably the Poverty and Social Exclusion studies by Gordon and colleagues in the UK). This involves collecting views from a representative sample of people about which items they regard as 'necessities', and taking the items so regarded by a majority or most people as representing a social consensus. With this in mind, the EU-wide Eurobarometer survey carried out in 2007 probed which in a list of items were considered necessary for people to have an 'acceptable' standard of living in their country. The responses, as described in Guio, Fusco, and Marlier (2009), showed that a personal computer, for example, was regarded as necessary by only about 30% of the population in the EU27, and for that reason was dropped from the set of deprivation indicators they employ. However, even in a national context the extent of consensus that actually exists across different social groups within a country may be limited (see the discussion in McKay, 2004; Pantazis et al., 2006). In seeking to apply the approach across countries, this becomes even more problematic: the Eurobarometer results show, for example, that an annual holiday and a car (retained by Guio et al.) are regarded as necessities by less than half the population in a substantial number of EU countries, and by only a bare majority across the EU27 as a whole: it seems unreasonable to take this as representing a social consensus across the EU that they are necessities. To justify retaining these items (including a PC) in the set of indicators we would instead hark back to Townsend's reference, quoted earlier, to living conditions and amenities that are customary, or at least widely encouraged, or approved, in the societies to which they belong. From our perspective, the justification for individual indicators and combinations of them rests essentially in their discriminatory power in helping to identify those excluded from such participation by lack of resources.

The deprivation indicators from the ECHP and EU-SILC will serve as the bedrock for our analysis of poverty and deprivation throughout the rest of this volume. Before proceeding to our own analysis, though, the next chapter deals with a key aspect of the context for this research, namely the development of indicators in the EU's Social Inclusion Process and the role played by non-monetary deprivation indicators in particular.

3

Deprivation and the EU's Social Inclusion Indicators

3.1 Introduction

While we focused in the previous chapter on the evolution of research using non-monetary indicators of life-style and deprivation, in parallel to that non-monetary deprivation indicators have come to play an important role in the way the European Union frames and monitors efforts to reduce poverty and promote social inclusion. This culminated in 2010 with the adoption of a high-level poverty reduction target for the Union for 2020, with direct measures of material deprivation as well as income (and joblessness) incorporated into the definition of that target. In this chapter we examine the development of social inclusion processes and indicators in the EU and how the role played by non-monetary deprivation indicators in that context has evolved. In doing so, our aim is to bring out the rationale(s) underlying this development, and the analytical and practical challenged it faces. This serves to set the stage for our subsequent in-depth analysis of deprivation and the role of deprivation indicators in the rest of the book.

We begin with a brief review of the development of the EU's engagement with social policy, then focus on the processes it developed around 2000 to engage more actively with poverty and social inclusion, and against this background focus on the adoption of a set of common indicators, on the way deprivation indicators have recently been incorporated into that set of indicators, and finally how even more recently they have formed one element in the EU's 2020 poverty reduction target.

3.2 Social Policy and the EU

The development of poverty monitoring in the EU must be seen in the light of the evolution of the broader EU social policy context in which it is set.[1] From the early days of the European Communities, the predominant focus was economic rather than social, the core aim being to enhance economic growth by promoting free movement of goods, services, capital, and labour. Social policy received little attention and Community institutions had very few powers relating to that domain, which under subsidiarity remained the province of the member states. However, the 1970s saw the EEC begin to develop and implement policies and programmes related to poverty and social exclusion. In 1974 the Council of Ministers adopted a 'Resolution concerning a social action programme' (European Council, 1974), which led to the establishment of a programme of pilot schemes and studies to combat poverty, which was subsequently extended through two further Poverty Programmes until 1994.

More generally, the social dimension enjoyed a significantly enhanced profile from 1985 when Jacques Delors became President of the European Commission. He launched the ambitious Single Market project to abolish barriers to free movement within the Community, to create by 1993 a large, unified economic area on a scale with the USA. The Single European Act, the first major revision to the 1957 Treaty of Rome, came into force in July 1987. The recognition that this might have negative effects on some groups was an important motivation behind the extension of the powers of the Community in the social policy area. Important landmarks in the development of that competence were the 1989 Social Charter and the Social Protocol of the Maastricht Treaty, which came into force in 1993 (at which point the EEC became the European Union). Progress towards European Monetary Union was an important part of the context, with the Stability and Growth pact agreed in 1997. In the same year, 'Modernising and Improving Social Protection in the European Union' (European Commission, 1997) argued that social protection systems can act as a productive factor that can contribute to economic and political stability and help EU economies to perform better. This contributed to the acceptance of a new legal base for the fight against social exclusion incorporated in the Treaty of Amsterdam, which came into force in 1999 and required the Community to support member states' action to combat social exclusion, assigning the fight against social exclusion a central role in the social policy agenda. The Council endorsed four broad objectives identified by the Commission in its Communication on 'A Concerted Strategy for Modernising Social Protection' (European Commission, 1999): to make work pay and to provide secure income, to make pensions safe and pensions systems sustainable, to promote social inclusion, and to ensure high quality and sustainable health care.

---

[1] We draw here on the detailed treatment in Marlier et al. (2007), chapter 2.

With eleven of the then 15 member states moving towards adoption of the common currency that came fully into operation from the start of 2001, the promotion of economic growth, notably by addressing structural impediments to flexibility that were seen to place Europe at a competitive disadvantage, remained centre stage. However, the linkage between economic and social areas was increasingly seen as important, as highlighted in the 2000 Lisbon European Council's goal that Europe become by 2010 'the most competitive and dynamic knowledge-based economy in the world capable of sustainable economic growth with more and better jobs and greater social cohesion'. That Council explicitly stated that the extent of poverty and social exclusion in the Union was unacceptable, and that building a more inclusive European Union was an essential element in achieving the Union's ten-year strategic goal. The common objectives on poverty and social exclusion subsequently agreed by the Nice European Council in December 2000 included facilitating participation in employment and access to resources, rights, goods, and services for all, preventing the risks of exclusion, helping the most vulnerable, and mobilizing all 'relevant actors'. A guiding principle of the Social Policy Agenda also adopted in 2000 was strengthening the role of social policy as a productive factor via a positive interaction between economic, employment and social policies.

From this point onwards, not only were promoting competitiveness, employment and social cohesion clearly identified as the central aims of European policy, but social protection and inclusion become specific policy areas for EU cooperation. The 2001 Nice Treaty included articles stating that in various fields relevant to social policy, including social security and social protection, combating social exclusion and modernization of social protection systems, the Council, while taking into account 'the diverse forms of national practices' under subsidiarity, is entitled to 'adopt measures designed to encourage cooperation between member states through initiatives aimed at improving knowledge, developing exchanges of information and best practices, promoting innovative approaches and evaluating experiences'. This underpinned the development of the Union's Social Inclusion Process in which the monitoring of poverty and social inclusion is embedded, to which we now turn.

3.3 The Social Inclusion Process and the Open Method of Coordination

In deciding in 2000 that social policy should be a distinct focus of attention for EU cooperation, the European Council also agreed on the process by which this should be implemented. Up to that point policy coordination at EU level had mostly applied to economic policy, and to employment via the so-called Luxemburg Process formalized by the Amsterdam Treaty, a peer review exercise involving the Commission and the member states through which countries were intended to learn from one another and therefore be able to improve their policies. This served to demonstrate the role that coordination, with agreed objectives and monitoring procedures, could play and that approach was in effect now extended to poverty and social exclusion. This was to be done through what is known as the Open Method of Coordination (OMC), with key elements being the agreement of common objectives, the preparation of National Action Plans and a regular Joint Report on Social Inclusion by the Commission and the Council, and the adoption of common indicators to monitor progress towards the common objectives and comparing best practice across member states. A group of high-level officials from the relevant ministries in each Member State, the Social Protection Committee (SPC), was assigned an important guiding and coordinating role together with the EU Commission.[2]

The 2000 Nice European Council provided common objectives in relation to the fight against poverty and social exclusion, as already noted, so the next step was to adopt a set of common indicators against which progress could be concretely measured. This was done during the Belgian Presidency of the European Council in the second half of 2001, and we will describe the set of indicators this produced in detail in the next section. The preparation and submission of national action plans on social inclusion got under way, with a further round in 2003 (European Commission, 2004). The year 2004 saw the enlargement of the Union to include eight new members from formerly communist Eastern Europe together with Cyprus and Malta, with Bulgaria and Romania becoming members in 2007. This enlargement fundamentally altered the pattern of poverty in the EU, as we shall see, and had significant implications for measuring and monitoring progress in tackling it. A mid-term review of the Lisbon strategy in 2005 included a major assessment of the OMC in the field of social inclusion, and emphasized the need to strengthen interaction with the renewed Lisbon Strategy on growth and jobs and to strengthen the mainstreaming of social inclusion objectives in national economic strategies. Around the same time the Union's objectives in the social inclusion field were reformulated in terms of the overarching aim of making a decisive impact on the eradication of poverty and social exclusion, together with more specific objectives such as ensuring access for all to the resources, rights, and services needed for participation in society, promoting participation in the labour market and fighting poverty and exclusion, and mobilizing

---

[2] For analysis of the OMC and its operation, see, for example, Ferrera, Matsaganis, and Sacchi (2002); Frazer, Marlier, and Nicaise (2010); Ferrera (2010); and Vanhercke (2010).

all stakeholders and relevant actors and mainstreaming social inclusion goals into national policy-making.[3]

The OMC has been expanded over time to cover not just social inclusion but also pensions and health care and long-term care, as well as the exchange of information in the field of what is termed 'making work pay'—that is, seeking to ensure that there is a significant financial incentive to work rather than remain unemployed on benefits. In 2006 these different areas were streamlined into one integrated 'Social OMC' built around 12 commonly agreed EU objectives, three for each main strand as well as three 'overarching' objectives addressing issues that cut across them.[4] Member states now prepare National Strategy Reports on Social Protection and Social Inclusion (incorporating their national action plans on poverty and social inclusion) in a regular cycle, aligned with the revised Lisbon process on jobs and growth, and the joint analysis of these by the Commission and the member states has been presented in the *Joint Reports on Social Protection and Social Inclusion*.

The Social OMC is essentially a 'soft' process, in the sense that it is based on voluntary cooperation without externally imposed frameworks or sanctions, with responsibility for developing and implementing policies remaining with the member states, and with much of the emphasis on information exchange and mutual learning. Agreed indicators play a vital role in that context, and we will discuss their evolution in detail in the next section. The process as a whole has been seen as productive in keeping poverty and social exclusion on the EU agenda, and generating useful learning, but the onset of the economic crisis has highlighted the need to strengthen linkages between social goals and processes and the Union's growth and jobs agenda. The European Commission's own assessment of the OMC was that while it can be used as a source of peer pressure and a forum for sharing good practice, most member states have used it as a reporting device rather than for policy development (European Commission, 2010).[5]

This limited success in relation to social inclusion processes and impact makes all the more striking the importance assigned to social inclusion in the *Europe 2020 Strategy for Growth and Jobs*, which set out the Union's response to the limited progress made in reaching the goals set out in Lisbon ten years earlier and to the challenges posed by the financial and economic crisis from late 2007. Crucially, this strategy includes among its five headline targets a concrete target for the reduction of poverty. In framing that target relative income poverty and material deprivation are taken into account,

---

[3] See Social Protection Committee and Economic Policy Committee (2006).
[4] For the 12 EU objectives for the streamlined Social OMC adopted by the EU in March 2006 see: http://ec.europa.eu/employment_social/spsi/docs/social_inclusion/2006/objectives_en.pdf
[5] See also Frazer, Marlier, and Nicaise (2010) for a discussion of the strengths and weaknesses of the process and proposals for enhancing its effectiveness.

together with household joblessness. This is clearly of critical importance for this book, where our focus is on the ways in which non-monetary indicators can be used to capture and understand poverty, and we describe the way this poverty target is framed in Section 3.6 and come back to the implications at various points subsequently, most centrally in our final chapter. First, though, it is necessary to discuss the development of the EU's set of agreed social indicators and the incorporation of indicators based on non-monetary deprivation measures into that set.

3.4 Commonly Agreed Social Inclusion Indicators

The fact that the EU set out common objectives in the area of social inclusion in 2000 had far-reaching implications for its measurement and monitoring of poverty and social exclusion. The task of developing a set of indicators to enable the member states and the Commission to monitor progress towards these common objectives was assigned to the SPC, which set up a technical Indicators Sub-Group (ISG) to assist it. As a contribution to this exercise being carried out during its Presidency of the EU, the Belgian Government sponsored a study, subsequently published as Atkinson, Cantillon, Marlier, and Nolan (2002). This emphasized that the portfolio of indicators should command general support as a balanced representation of Europe's social concerns, and that they should focus on social outcomes rather than the means by which they are achieved—which cohered with the principle of subsidiarity, with member states left free to choose the methods by which the common objectives are realized. It recommended that individual indicators should have a clear accepted normative interpretation, be robust and statistically validated, be measurable in a sufficiently comparable way across EU countries, be timely and susceptible to revision, and be responsive to policy interventions but not subject to manipulation. In addition, the portfolio should be balanced across the different dimensions, mutually consistent, and as transparent and accessible as possible to the citizens of the European Union. It went on to examine the various domains that one would wish to cover and made concrete proposals for indicators in the light of the data then available, as well as pointing towards areas where information deficits most urgently needed to be addressed.

Drawing on this study, the SPC's 'Report on indicators in the field of poverty and social exclusion' (2001) laid out methodological principles and recommended a set of 18 common indicators, subsequently endorsed by the December 2001 European Council held in Laeken.[6] These comprised 10 Primary

---

[6] On the process that led to this agreement, see *inter alia*, *Politica Economica* (2002), Marlier (2003), and Atkinson, Marlier, and Nolan (2004).

indicators to cover the most important elements leading to social exclusion, together with 8 Secondary indicators supporting them and covering other dimensions. The agreed social indicators have evolved significantly since then but continue to be referred to as the Laeken indicators, a practice we will follow. The original list of indicators is described and discussed in detail elsewhere (see Atkinson et al., 2002; Marlier et al., 2007), but here it is worth emphasizing first that they relied heavily on information about income and labour force status where comparative data were already relatively well developed, with indicators based on relative income poverty thresholds playing a particularly important role.

The percentage falling below a relative income threshold set at 60% of median equivalized income in the country in question was the first indicator in the original Primary set. The labelling of this indicator is noteworthy: rather than poverty, it is described as capturing those 'at risk of being poor'. This reflects an acceptance that low income on its own may not always be a reliable indicator of poverty and social exclusion—based partly on the research then available on the relationship between poverty and deprivation that we described in Chapter 2. (This logic underpinned the use of the 'risk of poverty' term in Atkinson, Cantillon, Marlier, and Nolan, 2002, and is also clearly articulated in the foreword by Frank Vandenbroucke, then Minister for Social Affairs and Pensions in Belgium, who initiated the study.) Partly for this reason, it was complemented by indicators reflecting how far people fell below the threshold, the numbers falling below it for a significant period of time, and the numbers falling below alternative thresholds set at 40, 50, and 70% of median income. Two measures of income inequality—the ratio of the income share going to the top versus the bottom quintile and the Gini coefficient—were also included. However, it was stressed in the study by Atkinson et al. and the SPC's 2001 Report that the portfolio of indicators should be comprehensive and cover all key dimensions of the common objectives, be balanced across the different dimensions, and enable a synthetic and transparent assessment of a country's situation in relation to the common objectives, and should thus not be restricted to income-based measures but should also cover other important dimensions. Thus, indicators relating to employment, education, and health were also included, although particularly in the area of health data availability seriously constrained the capacity to produce indicators directly related to poverty and exclusion.

Since that original set was adopted in 2001 the EU's social inclusion indicators have been refined and extended in various ways. When the various elements of the EU's social processes were being streamlined in 2006 into one integrated 'Social OMC', a comprehensive review and reorganization of indicators produced a new monitoring framework, with a set of indicators for each of social inclusion, pensions, and health as well as an 'overarching' set

Table 3.1. EU Social Inclusion Process Primary Indicators

At-risk-of-poverty rate (below threshold set at 60% of the national equivalized median income)
At-risk-of-poverty threshold
Persistent at-risk-of-poverty rate
At-risk-of-poverty gap
Long-term unemployment rate
People living in jobless households
Early school leavers not in education or training
Employment gap of immigrants
Material deprivation rate
Housing (to be developed)
Self-reported unmet need for medical care
Utilization of medical care services
Child well being (to be developed)

Table 3.2. EU Social Inclusion Process Secondary Indicators

At-risk-of-poverty rate by gender and age groups
At-risk-of-poverty rate by household type
At-risk-of-poverty rate by work intensity of household
At-risk-of-poverty rate by most frequent activity status
At-risk-of-poverty rate by accommodation tenure status
At-risk-of-poverty rate with thresholds at 40, 50, and 70% of national equivalized median income
Persons with low educational attainment
Low reading literacy performance of pupils
Depth of material deprivation
Persons in households with heavy housing costs burden (by gender, age group, poverty status, income quintile, tenure status, degree of urbanization, and household type)
Persons in overcrowded households (by gender, age group, poverty status)

and a set of 'context' indicators.[7] Some more specific changes have also been introduced subsequently, so that at time of writing the social inclusion portfolio now comprises the Primary Indicators, Secondary Indicators, and Context Information statistics shown in Tables 3.1, 3.2, and 3.3, respectively. We see that the Primary indicators now encompass income poverty risk, unemployment and joblessness, low educational qualifications, the employment situation of migrants, access to healthcare, and—most significantly for our focus here—material deprivation, together with indicators relating to housing and child well being that are currently being developed. The Secondary indicators include poverty risk by different breakdowns and with alternative thresholds, low educational attainment and reading literacy, the depth of material deprivation, and housing costs and overcrowding. The Context Information statistics include income inequality, regional unemployment,

---

[7] See Indicators Sub-Group (2006).

Table 3.3. EU Social Inclusion Process Context Indicators

Inequality of income distribution—Income quintile share ratio
Inequality of income distribution—Gini coefficient
Dispersion of regional employment rates
Healthy life expectancy and life expectancy at birth and at 65
At-risk-of-poverty rate anchored at a moment in time
At-risk-of-poverty rate before social transfers (other than pensions)
Persons living in jobless households by main household types
In-work poverty risk
Unemployment trap, inactivity trap, low-wage trap
Net income of social assistance recipients as a % of the at-risk-of-poverty
    threshold for 3 jobless household types
Self-reported limitations in daily activities by income quintiles, sex, and age
Housing deprivation by item
Housing deprivation by number of items by gender and age group
Housing costs share (median share of housing costs in total disposable income) by
    gender, age group, poverty status, and degree of urbanization

life expectancy, poverty risk using a threshold anchored in real terms, in-work poverty risk, poverty risk before social transfers, jobless households, indicators of the severity of unemployment and poverty 'traps', adequacy of social assistance, life expectancy, and housing deprivation and housing costs.

This description of the social inclusion indicators now in use at EU level is completed by reference to the separate but related set of 18 core overarching indicators and 10 context indicators used to monitor progress vis-à-vis overarching objectives of social cohesion, interaction with the objectives of Lisbon and Sustainable Development Strategies, and good governance. The majority of these are drawn from the indicators listed above, combined with measures such as projected social expenditure, health expenditure per capita, the labour market activity rate, public debt as a percentage of GDP, and the old age dependency ratio, current and projected.[8]

We see that non-monetary deprivation indicators, on which this book is focused, now feature in the common EU portfolio of social inclusion indicators in a number of different forms: in the material deprivation indicator including among the Primary set, the depth of deprivation indicator included in the Secondary set, and in two housing-related deprivation indicators included in the Context set. These were incorporated into the agreed indicators only in 2009 after considerable analysis and debate, and we bring out the issues at stake, to which we will be returning throughout the book, in the next section.

---

[8] See http://epp.eurostat.ec.europa.eu/portal/page/portal/employment_social_policy_equality/omc_social_inclusion_and_social_protection/overarching

3.5 Incorporating Material Deprivation into the Social Inclusion Indicators

At the time the adoption of agreed social inclusion indicators was being considered, as well as national research some comparative studies of poverty and social exclusion in the EU using non-monetary indicators were already available, based on data from the ECHP. As described in some detail in Chapter 2, this included our own research, studies by Muffels, Tsakloglou, and others, and Eurostat's first *European Social Statistics: Income, Poverty and Social Exclusion* (2000). In considering the role that deprivation indicators might play in the monitoring of social inclusion in the EU, Atkinson et al. (2002) were able to draw on that research. They emphasized that while the use of non-monetary indicators to study poverty and exclusion in an individual country involved difficult choices in how best to select and employ such items, even more complex issues must be faced when using them in a comparative context. In general terms, they set out some options for how deprivation indicators could be used in a comparative EU context:

- One could take a common set of what are considered key indicators, look at deprivation levels in terms of these indicators across each of the member states, and see how those levels change over time;
- One could take a common set of indicators across all the member states, but employ them in a way that takes average levels of living in the country in question into account, for example by constructing a summary deprivation index in which each item is weighted by the percentage not deprived of the item in the country in question;
- One could try to use indicators specific to the country in question, but designed to capture the same underlying condition of exclusion due to lack of resources;
- One could combine deprivation indicators with income to identify those both falling below relative income thresholds and reporting enforced lack of a common set of items, held fixed over time; and
- One could alternatively combine relative income thresholds with a set of items using weights that vary across countries and over time.

Atkinson et al. emphasized that the best approach to adopt depends on the object of the exercise, on precisely what it is intended to capture—which, as we shall see, continues to be both critical and under-examined in considering how deprivation across the EU is to be measured. Their conclusion at that point was that non-monetary indicators could serve in country-specific efforts to identify those experiencing exclusion due to lack of resources, and in a comparative context to bring out differences across countries in living standards on average or for those falling below relative income lines; there was, however, no simple generally accepted approach to using such indicators—either on their own or together with income—to measure relative poverty in different countries in the same way. They therefore recommended that non-monetary indicators of deprivation should, where possible, be included by member states in their own analysis, and that a significant investment should be made in developing these indicators in a comparative context for use in the EU monitoring process.

The SPC in its 2001 Report underpinning the original set of indicators recommended examining *inter alia* the possibility of developing additional commonly agreed indicators in a number of areas including 'living conditions'. Eurostat thus pursued the topic using data from the ECHP, notably Eurostat (2003), which (as we saw in Chapter 2) compared deprivation levels across countries using the same items without any weighting, and contrasted this with assigning greater weight to being deprived of an item or activity that most people in one's country have. The expansion of the EU from 2004 added significant impetus to the analysis of non-monetary indicators and consideration of their potential role in the Social Inclusion Process. Differences in average income per head from richest to poorest member states were now very much wider than before, so that relative poverty thresholds in the more affluent member states were above average income in the poorest member states, while those below the threshold and thus 'at risk of poverty' in some rich countries have higher standards of living than the well-off in some of the poorer ones. This helped to motivate interest in the potential of non-monetary indicators as a complement to purely relative income-based poverty measures (see, for instance, Guio and Marlier, 2004).

The Indicators Sub-Group of the SPC was charged with pushing forward this line of investigation, and the possibility of using non-monetary deprivation indicators to produce one or more common indicator for use at EU level was the subject of extensive discussions in the ISG around this time (see, in particular, ISG, 2005 and 2006). It is worth noting the rationale which its secretariat advanced in 2004 for pursuing ways in which indicators of material deprivation could usefully complement the relative poverty measures in the list of indicators of poverty and social exclusion:

- Questions are raised concerning the ability of the existing Laeken portfolio of indicators to fully reflect the situation in new member states and candidate countries, as well as differences between them and the 'old' member states. When comparing national situations in an enlarged Union, the performance in terms of exposure to monetary poverty risk is very similar between old and new member states but living standards are very different.

- Lack of essential durables or difficulties in payments were seen as a good proxy of persistent poverty, since they reflect absence of sufficient (permanent) resources rather than of adequate current income.

- Some of the items of material deprivation proposed by Eurostat capture aspects of poverty that are not well covered in the definition of relative poverty measures based on current income, notably poor housing.

- It is not always possible to measure income with accuracy, notably for certain groups of the population like the self-employed. In this case, the joint analysis of relative income poverty measures and material deprivation indicators is particularly useful.

So in essence the rationales advanced related to limitations of current income per se—in terms of reliability in measurement, change over time, and difficulty in capturing certain dimensions of poverty—but also to the relative nature of the at-risk-of-income-poverty indicators in a context where living standards now vary widely across the member states.

By this point data were beginning to emerge from EU-SILC, and the non-monetary indicators available from that source were investigated in studies such as our own (Whelan and Maître, 2005a, b; Nolan and Whelan, 2007), as well as by Guio (2005), Guio and Museux (2006), and Guio and Engsted-Maquet (2007) in association with Eurostat with a particular eye to the use of deprivation indicators in the EU's Social Inclusion Process. Guio's results pointed to the grouping of 11 deprivation items in EU-SILC into three dimensions, termed 'economic strain', enforced lack of durables, and housing; a combination of the first two dimensions was also analysed. (In Chapter 5 below we look in detail at these studies and their analysis of the grouping of deprivation items, but at this point we focus on their role in the development of the non-monetary indicators for the EU's social inclusion set.) The proportion affected by deprivation in each dimension was compared across countries, as was the proportion over a threshold, and this was compared with the cross-country pattern in terms of relative income poverty risk. While this was based on simply counting deprivation in the same way from one country to the next, the difference made by weighting each deprivation item by the proportion possessing it in the country was considered, and the proportion facing both relative income poverty and deprivation—in 'consistent poverty', as it was originally labelled in our own studies—was also examined.

Marlier, Atkinson, Cantillon, and Nolan (2007), based on a report originally produced in 2005, also considered the potential value of non-monetary indicators in the social inclusion set in some depth. Reasons for their inclusion were that they can supplement information about income, which is subject to mis-measurement and may not always be a reliable guide to 'permanent

47

income'; and that they can help to capture the multidimensional nature of poverty and social exclusion. While combining deprivation with low income to measure 'consistent poverty' was seen as potentially fruitful, the main focus was on the role non-monetary indicators can play as a complement to other social inclusion indicators, in particular in capturing differences in absolute levels of deprivation and in tracking change over time, and on alternative ways of employing them for that purpose. The most straightforward approach was seen to be taking a set of suitable non-monetary items, look at deprivation levels in terms of these items and a summary index across each of the member states, and see how those levels change over time. Such an 'absolute' approach, applying the same standard to countries with very different levels of income and living standards, was not regarded as suitable as the only, or even the main, measure of poverty and social exclusion, but as one in a set it was seen as having a real added value. It could be complemented in time by more relative approaches weighting items by the percentage not deprived of it in the country in question, perhaps with the set of items varying, but the introduction of the more straightforward indicator first seemed the best way to make progress. It was suggested that an index combining Guio's first two dimensions (economic strain and durables) could be the central focus in capturing deprivation broadly conceived, while a separate indicator would focus specifically on housing conditions. Each of these indicators would reflect both current differences across countries and trends over time in living standards.

In 2006 a task force was set up drawn from the ISG and Eurostat's 'Income and Living Conditions Statistics working group' to propose indicators for material deprivation and housing, based on the items currently available in EU-SILC.[9] Obtaining agreement on appropriate indicators and how best to use them took several years. As the ISG, assisted by the task force, moved towards concrete recommendations, it also drew on the analysis of data from EU-SILC 2006 for 26 countries in the study it commissioned from Guio (2009) reviewing the range of issues to be addressed and choices made, as well as the results of a Eurobarometer survey carried out in 2007 exploring which non-monetary items citizens in the different member states consider to be necessary for people to have an 'acceptable' standard of living in the country where they live. Guio, Fusco, and Marlier (2009) brought these together to discuss a similar range of issues and compare material deprivation and income-based poverty measures. In February 2009 the ISG recommended that two new indicators of material deprivation be included in the social inclusion portfolio, the 'material deprivation rate' as a primary indicator and the 'depth of deprivation' as a secondary indicator. The former is measured as the percentage of

---

[9] One of the present authors (Nolan) assisted in the work of this task force.

the population living in households that could not afford at least 3 of the following 9 items:

- To face unexpected expenses;
- One week's annual holiday away from home;
- To pay for arrears (mortgage or rent, utility bills, or hire purchase instalments);
- A meal with meat, chicken, or fish every second day;
- To keep home adequately warm;
- A washing machine;
- A colour TV;
- A telephone;
- A personal car.

The depth of deprivation indicator is constructed as the average number of these items lacked by those reporting some deprivation.

In relation to housing, the ISG decided that further consideration and improvement in the data available was needed before a primary indicator in that area could be recommended, but two new secondary indicators were agreed, relating to households overburdened by housing costs and to over-crowding. Two further housing-related indicators were agreed for inclusion in the 'context information' element of the social inclusion indicator set, namely the mean share of housing costs in total disposable household income and the percentage deprived of each of four housing deprivation items from EU-SILC:

- Leaking roof, damp walls/floors/foundation, or rot in window frames or floor;
- Lack of bath or shower in the dwelling;
- Lack of indoor flushing toilet for sole use of the household; and
- Dwelling too dark, not enough light.

These recommendations were adopted and each of these indicators was included in the revised description set out in EU Commission (2009) of the full suite of indicators for social protection and social inclusion, including the set of overarching indicators and those relating to social inclusion, pensions, and health care and long-term care.[10]

In both the case of material deprivation and housing, further development of these indicators is planned as further data become available. The list of non-monetary deprivation items included in EU-SILC is itself to be re-considered in the light of the results of a special module on material deprivation included in the 2009 round, testing some 40 items, including 20 relating to children. The

---

[10] See the discussion in Marlier, Cantillon, Nolan, Van den Bosch, and Van Rie (2009).

possibility of building a specific indicator for children based on such items is to be considered. A further Eurobarometer survey is also to be run in 2011/12 on attitudes towards these items. On housing, further analysis of data gathered in a special EU-SILC module in 2008 is intended to help improve the comparability of the data in relation to overcrowding and housing costs in particular.

We will be looking in detail at these EU indicators based on non-monetary deprivation items in subsequent chapters, but it is worth concluding this description of their evolution by highlighting the rationale advanced for adopting them. In relation to housing, this is clearly seen as a distinct dimension of living standards and deprivation, which might not be captured adequately by measures of a household's income or financial resources. This in effect is an argument about multidimensionality (see also Guio and Engsted-Macquet, 2007). In the case of the material deprivation indicator, the justification advanced for their relevance[11] can be seen as having two distinct elements:

- Some of those on low income in terms of the at-risk-of-poverty measure might have significant savings, access to credit, or other sources, whereas the material deprivation measure captures those unable to afford the items it includes;

- Moreover, by measuring deprivation using a threshold and list of items that are common to all member states, material deprivation indicator is more sensitive to differences in living standards across countries than the poverty risk rate with its nationally defined poverty threshold.

The first of these elements, in effect the limitations of current income as a comprehensive measure of financial resources and living standards, is at the core of the rationale advanced in national studies—including our own—for complementing income-based poverty measures with direct measures of inability to afford specific non-monetary items. The second element clearly has relevance only in a comparative context, and relates to (what are seen as) the limitations not of income per se but of purely relative income thresholds in capturing poverty in a context where there are substantial differences in average living standards across the countries covered. It is the desire to address *both* these issues at the same time via the material deprivation indicator that has driven the approach taken, a point to which we will be returning throughout this book.

---

[11] See, for example, on the valuable website created by the University of Antwerp, commissioned by the European Commission's Directorate-General for Employment, Social Affairs and Equal Opportunities, to serve as a 'vademecum' for the agreed social protection and social inclusion indicators: http://www.ua.ac.be/main.aspx?c=.VADEMECUM&n=86535&ct=78951&e=234756

3.6 The 2020 Poverty Target

Once a set of common indicators relating to social inclusion had been adopted by the EU, setting targets framed in terms of some of those indicators—as was the practice in the EU's Employment Strategy—became a possibility and did receive some consideration. The March 2002 Barcelona European Council invited member states to set targets in their National Action Plans for significantly reducing the number of people at risk of poverty and social exclusion by 2010, and the way this might be approached was discussed in the Common Outline for the 2003–5 NAPs/inclusion agreed upon between the SPC and the Commission (Social Protection Committee, 2003). The 2005 report by Marlier et al. (2007) argued for a more intensive use of the indicators in a variety of ways, including in target setting, and the guidelines for the preparation of the 2006–8 National Reports on Strategies for Social Protection and Social Inclusion (Social Protection Committee, 2006) suggested that member states set clear specific quantified targets for the reduction of poverty and social exclusion by 2010. These were to draw as appropriate on the work of the SPC on commonly agreed indicators and on that report, but using national indicators/data when these better reflect aspects of poverty and social exclusion that are a priority for a Member State. In practice, however, only a minority of member states set concrete targets focused on high-level outcome measures in their national plans, and even fewer employed the common indicators—mostly the at-risk-of-poverty rate—for that purpose.

It was therefore a radical departure when a poverty target set at EU level, and framed in terms of common indicators, was put on the Union's agenda at the highest level in 2010, initially by the President of the European Commission, Jose Manuel Barroso. The economic crisis created the impetus for the development of the 'Europe 2020' strategy for jobs and growth, intended to provide a coherent framework to help Europe recover from the crisis and introduce medium- to longer term reforms to boost competitiveness, productivity and growth, but also social cohesion and economic convergence. The European Council formally adopted this Strategy in June 2010, and in doing so set five headline targets constituting shared objectives guiding the action of member states and the Union as regards:

- Promoting employment;
- Improving the conditions for innovation, research, and development;
- Meeting climate change and energy objectives;
- Improving education levels, and
- 'Promoting social inclusion in particular through the reduction of poverty'.

These headline targets are seen as a package, interrelated and mutually reinforcing. The implementation of the targets is supported by a set of integrated guidelines, which will be reported upon annually under a national reform programme.[12]

The target in relation to social inclusion is 'to lift at least 20 million people out of the risk of poverty and exclusion'. This target, and the way in which the population 'at risk' is identified, was developed following a process of discussion and debate between the Commission and member states under the auspices of the SPC (and in particular its Indicators Sub-Group). The original formulation proposed by the Commission when the idea of a poverty reduction target was first mooted in concrete form earlier in 2010 focused on those 'at risk of poverty' as captured simply by the relative income poverty measure, which as we have seen has been prominent among the Social Inclusion Process indicators since they were adopted in Laeken. The figure of 80 million people in the Union 'at risk of poverty' on this basis—that is, falling below an income threshold of 60% of the median in their own country—was widely cited as the headline figure, by the President of the Commission among others, and the target of reducing this by one-fifth was the initial proposal. However, various member states were not happy with a target framed that way, and the formulation eventually agreed is rather different.

The population at risk of poverty and exclusion for the purpose of the target is defined on the basis of three indicators:

- The relative income measure of at-risk-of poverty;
- Material deprivation; and
- Jobless households.

Focusing on the specifics of how each of these elements is measured, the at-risk-of-poverty measure is persons living with less than 60% of the national median income. Material deprivation is captured by the nine items included in the common material deprivation indicator adopted in 2009 (and described in detail in the previous section), but importantly with a higher threshold: whereas the common indicator employs a threshold of 3 to distinguish those to be counted as deprived, this element in the target counts only those reporting at least 4 out of 9 as deprived. The element relating to household joblessness is based on the pre-existing common indicator of 'work intensity', based on the number of months spent at work over the previous 12-month

---

[12] See European Council (2010). The first four targets can be summarized as raising the working-age employment rate to 75%; raising public and private R&D spending to 3% of GDP; reducing greenhouse gas emissions by 20% compared to 1990 levels, increasing the share of renewables in final energy consumption to 20%, and moving towards a 20% increase in energy efficiency; and reducing school dropout rates to less than 10% and increasing the share of 30–34 year olds having completed tertiary or equivalent education to at least 40%.

period by household members aged 18 to 59 (excluding students); for the purpose of the target a threshold of 20% has been adopted, that is household members were in work for a fifth or less of the available time in aggregate. Neither the selection of this specific threshold nor the increase in the threshold on the material deprivation element from 3 to 4 items has a clearly articulated rationale; they seem to have been designed to produce a total that was acceptable from a political perspective. In the EU as a whole, 17% of the population are at risk of poverty in terms of the 60% of national median threshold, 8% are above that material deprivation threshold, and a similar figure is counted by this low work intensity measure. With some people captured by more than one of the three indicators (as we will examine in depth subsequently), the aggregate EU figure for those 'at risk of poverty and exclusion' is less than the sum of the three indicators, 24.5% of the total population, 120 million people. The agreed target is then to lift at least 20 million of these people out of 'the risk of poverty and exclusion'.

We will return to the way this overall target for the EU has been framed and its implications in subsequent chapters, but in concluding this chapter it is important to stress the precise nature of the political commitment made by the member states in adopting it. Member states are to set national targets to contribute to the achievement of the EU target, but are free to set those targets on the basis of the most appropriate indicators, taking into account their national circumstances and priorities. There will be a dialogue between the Commission and member states as to how the national targets will contribute to the achievement of the EU target, but the targets member states set—in terms of both the indicators on which they are based and how much progress they aim for—remain strictly under national control. There will be a supporting process at EU level, with specific guidelines for reporting on member states' actions to tackle poverty and social exclusion and a mid-term review of the EU headline target, including indicators and improved measurement instruments, to take place in 2015 under the aegis of the SPC. (There is also to be a flagship 'European Platform against Poverty' initiative at EU level, details of which are yet to be finalized.) None the less, the fact that an overall poverty reduction target has now been agreed for the Union is of fundamental importance to any consideration of poverty in Europe, and the way it has been framed serves to highlight the salience of the issues addressed in this book.

4

Income Poverty and Deprivation in an Enlarged Europe

4.1 Introduction

The EU's current set of social inclusion indicators, while still assigning a central role to income-based measures of poverty and exclusion, has gone a considerable distance in complementing them with other types of indicators, including direct measures of deprivation. There have also been significant moves in the same direction in official practice in some individual member states, and in academic research on poverty as we saw in Chapter 2. Why is relying entirely on income increasingly seen as problematic, how do patterns of income poverty and deprivation compare with each other, and what light do these patterns shed on the way poverty should be measured? These are the question addressed in this chapter, with the implications being teased out in the remainder of the book.

The chapter starts by describing the conventional approach to setting and employing income poverty lines framed in relative terms, with average or median income in the country in question as the point of reference. It presents the patterns of poverty this approach produces for the countries of the EU, and discusses their interpretation and robustness. If these measures of poverty are judged to be unsatisfactory, as many believe they are (in ways to be discussed), one option is to continue to rely on income as the measure of living standards but adopt a different approach to setting poverty thresholds. An obvious alternative, for example, is to apply a threshold that is common (in purchasing power terms) across all EU countries. Results on this basis are also presented and discussed.

We then provide an alternative perspective on poverty in Europe by making use of the information on non-monetary indicators of deprivation obtained by the ECHP and EU-SILC. We construct summary deprivation indices employing these indicators, and describe the patterns of deprivation across countries that these display. These can then be contrasted with income-based poverty measures.

We then ask whether it is reliance on income per se, rather than the choice of income poverty thresholds, that needs to be questioned. We put forward evidence that strongly suggests this is indeed the case. This relates first to the relationship between low income and measures of deprivation, which our analysis of comparative European data shows to be much weaker than is commonly assumed. This is supported by our analysis of respondents' subjective assessments of their own circumstances, and by evidence from elsewhere on the relationship between low income and deprivation, subjective evaluations, expenditure, and assets. We discuss why the overlap between low income and deprivation is relatively weak, and tease out the implications.

If income as currently measured does fail to distinguish satisfactorily those experiencing poverty and exclusion, one response is to seek to improve the measure of financial resources employed for that purpose, and we discuss how this is being pursued in academic and official practice. In conclusion, though, we outline the case for also seeking to broaden the information set to be used beyond income to include non-monetary indicators, which can add substantially to our ability to measure, understand, and combat poverty and exclusion.

4.2 Poverty in Europe with Country Relative Income Poverty Lines

Current practice in many academic studies on poverty in European countries, especially those that are comparative in nature, is to use household income as the measure of living standards and well being, and to employ an income poverty threshold derived as a proportion of the average (or median) income in the country in question. The income concept is income after receipt of cash transfers and deduction of income taxes and social insurance contributions. The accounting period used for income can vary with the data source being used: in the ECHP and EU-SILC, on which we rely here, the main measure employed is generally income received in the previous calendar year (not last week or month).[1] The income recipient unit employed is generally the household,[2] so everyone in a particular household is assumed to have the same standard of living, but with persons rather than households being counted

---

[1] In EU-SILC, for Ireland and the UK the accounting period for annual income is the 12 months prior to the date of interview rather than the previous calendar year.

[2] This is defined in the ECHP as comprising 'either one person living alone or a group of persons, not necessarily related, living at the same address with common housekeeping—i.e. sharing a meal on most days or sharing a living or sitting room'.

since it is the proportion of persons in poverty that is the ultimate source of social concern.

Since the living standard associated with a given level of household income depends on how many adults and children are depending on it, household income is adjusted to take differences in size and composition into account, by a process generally referred to as 'equivalizition'. The particular equivalence scale employed in this process can affect the results: here we focus primarily on the one now most commonly used in European comparative poverty measurement—often termed the 'modified OECD scale'—where the first adult in the household is attributed a value of 1, each additional adult is given a value of 0.5, and each child a value of 0.3. In this instance, a couple with 2 children make up 2.1 'equivalent adults', and household income is divided by that number to produce equivalized income. In effect, then, a couple with 2 children is assumed to need 2.1 times the income of a single adult to reach the same living standard.

The remaining, crucial, decision to be made in using income to measure poverty is how to set the income poverty threshold below which people will be taken to be poor. Various different ways of doing so have been developed and employed in research and official practice, as described in Chapter 2, but the most common approach in comparative European research has been to derive income poverty thresholds as a proportion of average or median income in the country in question. While initially the mean of the income distribution was often taken as the point of reference, more recently the median—the mid-point of the distribution—has been more widely employed for this purpose, because the mean is sensitive to fluctuations in incomes towards the very top of the distribution, which may have limited relevance to 'ordinary' living standards. The choice of which proportion of the median to take is essentially arbitrary, with thresholds ranging from 40 up to 70% used on occasion, but 60% of the median is the most commonly used in a European context (although 50% tends to be emphasized in US research and by the OECD). Frequently, given that there is no firm basis for selecting one proportion over the others, results based on several such thresholds are presented so that their sensitivity to the level chosen can be seen.

This is indeed the approach adopted in the relative income poverty measures that play a key role in the EU's social inclusion indicators, as described in Chapter 3. The indicators of 'poverty risk' incorporated into that set cover the percentage of persons below thresholds set at 40, 50, 60, and 70% of median income in the country, but the 'headline' figure included among the Primary indicators is based on the 60% threshold; this is also the basis for the income element of the measure on which the EU's 2020 poverty reduction target is focused.

Table 4.1. Relative Income Poverty Rates, EU Member States, 1996 and 2006

	Relative income poverty vis-à-vis 60% of median (%)	
	1996	2006
Austria	14	12
Belgium	15	15
Cyprus		16
Czech Republic		10
Germany	14	13
Denmark	10	12
Estonia		18
Spain	18	20
Finland	8	13
France	15	13
Greece	21	21
Hungary		12
Ireland	19	18
Iceland		10
Italy	20	20
Lithuania		20
Luxembourg	11	14
Latvia		23
Netherlands	12	10
Norway		11
Poland		19
Portugal	21	18
Sweden		12
Slovenia		12
Slovakia		11
UK	18	19
EU average	16	16

A natural starting-point for our analysis is therefore to examine the pattern of poverty (or 'poverty risk'—the rationale for employing that terminology at EU level having been discussed in Chapter 3) one finds using the percentage falling below 60% of median equivalized income in each country. Table 4.1 shows the estimates from EU-SILC produced by Eurostat on that basis for 2006 for all 27 member countries, together with Iceland and Norway. It also shows the corresponding figures for a decade earlier drawn from the ECHP and covering the 14 (out of 15) EU member states at that time who participated in that data-gathering exercise (Sweden being the exception).

We see that in 2006 poverty measured this way varied from a low of 10% in the Czech Republic, Iceland, and the Netherlands up to a high of 23% in Latvia. Countries towards the low end of the spectrum include all the Scandinavian countries (Denmark, Finland, Iceland, Norway, and Sweden), the Netherlands, France, and Germany, and also some of the eastern European transition economies—the Czech Republic, Hungary, Slovakia, and Slovenia. Countries with poverty rates well above the average, on the other hand, include Ireland and the UK, the southern European countries Spain, Italy, Greece, and Portugal, and from eastern Europe Estonia, Latvia, Lithuania, Poland, and Romania. The 'old' member countries for which corresponding figures are available from Eurostat for 1996 display a reasonably high degree of similarity in their rates between the two years, though the fact that different data sources (ECHP versus EU-SILC) are being used may limit the extent to which trends over time are reliably captured.

The choice of the proportion of median income used in deriving the poverty threshold makes a substantial difference to levels of poverty in each country, as comparison with corresponding figures based on, for example, the 50% of median threshold reveals. In terms of the pattern across countries, however, varying the threshold makes much less difference to which have below-average and which above-average poverty rates (though the precise ranking of particular countries can be affected). Instead, it is a consideration of the variation in average incomes across countries and how that relates to these poverty figures that highlights a significant source of concern about them. This is brought out in Table 4.2, which shows the poverty threshold for a single person household derived as 60% of median equivalized income in 1996 and 2006 in each of the countries covered by ECHP and EU-SILC, respectively, first expressed in common currency terms and then in terms of purchasing power parities (PPPs).

We see that in 1996, the variation in the level of the poverty threshold across EU countries was substantial. With France and the Netherlands being in the middle of the distribution, the poverty threshold in Portugal is less that 40% of their poverty thresholds in common currency terms, while Greece is at 46%. Luxembourg is an outlier at the other end of the spectrum at 170% of the French and Dutch thresholds, with Austria next highest at 125%. When we move to purchasing power parities, which seek to take differences in the cost of living into account, the range of values narrows somewhat because the cost of living is generally lower in the countries with lower average income per head. Still, the 1996 threshold in PPP terms in Portugal is only 56% of the threshold in France and the Netherlands and the Greek threshold is 65%. At the top, the threshold in Luxembourg is over 160% of the thresholds in France and the Netherlands, while that in Austria is 116%.

When we turn to 2006, however, we find a much wider range, much greater variation in the level of the poverty threshold, reflecting corresponding variation in median income across the enlarged EU. This is more pronounced towards the bottom rather than the top of the range: Luxembourg is still an outlier with a threshold about 175% of the thresholds in the middle countries, but Austria is still about 115% of their level, similar to 1996. At the bottom, though, countries such as Latvia, Lithuania, Poland, and Slovakia now have thresholds that are only one-third of the level of the middle countries in PPP

Table 4.2. Median Equivalized Income, EU Member States, 1996 and 2006

	Median equivalized income			
	1996		2006	
	€	PPP	€	PPP
Austria	8,887	7,880	10,713	10,452
Belgium	8,467	7,752	10,328	9,707
Cyprus			8,722	9,817
Czech Republic			2,881	4,956
Germany	8,714	7,601	9,398	9,100
Denmark			13,598	9,688
Estonia			2,183	3,377
Spain	3,748	4,357	6,888	7,560
Finland	7,674	5,916	11,007	8,906
France	7,913	6,703	9,726	8,989
Greece	3,279	4,419	5,910	6,697
Hungary			2,310	3,646
Ireland	4,946	4,825	11,854	9,563
Iceland			17,083	11,141
Italy	4,412	4,660	8,714	8,323
Lithuania			1,520	2,772
Luxembourg	12,099	10,953	17,688	15,851
Latvia			1,520	2,668
Netherlands	7,113	6,763	10,358	9,897
Norway			16,654	11,840
Poland			1,867	3,057
Portugal	2,788	3,808	4,348	5,157
Sweden			10,795	9,068
Slovenia			5,590	7,292
Slovakia			1,988	2,772
UK	6,113	6,868	11,707	10,587

terms. Estonia and Hungary are also relatively low at 37–40%, and even the Czech Republic, a relatively prosperous new EU member, has a threshold of about 56% of the middle countries, similar to Portugal, which was and continues to be the 'old' Member State with the lowest threshold/median.

So the striking difference made by enlargement of the EU in this context is that the countries of eastern Europe joining the Union have much lower average living standards—and that is before one takes into account Bulgaria and Rumania, which are not included here for data reasons but have even lower average incomes. This has cast a searching new light on the way poverty is to be measured in the EU, and how differences in living standards within versus across countries are to be taken into account. It means that many of those above relative income poverty thresholds in these new member states, and thus not counted as 'at risk of poverty', are on lower incomes (including in purchasing power terms) than some of those below the relative income thresholds in the richer 'old' member states, who will be counted as at risk.

By taking median income in the country in question as the sole benchmark in setting or deriving a relative income poverty threshold, differences across countries in the level of that median, reflecting (more or less) differences in living standards, are entirely discounted or ignored.

This can be justified from a conceptual perspective by arguing that the country is indeed the natural unit within which the ability to participate matters and is to be assessed, and that is why much—though not all—comparative research on poverty in Europe has indeed focused on relative income poverty thresholds. In an EU context, though, the limited nature of the Union's competence in social policy and the centrality of subsidiarity has also been important in underpinning the focus of social inclusion on country-specific poverty standards; differences in average living standards across member states have always been recognized as of central importance, but promoting convergence in those living standards is a matter for other (much better resourced) elements of the Union's activities, including broad economic policy as well as the Regional and Social Funds and the Common Agricultural Policy. However, the scale of the differences in living standards across the enlarged Union has made that distinction more difficult to preserve, at least insofar as ignoring cross-country differences in living standards in measuring poverty and social exclusion is concerned. One response, as we explore in the next section, is to continue to rely entirely on income but reframe the threshold against which poverty is measured so that the same level is used across countries, irrespective of the income level of that country.

4.3 Poverty in Europe with a Common Income Poverty Line

The application of a common income threshold across EU countries in measuring poverty has been investigated in various studies, notably Brandolini (2007) and Kangas and Ritakallio (2007). Kangas and Ritakallio employed data from the Luxembourg Income Study for 13 'old' EU member states, whereas Brandolini combined data from the ECHP for 'old' member states with data from the Luxembourg Income Study for some new EU countries. Since then this approach has been applied with data from EU-SILC, most recently in the study *European Inequalities* edited by Ward, Lelkes, Sutherland, and Toth (2009). In deriving such a threshold the same issues arise as must be faced in a national context, and given the arbitrariness of any specific choice an obvious route is to once again derive the threshold as a proportion of median income, say 60%, but now use median income across the EU as a whole rather than for the country in question. To take differences in purchasing power across countries into account, rather than simply converting incomes into a

Table 4.3. Relative Income Poverty Rates with a Common EU Income Threshold, 1996 and 2006

	Relative income poverty vis-à-vis 60% of EU median (%)	
	1996	2006
Austria	5.9	4.7
Belgium	7.1	8.2
Cyprus		8.5
Czech Republic		40.3
Germany	6.1	9.7
Denmark	3.1	5.9
Estonia		65.3
Spain	35.1	22.4
Finland	7.2	7.9
France	9.7	8.9
Greece	42.2	27.6
Hungary		66.6
Ireland	23.1	9.8
Iceland		3.4
Italy	24.7	18.3
Lithuania		76.6
Luxembourg	1.1	1.2
Latvia		75.5
Netherlands	9.3	4.8
Norway		3.5
Poland		73.5
Portugal	47.2	46.5
Sweden		9.2
Slovenia		14.7
Slovakia		69.7
UK	12.5	9.8
EU average	20.3	21.5

common currency using prevailing exchange rates such a common threshold should be expressed in PPP terms.[3]

This is what we do in deriving the poverty rates presented in Table 4.3 for the 14 countries covered by the ECHP in 1996 and the 26 countries in EU-SILC in 2006, using thresholds derived as 60% of median income across the EU in PPP terms. We see that—unsurprisingly—there is a much wider span of rates than with the national poverty thresholds employed in Table 4.1. Looking first at the narrower set of countries in 1996, the range with national thresholds was from 8–10% in Finland and Denmark to 21% in Portugal and Greece; now, the lowest rates are 1% in Luxembourg and 3% in Denmark, while the highest are 42% in Greece and 47% in Portugal. When we turn to 2006 and the broader set of 26 countries the contrast is even greater: the range with national thresholds was no wider than for the 14 countries, but with the

---

[3] The use of PPPs is far from problematic, as brought out in, for example, Brandolini (2007), with a variety of methods and sources; here we simply rely on the PPPs produced by Eurostat.

common European line the lowest rate is again 1% in Luxembourg but in the countries at the other end of the spectrum—Latvia, Lithuania, Poland, and Slovakia—70% or more of their population is below the threshold.

The overall extent of poverty produced by this approach is somewhat greater than national relative income lines, at about 21% compared with 16–17% of the overall EU-SILC sample. However, the more substantial and potentially significant difference is in the distribution of the people in question across countries. About half of all persons falling below the common threshold are in countries of the 'old' EU-15, because these include countries with very large populations. However, 28% of those below the common threshold live in Poland, and many of the other new member states have a much greater proportion of the total when a common threshold is applied rather than country-specific ones.

4.4 Levels of Deprivation in Europe

We now want to set these competing income-based pictures of poverty in Europe against the pattern of deprivation one sees based on non-monetary indicators. While one could look at the individual non-monetary indicators available for this purpose, an overview can be obtained by combining them in some way. The simplest approach to doing so is to construct a single summary deprivation index using all the available items, simply adding up the number of items on which each person or household reports being deprived. So we assign a value of 1 for each item where the household reports enforced deprivation and zero where it does not, and aggregate those scores into the overall deprivation measure or index. We now construct and analyse such a summary deprivation index using the range of indicators available to us from the ECHP and then EU-SILC.

For the ECHP we use the 24 items described in Chapter 2 and listed in Table 2.1.[4] Table 4.4 shows mean deprivation scores on this summary index for the 14 EU members that participated in the ECHP in 1996.[5] We see that the mean deprivation score ranges from 2 or below for countries like Denmark, the Netherlands, and Luxembourg up to nearly 7 for Portugal and Greece. While there is a strong relationship between average income per head in PPP terms—also shown in the table—and the average deprivation level, there are

---

[4] Where the format of the question sought to identify where respondents were doing without the item due to lack of money/because they could not afford it rather than because they did not want it, as discussed in Chapter 2, only those cases are counted as deprivation in constructing these indices.

[5] Not all these countries participated in 1994 and 1995, so this represents the first observation for the maximum number of countries; Sweden did not participate in the ECHP.

Table 4.4. Mean Deprivation Score (24-Item Summary Index) and Mean Income, ECHP 1996

	Mean deprivation score	Mean equivalized income (ppp)
Austria	2.27	14,178
Belgium	2.28	14,384
Germany	2.14	14,675
Denmark	1.62	14,220
Spain	4.37	9,191
Finland	3.00	11,337
France	2.66	13,388
Greece	6.81	8,300
Ireland	2.52	11,695
Italy	3.45	10,490
Luxembourg	1.54	22,337
Netherlands	1.96	12,910
Portugal	6.85	7,798
UK	2.56	13,659
EU average	3.41	10,873

some differences in the rankings these produce. For example, Denmark has similar mean income but lower deprivation scores than Belgium, France, or Germany. Greece and Portugal have the lowest average income levels of the EU-15, but the gap between them and the other 'old' member states in terms of deprivation level is very much greater.

It is then particularly interesting to look at similar results from EU-SILC, which as noted in Chapter 2 contains a narrower set of non-monetary indicators, but covers the enlarged EU (plus Iceland and Norway), with a much wider span across countries in terms of average income per capita. From that source we construct a summary index using the 17 items listed in Table 2.2. Table 4.5 shows mean levels on that summary deprivation index, and we see that there is indeed now considerably more variation in mean deprivation levels. The range within the 'old' EU-15 is now from 1.3–1.5 in the case of Denmark, the Netherlands, and Luxembourg up to 2.5–2.8 in Greece and Portugal, but in Latvia it reaches 4.7. Again this partly reflects differences in average income, but the gap in deprivation levels between, for example, Latvia and Lithuania is wider than that in average income.

So non-monetary indicators, used in this fairly straightforward way, allow for a comparison of the extent of deprivation across countries that gives a very different picture to the 'at-risk-of-poverty' rates based on relative income poverty lines that are widely used in comparative poverty research in Europe. They also add to what we learn from comparisons of average income levels across countries: it is the combination of differences in average income levels and how those are distributed within countries that underpins variations in deprivation.

Table 4.5. Mean Deprivation Scores (17-Item Summary Index) and Mean Income, EU-SILC 2006

	Mean deprivation score	Mean equivalized income (PPP)
Austria	1.43	19,269
Belgium	1.82	17,962
Cyprus	2.90	18,840
Czech Republic	2.23	10,142
Germany	1.94	16,470
Denmark	1.31	17,156
Estonia	2.95	7,753
Spain	1.89	14,518
Finland	1.55	16,667
France	1.78	17,309
Greece	2.50	13,919
Hungary	3.20	7,975
Ireland	1.63	18,915
Iceland	1.21	21,169
Italy	2.02	15,937
Lithuania	3.95	6,419
Luxembourg	1.14	30,498
Latvia	4.70	6,576
Netherlands	1.51	18,812
Norway	0.96	22,357
Poland	3.72	6,817
Portugal	2.77	11,156
Sweden	0.97	15,893
Slovenia	2.10	13,735
Slovakia	2.90	7,686
UK	1.65	20,343
EU average	2.04	15,540

While these deprivation indices are constructed by simply adding up the number of items on which someone is deprived, in an identical way across indicators and countries, more complex approaches to such indices are also common. These, employed in various national and comparative studies mentioned in Chapters 2 and 3, involve most importantly introducing variation across indicators and countries in the weight accorded to doing without different items, rather than counting all items as equivalent to one another. It can be argued that doing without an item or activity that almost everyone has represents a more extreme form of deprivation than doing without something a significant minority does not have. The most widely used approach to taking this into account is to use the prevalence of the item as the basis for a varying set of weights, so the individual's or household's score on the deprivation index is now not simply the sum of the number of items on which they report enforced deprivation, but the sum of that item count with each multiplied by the proportion 'not deprived'.

We can illustrate the impact of using weights that vary across deprivation items first by taking the EU as a whole as the point of reference and using the proportion 'not deprived' across the entire Union as the basis for these

Table 4.6. Mean Deprivation Scores on 24-Item Summary Index without and with Item Prevalence Weighting, ECHP 1996

	Mean deprivation score		
	Items weighted equally	Items weighted by prevalence in EU	Items weighted by prevalence in country
Austria	2.27	1.75	1.85
Belgium	2.28	1.80	1.92
Germany	2.14	1.70	1.81
Denmark	1.62	1.28	1.44
Spain	4.37	3.40	2.94
Finland	3.00	2.32	2.29
France	2.66	2.08	2.16
Greece	6.81	5.48	3.42
Ireland	2.52	2.02	2.11
Italy	3.45	2.63	2.45
Luxembourg	1.54	1.21	1.37
Netherlands	1.96	1.55	1.65
Portugal	6.85	4.75	4.09
UK	2.56	2.00	2.07
EU average	3.41	2.69	2.39

weights. This still assumes that a common standard is appropriate across countries, but that items should be differentially treated in constructing/applying this standard. These results can then be usefully contrasted with those produced by looking at deprivation in relative terms and using the country as the frame of reference. Prevalence weights are again employed, but it is the proportion 'not deprived' in the country in question rather than the EU as a whole that matters: this means that, now, more weight is given to having to do without something in a country where almost everyone has it than doing without the same item in a country where many others cannot afford it. These approaches are illustrated using the 24 deprivation items in the ECHP in Table 4.6, and the 17 items in EU-SILC across the wider set of countries in Table 4.7.

Looking first at the ECHP-based results for the pre-Enlargement EU in Table 4.6, we see that switching from equal weighting of deprivation items to weighting by prevalence in EU reduces average scores on the aggregate deprivation index but has little impact on the extent of variation across countries. In either case, the countries with the highest average deprivation scores (Greece and Portugal) are at about twice the EU average, while the countries with the lowest scores (Denmark and Luxembourg) are below half that average. The impact of switching to country-specific prevalence weighting, though, is to markedly reduce the variation in measured deprivation levels across countries. The highest scores are now about 175% of the average, while the lowest scores are about 60%. Countries with below-average scores rise towards the average while those above it see their scores fall, as being

Table 4.7. Mean Deprivation Scores on 17-Item Summary Index, without and with Item Prevalence Weighting, EU-SILC 2006

	Mean deprivation score		
	Items weighted equally	Items weighted by prevalence in EU	Items weighted by prevalence in country
Austria	1.43	1.12	1.20
Belgium	1.82	1.46	1.51
Cyprus	2.90	2.28	1.92
Czech Republic	2.23	1.76	1.70
Germany	1.94	1.51	1.48
Denmark	1.31	1.04	1.11
Estonia	2.95	2.40	2.09
Spain	1.89	1.47	1.46
Finland	1.55	1.23	1.28
France	1.78	1.39	1.42
Greece	2.50	1.99	1.83
Hungary	3.20	2.55	2.10
Ireland	1.63	1.28	1.31
Iceland	1.21	0.95	1.02
Italy	2.02	1.59	1.57
Lithuania	3.95	3.24	2.52
Luxembourg	1.14	0.90	0.97
Latvia	4.70	3.85	2.81
Netherlands	1.51	1.18	1.22
Norway	0.96	0.75	0.83
Poland	3.72	3.01	2.36
Portugal	2.77	2.25	1.94
Sweden	0.97	0.77	0.87
Slovenia	2.10	1.64	1.58
Slovakia	2.90	2.30	1.89
UK	1.65	1.30	1.34
EU average	2.04	1.61	1.54

deprived of a given item is accorded more weight in countries where deprivation is low/prevalence is high.

A similar pattern can be seen, in a more pronounced form, when we look at the EU-SILC-based results for the post-Enlargement EU in Table 4.7. Switching from equal weighting of deprivation items to weighting by EU prevalence once again reduces average scores on the deprivation index but has little impact on the extent of variation across countries. The country with the highest average deprivation score (Latvia) is now at more than twice the EU average, while the countries with the lowest scores (Iceland and Luxembourg) are at about 55% of that average. Switching to country-specific prevalence weighting reduces this variation so that the highest scores are now about 180% of the average, while the lowest scores are about 62%. While this is happening to the extremes, another illustration of the narrowing of gaps brought about by country-specific prevalence weighting is that a relatively high-deprivation country such as Poland moves from having a mean deprivation score that is 2.6 times higher than that of a relatively low-deprivation country such as Austria to about twice its level.

The use of country-specific weights for deprivation items, rather than a common set of weights, can thus make a considerable difference to the patterns of deprivation across the EU one will find. While we have illustrated this using weights based on prevalence, there are other ways of differentiating between more versus less important items, one being to take views in the population about which items represent 'necessities' as the basis for such varying weights: doing without items more widely seen as necessities can be counted as more serious than being deprived of ones on which there is a less pronounced consensus. This has been the approach adopted in some national studies, and the results of the Eurobarometer 2007 survey on attitudes to a range of items constituting necessities (mentioned in Chapters 2 and 3) could provide a basis for its application in an EU context. However, there are significant conceptual issues involved in relying on such attitudes rather than the underlying realities of what people have and lack. Using the results from the Eurostat survey, for example, items such a television or a telephone would be given rather lower weight on the basis of the proportion stating they are a necessity than the proportion actually possessing them. (See Guio, Marlier, and Fusco, 2009 for a useful comparison of the two approaches applied to EU-SILC data.)

While different approaches to deriving country-specific weights may have some impact on measured deprivation levels, the fundamental choice, and the one making a major difference to the pattern of variation, will be whether to use country-specific or common weights for items in the first place. Whether differential weighting of items across countries is appropriate depends on the question being asked—whether the focus is on 'absolute' differences in living standards versus relative deprivation within countries—and we will bring out the contrast between the two and the complementary value of each at various points throughout this book.

4.5 The Relationship between Low Income and Deprivation

While serious questions can be raised about whether country-specific relative income measures adequately reflect the variation across EU countries in what would generally be regarded as poverty, a more fundamental question can also be asked: do such measures even succeed in distinguishing the worst off within a given country? The evidence has been accumulating for some time that they in fact significantly fail to do so. This relates in particular to what non-monetary indicators of deprivation reveal about the situation of those on low incomes/below relative income thresholds, as well as their own subjective

Table 4.8. Mean Score on 24-Item Summary Deprivation Index by Income Decile across Countries, ECHP 1996

	Bottom	2	3	4	5	6	7	8	9	Top
Germany	4.4	3.7	2.8	2.4	1.9	1.6	1.5	1.1	1.2	0.9
Denmark	2.5	1.9	2.0	1.9	1.7	1.8	1.3	1.2	0.9	0.9
Netherlands	3.9	3.6	2.3	2.0	1.8	1.6	1.3	1.1	1.0	1.0
Belgium	4.0	3.6	2.9	2.5	2.1	1.7	1.6	1.3	1.5	1.2
Luxembourg	3.4	2.4	1.6	1.4	1.4	1.3	1.0	0.7	1.0	1.0
France	5.0	4.2	3.7	2.9	2.6	2.2	1.9	1.6	1.3	1.1
UK	4.2	4.1	3.7	3.4	2.4	2.1	1.7	1.6	1.3	1.1
Ireland	4.7	4.0	3.7	3.2	2.5	1.6	1.7	1.1	0.9	0.8
Italy	5.9	4.9	4.7	3.6	3.3	3.0	2.8	2.2	2.0	1.6
Greece	9.0	8.6	7.8	7.6	7.2	6.6	6.2	5.6	5.0	3.9
Spain	6.8	5.9	5.4	5.1	4.8	4.0	3.5	3.2	2.5	1.7
Portugal	9.9	9.2	8.7	8.3	7.2	6.7	5.8	4.9	3.7	2.4
Austria	3.7	3.5	2.7	2.4	2.1	1.9	1.9	1.5	1.5	1.3
Finland	5.0	3.6	3.6	3.5	3.2	2.8	2.5	2.1	1.9	1.4
Total	5.5	4.9	4.3	3.9	3.4	3.0	2.7	2.3	2.0	1.5

assessments of their financial position. To bring out the strength and nature of this evidence we now look at the relationship between income poverty, deprivation, and subjective assessments across EU countries, using data from the European Community Household Panel Survey and EU-SILC.

To investigate the overall relationship between low income and deprivation within EU countries, we again employ the summary indices using the range of indicators available to us from EU-SILC and the ECHP. We constructed our index from the data in the ECHP using the 24 items it contains, which were listed in Table 2.1, where 1 is added to the index for each item the household lacks or was doing without. EU-SILC contains a narrower set of non-monetary indicators, as noted in Chapter 2, but covers more countries, and from that source we constructed our index using the 17 items listed in Table 2.2. To look at the relationship between scores on these deprivation indices and income, we rank persons by their position in the (equivalized) income distribution in terms of successive one-tenths or deciles—that is, whether the person was in the bottom 10% of the distribution, the next 10%, ... up to the top 10%. Table 4.8 then shows for each country in the ECHP how the average deprivation score varies as we move up the income deciles. Table 4.9 shows the corresponding results for the larger set of countries covered by EU-SILC.

We see in each case that mean deprivation levels generally decline as one moves up the distribution, but often rather modestly across deciles 2–5, and even towards the top some deprivation is being reported;

Table 4.9. Mean Score on 17-Item Deprivation Index by Income Decile across Countries, EU-SILC 2006

	Bottom	2	3	4	5	6	7	8	9	Top
AT	2.8	2.3	1.8	1.5	1.3	1.1	1.1	0.9	0.9	0.7
BE	3.5	3.1	2.4	1.9	1.8	1.5	1.2	1.1	1.0	0.9
CY	4.3	4.1	3.6	3.4	3.0	3.0	2.6	2.1	1.6	1.3
CZ	4.7	3.2	2.8	2.3	2.1	2.0	1.6	1.4	1.2	0.9
DE	3.4	3.0	2.4	1.9	1.8	1.6	1.6	1.5	1.3	1.1
DK	2.6	1.9	1.6	1.7	1.5	1.0	0.9	0.8	0.7	0.5
EE	5.0	4.4	4.0	3.5	3.2	2.9	2.4	1.9	1.5	1.0
ES	2.8	2.5	2.4	2.3	2.0	1.9	1.5	1.5	1.2	1.0
FI	3.0	2.8	2.1	1.8	1.4	1.2	1.1	0.9	0.8	0.6
FR	3.2	2.8	2.4	2.1	1.9	1.6	1.2	1.0	0.9	0.7
GR	4.0	3.6	3.4	3.0	2.7	2.6	2.2	1.5	1.2	0.8
HU	5.6	4.6	4.0	3.6	3.3	2.9	2.6	2.2	1.8	1.4
IE	3.1	2.5	2.2	1.9	1.8	1.4	1.1	0.8	0.8	0.7
IS	2.0	1.7	1.6	1.5	1.2	1.3	1.0	0.9	0.6	0.5
IT	3.6	3.0	2.5	2.1	2.0	1.7	1.6	1.4	1.2	1.1
IT	7.2	5.5	5.1	4.3	4.1	3.9	2.9	2.9	2.1	1.5
LU	2.4	1.8	1.5	1.1	1.0	0.9	1.0	0.6	0.6	0.6
LV	7.4	6.2	5.8	5.5	5.1	4.6	4.0	3.5	2.8	2.1
NL	2.5	2.6	1.9	1.8	1.4	1.3	1.1	0.9	0.9	0.8
NO	1.7	1.5	1.4	1.1	0.9	0.8	0.8	0.7	0.6	0.4
PL	6.1	5.2	4.9	4.4	3.9	3.6	3.1	2.6	2.1	1.4
PT	4.3	3.8	3.5	3.4	2.9	2.8	2.4	1.9	1.5	1.1
SE	1.6	1.6	1.5	1.2	0.9	0.9	0.7	0.6	0.6	0.4
SI	3.7	3.1	2.6	2.4	2.0	1.9	1.7	1.5	1.2	0.9
SK	4.4	3.6	3.3	3.4	3.1	2.8	2.7	2.2	2.0	1.5
UK	2.5	2.4	2.0	1.9	1.7	1.5	1.4	1.2	1.1	0.9
Total	3.5	3.0	2.6	2.3	2.1	1.8	1.6	1.4	1.2	1.0

substantial differences between the richer and poorer countries persist right across the distribution.

For reasons to be discussed in depth in the next chapter, simply aggregating deprivation items into a single index regardless of their inter-relationships may not be the most satisfactory or revealing way to employ them. We will show there that different dimensions of deprivation can usefully be distinguished and captured by the indicators available in the ECHP and EU-SILC. For the purpose of this chapter, though, while the relationship with income is consistently stronger for some indicators and some dimensions than others, as will be demonstrated, even selecting the types of indicators/aspects of deprivation most strongly associated with income the overlap between low income and deprivation is limited.

In the remainder of this chapter we provide a brief descriptive account of the scale of the 'mismatch'. In Chapter 6 we address this issue more systematically and consider not just the different combinations of income poverty and deprivation (low income with high deprivation, low income without high deprivation, etc.) but also the socio-economic factors associated with

Table 4.10. Percentage of Persons below 60% of Median Income Who Are above Corresponding Deprivation Threshold, ECHP

	% above corresponding deprivation threshold
Germany	31.9
Denmark	17.0
Netherlands	39.2
Belgium	33.3
France	39.3
UK	47.2
Ireland	44.3
Italy	42.2
Greece	45.7
Spain	46.1
Portugal	52.2

particular outcomes, and how both comparative and longitudinal perspectives can contribute to our understanding of the underlying processes.

We can illustrate the extent of the mismatch first with figures from the ECHP, now measuring deprivation in terms of a summary index employing a subset of the available items, which is relatively strongly correlated with income. (These are the items that, as we will see in Chapter 5, capture what we term 'basic' and 'secondary' dimensions of deprivation, which are more strongly associated with current income than items related to housing quality or local neighbourhood problems.) As we shall see in Chapter 6, the figures from EU-SILC tell a very similar story. To examine the degree of overlap with deprivation, we distinguish a group in each country that is equal in size to the number below the 60% income poverty threshold in that country, but selected instead as having the highest deprivation score on this sub-index. Table 4.10 then shows how much these two groups overlap: if those below the income poverty threshold were also all among the most deprived (on this index), the figure would be 100%.

We see that the extent of overlap ranges from 17 up to 52%. It tends to be high in the countries with relatively low average income and those with high income poverty rates. It is very low indeed in Denmark, a high-income country with a very low income poverty rate. Treating Denmark as an outlier, the overlap otherwise ranges from about 33 to 50%. So only from one-third to one-half of those identified as poor using the income poverty threshold in a given country would also be distinguished by an equally demanding deprivation threshold as among the most deprived.

The proportion of low-income households not reporting high levels of deprivation is particularly pronounced right at the bottom of the income distribution. Levels of deprivation are often much lower for those in the bottom 2 or 5% than the rest of the bottom decile, for example. However, the mismatch between income and deprivation is by no means confined to such very low-income households: while average derivation levels are often at their highest for the households with incomes between say 40 and 60% of the median, a significant minority of these households still report intermediate or even low levels of deprivation compared with others in the country in question.

While a substantial proportion of the income-poor may not register as highly deprived, it is also the case that a substantial proportion of those reporting high deprivation—compared with others in their country—are often not below conventional relative income poverty thresholds. While many of these are on incomes not far above the poverty thresholds—for example, between 60 and 80% of the median—some are well above. It should be recalled that this is so despite the widespread use of questions about deprivation that seek to focus the respondent's mind on things they must do without because they cannot afford them.

What significance should we attribute to this degree of overlap—and more significantly of non-overlap—between low income and deprivation to be interpreted? A valuable perspective on this key question can be obtained by seeing how each relates to people's subjective evaluations of their own financial situation.

4.6 Low Income, Deprivation, and Subjective Evaluations

Surveys have for some time sought to measure respondents' subjective evaluations of their own situation, including levels of satisfaction with their work, their relationships, their housing, and their life more broadly. The data obtained in this way have underpinned the burgeoning research literature on 'happiness', and how such subjective evaluations relate to objective life circumstances including age, marital status, unemployment, ill-health, and income level. Studies focusing on people's own evaluations of the adequacy of income, and of poverty status, also represent a significant element in poverty research.[6]

A widely used measure of self-assessed economic circumstances or pressures, included in the ECHP and EU-SILC, is derived from responses to the following question: 'Thinking now of your household's total income, from all sources and from all household members, would you say that your household is able to make ends meet?', with respondents offered responses ranging from 'with great difficulty' to 'very easily'. Levels of self-assessed economic strain as measured by this question are generally found to be considerably higher for

---

[6] See Van den Bosch (2001) for an in-depth discussion of subjective assessments of income adequacy.

Table 4.11. Percentage Experiencing Economic Stress among Those Falling below the 60% Median Income Line and above the Corresponding Deprivation Threshold, ECHP 1996

	Below 60% income line	Above corresponding deprivation threshold
Germany	16.4	32.3
Denmark	22.5	55.4
Netherlands	40.8	65.5
Belgium	28.0	47.1
France	42.3	61.0
UK	43.1	61.8
Ireland	53.8	69.6
Italy	44.5	59.6
Greece	78.1	91.5
Spain	62.3	74.5
Portugal	57.0	71.5

those above the deprivation threshold than for those in income poverty. For example, Table 4.11 compares the percentage in the ECHP reporting great or some difficulty among those below the 60% relative income poverty line with those above a deprivation threshold distinguishing the same proportion of the sample (Whelan et al., 2001). In every country levels of self-assessed economic stress are considerably higher for those above the deprivation threshold than for those in income poverty.

4.7 Conclusions and Implications

It is reasonable to conclude, on the basis of both comparative and national studies, that measured income and material deprivation each contain valuable information about the situation of households, reflecting their resources and needs and how these have evolved, with income not an adequate substitute for deprivation or vice versa. This conclusion is underpinned when one looks at how income and deprivation levels relate to people's overall subjective evaluations of their own situation.

If the limitations of income-based poverty measures are recognized, one response is to seek to improve the measure of financial resources employed. This involves, for example, using panel data to capture income over a longer period, trying to measure stocks of assets and liabilities as well as income flows, incorporating non-cash benefits into 'income', and exploring ways of capturing needs associated with, for example, disability into a better needs-adjusted measure of income. These avenues are being pursued in both academic studies and official practice, and are extremely worthwhile, but we would argue that they should be regarded as a complement to rather than a substitute for making use of non-monetary indicators as another source of valuable information about living standards and poverty.

They do not invalidate the case for also seeking to broaden the information set beyond income—both to be able to identify with more confidence the 'truly poor and excluded' and to provide ways of capturing the multidimensional nature of that poverty and exclusion. This can also provide new and more satisfactory ways of dealing with the problems created for conventional purely relative income-based measures by the fact that average living standards now vary so widely across the countries of the expanded EU. This is by no means intended to downplay the importance of financial resources or imply that non-monetary measures are to be preferred. Instead, the argument is that combining monetary and non-monetary indicators with appropriate methods and care adds substantially to our ability to measure, understand, and combat poverty and exclusion. This is the argument we develop in the rest of this book.

5

The Dimensionality of Deprivation in Europe

5.1 Introduction

To use non-monetary indicators in research on poverty in an individual country, a variety of analytical challenges must be faced, both in selecting appropriate indicators and in deciding how best to employ them. These challenges are even more severe when, as here, the central aim is to use these indicators in a comparative cross-country context, where one of the core objectives is to be able to draw meaningful conclusions about the extent and nature of poverty in one country versus another as well as over time. As already noted, reliance on relative income poverty thresholds is even more problematic than it might otherwise be when the countries being examined are at very different average income levels. However, employing non-monetary indicators in such a context also raises additional issues in terms of methods and interpretation. This chapter explores these issues using the deprivation items included in the ECHP and in EU-SILC, focusing in particular on the use of non-monetary indicators to identify and analyse different aspects or dimensions of deprivation.

The chapter first investigates the most satisfactory dimensional structure for the analysis of material derivation—that is, a grouping of items into different sets that reflect distinct aspects of living standards and deprivation, such as the capacity to afford basic requirements, possession of consumer durables, housing conditions, and quality of neighbourhood environment. We assess the levels of reliability associated with the dimensions proposed, and discuss how our dimensional structure and indices relate to those advanced in other EU-level studies on this topic. We then document the variation across countries in terms of the deprivation dimensions identified, taking into account alternative ways of assigning importance or weight to different items. We then examine the relationship between different dimensions of deprivation, income, and social class, arguing that the particular form of deprivation that we label 'consumption deprivation' is most suitable if one is seeking to capture generalized deprivation. Finally, we look at the extent to which different dimensions of deprivation are correlated with each other and how frequently they are to be found together in households experiencing multiple deprivation.

5.2 Distinguishing Dimensions of Deprivation

Non-monetary indicators of life-style and deprivation offer a window into what people have and can do, and what they must do without. From this perspective individual non-monetary indicators are of significant interest in themselves. Knowing, for example, how many and which types of household are unable to heat their house or buy new clothes is of substantive importance. Guio (2009), for example, shows that the number having to do without an annual holiday ranges from 10% in Denmark up to two-thirds or more in Hungary, Latvia, Lithuania, and Poland; the number having to do without a television, by contrast, varied from 0 up to 4% (Annex 4, p. 32). More often, though, such indicators are combined into indices of life-style or deprivation, intended to capture what is believed to be an underlying or latent phenomenon. The individual indicators are not then of value primarily for their own sake, but rather for the contribution they make to capturing that latent variable.

All the available indicators can be combined into overall summary indices of the type used in Chapter 4, and as demonstrated there this has a clear value in comparing levels of deprivation across socio-economic groups or countries. Studies adopting this approach with data from the ECHP include, for example, Eurostat (2002, 2003) and Muffels and Fouarge (2004). In the Eurostat (2003) study, for example, a team including one of the present authors (Whelan) constructed a summary deprivation index from the same 24 ECHP items that we employ here, and looked at variation across countries in that index. However, as that report indicated and as we now go on to argue and demonstrate, these indicators can be more revealing when used to distinguish and analyse different aspects or dimensions of deprivation.

Suppose that the types of deprivation experienced differ systematically across different socio-economic groups—for example, many older people are in bad housing, while younger families are generally in better housing but some are unable to buy new clothes. In those circumstances, despite the fact that an overall index may still be useful for some purposes, simply combining all the indicators into one single index would mask those differences and make it more difficult to understand and tackle these kinds of deprivation. The recognition that poverty and disadvantage manifest themselves in different ways for different people is not new, but is central to the recent thrust towards a multidimensional perspective and multidimensional measures. As

75

we shall see, the nature of this multidimensionality needs careful teasing out, and some dimensions may be of more central interest than others, but the case for seeking to distinguish them in the first place is clear.

Studies investigating how different items relate to each other and cluster into dimensions generally employ the statistical techniques of exploratory or confirmatory factor analysis. The results of national studies applying these to the types of non-monetary indicators employed here show that a better fit statistically is generally obtained when a number of different dimensions are distinguished, rather than treating all the indicators as if they related to a single underlying dimension of deprivation (see, for example, Nolan and Whelan, 1996, for Ireland; Gordon et al., 2000, for Britain; Saunders and Adelman, 2006, for Australia). We now show that this also applies to a comparative study of EU countries, focusing first on the data on non-monetary indicators available from the ECHP, and then turning to the data from EU-SILC with its more limited set of indicators but wider country coverage.

The dimensional structure of the non-monetary indicators in the ECHP was analysed in a number of studies we undertook with colleagues, already referred to in Chapter 2, notably Layte, Maître, Nolan, and Whelan (2001); Whelan, Layte, Maître, and Nolan (2001); Whelan, Layte, and Maître (2002a). The approach adopted there built upon our analysis of dimensionality using data from an earlier survey for Ireland, with a somewhat different but overlapping set of items (see Callan, Nolan, and Whelan, 1993; Nolan and Whelan, 1996). Factor analysis suggested that with the 24 non-monetary items in the ECHP described in Chapter 2, a 5-factor solution provided the best fit statistically, distinguishing the following dimensions:

- Basic life-style deprivation—comprising inability to afford food and clothing, a yearly holiday, replacing worn-out furniture, having friends or family over, keeping the home warm, and avoiding arrears.

- Secondary life-style deprivation—comprising inability to afford items such as a car, a phone, a colour television, a video, a microwave, and a dishwasher.

- Housing facilities—not having a bath or shower, an indoor flushing toilet, and hot and cold running water.

- Housing deterioration—having problems such as a leaking roof, dampness, and rotting in window frames and floors.

- Environmental problems—having problems including noise, pollution, vandalism, and inadequate space and light.

This conclusion is underpinned by a range of statistical findings and tests. Using the factor loadings produced by confirmatory factor analysis, Table 5.1 shows first that individual items generally load strongly onto the dimension in which we have placed them. The loadings on the first dimension range

Table 5.1. Confirmatory Factor Analysis Results (5-Factor Solution), ECHP

Item	Basic	Secondary	Housing facilities	Housing deterioration	Environment
Replacing any worn-out furniture	0.733				
A week's annual holiday away from home	0.733				
Buying new, not second-hand clothes	0.652				
Having friends or family for a meal once a month	0.645				
Keeping home adequately warm	0.635				
Meat, chicken, or fish every second day	0.512				
In arrears on rent, utilities, and HP	0.364				
Microwave oven		0.696			
Dishwasher		0.676			
Video recorder		0.645			
Car		0.497			
Telephone		0.425			
Colour TV		0.367			
Bath or shower			0.853		
Indoor flushing toilet			0.764		
Hot running water			0.729		
Damp home				0.653	
Rot in home				0.570	
Leaking roof				0.578	
Noise from neighbours					0.463
Pollution					0.418
Shortage of space					0.379
Not enough light					0.370
Vandalism					0.322

from 0.5 to 0.7 except for the arrears item, which is below 0.4. On the 'secondary' dimension only a television is below 0.4. On the two housing-related dimensions all the items have loadings above 0.55. Finally, loadings on the environment dimension are relatively low for all five items, in the range 0.3–0.5.

These factor loadings were estimated across the ECHP sample as a whole, but statistical models allowing the dimensions to differ across countries can also be tested, rather than assuming that the same dimensional structure applies across all the countries. Various measures of goodness of statistical fit are conventionally used in this context, and these show a consistent pattern here. For example, the root mean squared error of approximation (RMSEA) based on the analysis of residuals has a value of 0.05, indicating a very good fit, as does the comparative fit index (CFI) with a value of 0.89. Other measures such as the adjusted goodness of fit index, the normal fit index, and the parsimonious goodness of fit index confirm this conclusion. Furthermore, in each case, the model that is 'constrained' to employing a common set of dimensions across all the countries performs as well as one that is not constrained in this way. This is substantively very interesting and important: there is no reason to expect a priori that deprivation indicators would cluster together in the same way in different countries. It is also very convenient analytically, since it means that, in principle, one can employ the same dimensions for all the countries in making cross-country comparisons, although there are some complicating factors that need to be taken into account.

It may be helpful to relate these results on dimensions of deprivation to other studies using the ECHP and also distinguishing different dimensions. These generally focused on variants or combinations of those we have presented, depending on the breadth of coverage of the items they include. For example, Tsakloglou and Papadopoulolos (2002a) looked at what they term the domain of 'necessities of life', similar to our 'basic life-style deprivation', and the domain of living conditions, which combines indicators from across our other four dimensions; they also included the domain of social relations, which we have not included for the reasons explained towards the end of Chapter 2. As well as focusing on an overall summary index, the analysis in Eurostat (2003) distinguished the same five dimensions we have just described, and looked at the way deprivation rates on the relevant sub-indices varied across countries, and between those above and below the 60% of median relative income poverty threshold in each.

As we saw in Chapter 2, EU-SILC at present includes a more limited but still substantial set of non-monetary indicators, mostly drawn from the ECHP. We start once again with the 17 items described earlier and listed in Table 2.2. Factor analysis suggests that this set of indicators allows only three dimensions to be distinguished, as follows:

- Consumption deprivation—being unable to afford a meal with meat, chicken, or fish, heating, a holiday, a car, a PC, and unexpected expenses, and experiencing arrears on rent or utilities.
- Household facilities—not having a bath or shower, an indoor toilet, not being able to afford a telephone, a colour TV, and a washing machine.
- Neighbourhood environment—noise, pollution, crime, and violence.

This allowed 15 of 17 items be allocated: the remaining two—having rooms that are too dark, and having a leaky roof, damp, or rot—did not fit well into any of the dimensions distinguished.

Details of the confirmatory factor analysis underpinning this in terms of factor loadings are shown in Table 5.2. The loadings on the first dimension range from 0.8 to 0.9 for the holidays, inability to cope with unexpected

Table 5.2. Results of Confirmatory Factor Analysis for Deprivation Items, EU-SILC 2006

	Consumption	Household facilities	Neighbourhood environment
Unexpected expenses	0.824		
Meal with meat, chicken, fish (or vegetarian)	0.786		
A car	0.711		
To keep home adequately warm	0.680		
A PC	0.702		
Arrears on mortgage payments, rent, utility bills, hire purchase	0.565		
Bath or shower in dwelling		0.981	
Indoor toilet		0.969	
Telephone		0.840	
Washing machine		0.786	
Colour TV		0.757	
Noise from neighbours or street			0.797
Pollution, grime, or other environmental problems in area			0.817
Crime, violence, or vandalism in area			0.560

expenses, and meal with meat, fish, or chicken items, about 0.7 for inability to keep the home warm and a PC, and the lowest value of about 0.6 for arrears. On the household facilities dimension the bath or shower and indoor toilet items occupy the most prominent position, with loadings of close to 1, while for telephone, washing machine, and TV the coefficients are about 0.8. Finally, on the neighbourhood environment dimension both noise and pollution load at a level close to 0.8 while the crime, violence, or vandalism coefficient is somewhat lower at below 0.6. Once again conventional measures of goodness of fit for this model are satisfactory, with the RMSEA at 0.035 indicating a very good fit, while the CFI at 0.98 implies a good fit, and as with the ECHP the model that employs a common set of dimensions across all the countries performs as well as one not constrained in this way.

Having identified distinct clusters or dimension of deprivation, one can then combine items into scales or indices for each dimension. Standard statistical tests of reliability for the scales provide reassurance about the extent to which the individual items are tapping the same underlying phenomenon, the most widely used being Cronbach's coefficient alpha where values over about 0.5 are generally taken to indicate a reliable measure. For our ECHP-based indices, alpha is very high for the basic dimension with a value of 0.81, high for both the secondary and housing services dimensions at 0.71, and slightly lower for the housing deterioration dimension at 0.63. The lowest value for alpha, of 0.47, is observed for the environmental dimension, suggesting that this scale would benefit from the addition of further relevant items if available (see, for example, Layte, Nolan, and Whelan, 2001). The distinctive nature of these dimensions is made clearer by the analysis of the relationship between income and each measure conducted by Whelan et al. (2001). A number of conclusions emerged that were generalizable across country. The relationship between equivalized household income and the housing and environmental dimensions was generally weak although it is somewhat stronger in Greece and Portugal. It is likely that in most countries life-course locational and policy influences play a greater role for these dimensions than in the case of others.

The impact of income was consistently stronger for the basic and secondary deprivation dimensions than for the others. While the identification of common housing and neighbourhood dimensions across countries allows a number of interesting questions to be asked, such items do not appear suitable for inclusion as part of a measure of generalized deprivation that is hypothesized to arise from a lack of economic resources.

A relatively strong correlation between the basic and secondary deprivation dimensions, and their stronger association with income, suggested that where the primary interest was in the impact of resources-type variables on life-style deprivation and the consequences of such deprivation for subjectively experienced economic stress, rather than poverty per se, combining the basic and secondary dimensions in the ECHP into a summary index comprising 13 items labelled 'current life-style deprivation' was appropriate. This scale has a highly satisfactory alpha value of over 0.80.

For the EU-SILC-based results, these tests (for details see Whelan, Nolan, and Maître, 2008) suggest that the consumption deprivation dimension is particularly reliable, with a value of Cronbach's alpha of 0.74. For the household facilities dimension the reliability level is slightly lower but still satisfactory at 0.66. The neighbourhood environment dimension has a slightly lower overall level of reliability with alpha at 0.56, which is unsurprising given that it is made up of only three items, so once again additional items would be desirable in order to increase the level of reliability for that index.

5.3 Comparison with Deprivation Dimensions in Other Studies

Comparing our findings on the dimensionality of deprivation indicators in EU-SILC with other studies, the most relevant comparison is with Guio (2005, 2009); and Guio and Engsted-Maquet (2007). As noted in Chapters 2 and 3, these have been particularly important in the evolution of the material deprivation and housing indicators in the EU's set of social inclusion indicators. It is thus worth teasing out the similarities and differences between the dimensional structure we employ and theirs in some detail. The first point to make in this respect is that the 3 items in our 'neighbourhood environment' dimension—noise from neighbours; pollution, grime, or other environmental problems; and crime, violence, or vandalism—were included in their preliminary analysis, where the factor analysis again showed that they group together in a separate dimension. They were excluded from their subsequent analysis, together with a PC, for reasons we have already discussed towards the end of Chapter 2. Finally, they retain two items that we end up dropping from our analysis because they did not fit our dimensional structure, namely a leaking roof/damp in walls/floors/foundations, and rot in window frames/floor. So while we allocate 15 items to dimensions and they allocate 13, there are 11 items in common between the two dimensional structures.

Guio and Engsted-Maquet (2007) and Guio (2009) present detailed results of the factor analysis by which they arrive at three dimensions described as follows:

Economic strain. Could not afford:

- A week's annual holiday away from home;
- To avoid arrears (mortgage or rent, utility bills, or hire purchase instalments);
- A meal with meat, chicken, or fish every second day;
- To keep home adequately warm;
- To meet unexpected expenses.

Durables. Enforced lack of a:

- Colour TV;
- Telephone;
- Car;
- Washing machine.

Housing. Dwelling has:

- Leaking roof, damp walls/floors/foundations, or rot in window frames or floor;
- Accommodation too dark;
- No bath or shower in dwelling;
- No indoor flushing toilet for sole use of the household.

Comparing this with the set of dimensions we outlined above, there is a good deal of commonality but also some significant differences. In effect, with the items they retain we distinguish only two dimensions whereas they distinguish three. This reflects the fact that Guio et al. arrive at a distinct 'housing' dimension, which contains items relating to the physical condition of the house and to whether there is a bath and indoor toilet, and is distinct from the household durables dimension containing a TV, telephone, and washing machine as well as a car. By contrast, in our structure the 'household facilities' dimension includes three of the items they include under 'Durables'—TV, telephone, and washing machine—together with a bath and indoor toilet. In addition, our 'consumption deprivation' dimension includes the 4 they include under 'economic strain', together with a PC, which they do not use, and a car, which they have in their 'Durables' dimension.

Guio et al. point out that their first two dimensions are not very sharply differentiated and may be combined 'with little loss of information and some gain in simplicity' into what they term a 'Combined Strain + Durables' dimension. As they note, presenting only two aggregations of items, one based on a set of commodities and activities for which access is linked to the household's financial position and the other depicting housing conditions, has clear advantages in an EU context. This structure can be translated readily into one aggregate indicator capturing material deprivation and another focused on housing—which as we have seen in Chapter 3 is what the ISG decided to do, using these measures. The imperative to have an aggregate housing indicator is understandable from a policy and monitoring perspective. However, the housing dimension is not particularly distinct with the items currently available in EU-SILC. Furthermore, our primary interest here is in constructing the most robust and reliable measure of generalized deprivation possible with the available indicators, rather than prioritizing the ability to capture housing-related deprivation as in the EU process. In our analysis of individual levels of deprivation employing EU-SILC we therefore focus on the three dimensions relating to consumption deprivation, housing facilities, and neighbourhood environment described earlier, and pay particular attention to the consumption dimension as coming closest to a measure of generalized deprivation.

In this we have been guided by our earlier work that brought out the distinction between dimensions capturing generalized deprivation and those relating to more specific forms of deprivation or exclusion (Nolan and Whelan, 1996; Whelan et al., 2001). The available evidence analysed there first for Ireland and then comparatively with the ECHP pointed to the fact that rather different sorts of socio-economic influences were involved in shaping different forms of deprivation. EU-SILC does not allow us to make as detailed a set of distinctions as the ECHP, but in line with earlier analysis our expectation is that enforced absence of items in the consumption deprivation index will be influenced by broad factors tapping command over economic resource, such as labour force status, education, and social class, and, to a lesser extent, factors reflecting additional demands on resources relating to family and marital circumstances. On the other hand we would anticipate that dimensions such as housing facilities and neighbourhood environment will be significantly influenced by factors such as stage of the life-course, urban–rural location, home ownership, and housing-related institutions and structures.

The confirmatory factor analysis that we have reported is consistent with those expectations in the sense that it does indeed assign those items into different dimensions. However, the more limited range of deprivation indicators in EU-SILC compared with the ECHP means that a number of different factor analytic solutions are consistent with the statistical evidence. It is therefore useful to investigate in more detail the comparison between Guio's 'Combined Strain + Durables' dimension now widely used at EU level and our 'consumption deprivation' dimension. The two have 6 deprivation items in common, namely food, heat, a holiday, a car, avoiding arrears on rent or utilities, and being able to meet unexpected expenses. Our 7-item index is completed by adding enforced absence of a PC; their 9-item index instead adds items capturing enforced absence of a phone, a washing machine, and a colour TV.

Guio et al. (2009) exclude enforced absence of a PC because a majority of people do not consider it a necessity, as revealed by the results of the Eurobarometer survey mentioned earlier. However, the limited range of items available in EU-SILC means one cannot make the distinction between basic and secondary forms of deprivation that was possible with the larger set of items in the ECHP; we do not see a compelling argument that all of the items included in a broad consumption deprivation index (as opposed to a narrower index of 'basic' deprivation) must be regarded as necessities. Instead, given the challenge of constructing an adequate index of consumption deprivation with the limited set of items in EU-SILC, we consider that the fact that the PC item consistently loads with the remaining 6 items and contributes to enhancing the reliability of the index (as indicated by the change in the Cronbach's alpha measure when it is included) justifies its retention.

The key issue is then whether the addition of a telephone, a washing machine, and a colour TV, included in Guio's 9-item deprivation index, would enhance our consumption deprivation measure. Guio (2009) noted that in her analysis the highest value for the alpha reliability coefficient was actually obtained when these three items were excluded. She also noted that in most countries less than 1% of persons experienced enforced deprivation on these items. However, it was decided to retain these items because being deprived of such an item has a particularly stigmatizing effect.

This is not an argument that we find particularly persuasive, and it is worth spelling out the impact that adding these 3 items to our 7-item index would have on measured levels of reliability and on the numbers identified as above a deprivation threshold. When these 3 items—telephone, washing machine, and colour TV—are added to our 7-item consumption deprivation scale, the value of Cronbach's alpha falls from 0.729 to 0.715. Underpinning this is the fact that the average item-total correlation with our 7 consumption items is 0.45, whereas with the additional 3 items it falls to 0.21. It is also worth noting that the extent of this gap is generally widest in the more affluent countries. The reason for these country differentials becomes clear when one restricts

Table 5.3. Average Inter-Item Correlations for Telephone, TV, and Washing Machine Deprivation Items, EU-SILC

	Correlation
Austria	0.084
Belgium	0.217
Cyprus	0.109
Czech Republic	0.120
Germany	0.155
Denmark	0.034
Estonia	0.269
Spain	0.057
Finland	0.127
France	0.140
Greece	0.198
Hungary	0.264
Ireland	0.114
Iceland	−0.002
Italy	0.223
Lithuania	0.275
Luxembourg	0.384
Latvia	0.309
Netherlands	0.000
Norway	0.060
Poland	0.178
Portugal	0.247
Sweden	−0.001
Slovenia	0.246
Slovakia	0.315
UK	0.070
Average	0.145

one's attention to the relationships between the three additional items, as set out in Table 5.3. We see that the overall average inter-item correlation for these three items across the 26 countries is 0.145. However, in the affluent social democratic countries, such as the Netherlands, Norway, Iceland, and Denmark the figure tends towards 0, whereas at the other extreme in countries such as Latvia, Slovakia, Portugal, Hungary, and Estonia it ranges between 0.26 and 0.31. So in the richer countries where deprivation levels on these items are extremely low, the relationships between the items take on a random character. Only where levels of deprivation are higher do the items come closer to tapping a common underlying factor, although even then the correlations are much more modest than among our consumption deprivation items.

So what difference would including these 3 items make to measured deprivation levels across countries? In Table 5.4 we compare the percentages above a threshold level of 3 for our 7-item consumption deprivation index and for the 10-item index, which includes in addition the 3 extra items of a telephone, a washing machine, and a colour TV. These results make clear that the addition of these items actually has virtually no impact on the number found

Table 5.4. Percentage over Deprivation Threshold with Alternative Summary Indices, EU-SILC

	Consumption 7-item 3+ Threshold (%)	Consumption 7-item + 3 household facilities items 3+ Threshold (%)
Austria	10.9	11.0
Belgium	13.6	13.9
Cyprus	31.9	32.1
Czech Republic	21.7	22.0
Germany	14.1	14.2
Denmark	7.6	8.1
Estonia	20.6	21.3
Spain	13.4	13.5
Finland	10.8	11.2
France	14.3	14.5
Greece	26.4	26.9
Hungary	39.5	39.9
Ireland	14.1	14.4
Iceland	7.7	7.8
Italy	15.1	15.3
Lithuania	44.7	45.8
Luxembourg	3.5	3.5
Latvia	53.2	53.8
Netherlands	6.9	6.9
Norway	5.8	5.8
Poland	47.8	48.1
Portugal	24.7	25.9
Sweden	6.3	6.4
Slovenia	16.3	16.4
Slovakia	39.8	40.0
UK	11.5	11.6

above this threshold, even in the less affluent countries. This finding is not entirely surprising given that 7-items are common to the two indices. Everyone who is counted as above the threshold using the 7-item scale is necessarily so using the 10-item scale. The increase in the number above the threshold when we move from the 7-item to the 10-item scale is extremely modest, even in countries such as Denmark, Estonia, Finland, and Portugal.

Our final piece of analysis in relation to this issue examines whether including these 3 items would produce a deprivation index more strongly related to households' subjective assessments of their own financial situation, as reflected in how difficult they find it to 'make ends meet'. Consistent with our earlier analysis involving the deprivation dimensions, from Table 5.5 we can see that entering these 3 items reduces the odds ratio on being economically stressed for the 7-item consumption deprivation index only marginally from 2.630 to 2.617. The coefficients for a washing machine and a colour TV are close to 1, indicating no effect. The net effect of the telephone item is 1.770

Table 5.5. Logistic Regression of Economic Stress with 7-item Consumption Deprivation Index and Additional Deprivation Items, EU-SILC

	(i) Odds ratios	(ii) Odds ratios
7-item consumption deprivation scale	2.630	2.617^{a}
Telephone		1.770^{a}
Washing machine		0.992
TV		1.005
Reduction in log likelihood	178,039.7	178,243.7
Degrees of freedom	1	4
Nagelkerke R^2	0.429	0.429

^{a} $p < 0.001$.

and is statistically significant. However, the Nagelkerke R^2 remains unchanged at 0.429.

The evidence relating to reliability levels, inter-item correlations, levels of deprivation, and our ability to understand economic stress all confirm that there is nothing to be gained from incorporating the additional 3 items in our index of consumption deprivation. Where cross-national comparisons are critical it is preferable to operate with a deprivation index that we are confident operates in a relatively uniform manner across countries. We are then able to explore how a measure such as the consumption deprivation index relates to other forms of deprivation relating to factors such as housing, health, and neighbourhood. This is the strategy that we will adopt in our subsequent analysis.

It should be clear that choosing between the alternative consumption deprivation indices has relatively modest consequences for the conclusions we draw even though the 7-item scale is clearly superior in a number of respects. However, efforts to improve upon the current measures that are clearly necessary require that we understand the behaviour of individual items and take this knowledge into account in constructing scales that have desirable properties in terms of both reliability and construct validity.

5.4 Cross-Country Patterns of Deprivation by Dimension

On the basis of the dimensions we have distinguished, one can examine levels of deprivation across European countries and how these vary from one dimension to another. Looking first at the ECHP and the five dimensions of deprivation we can distinguish from that source, Table 5.6 shows mean levels of deprivation on the relevant summary indices for each of the countries covered, with each item counted equally in constructing these indices. Interesting

Table 5.6. Mean Deprivation Scores by Dimension of Deprivation across Countries, ECHP 1996

	Basic deprivation	Secondary deprivation	Housing facilities	Housing deterioration	Environmental problems
Austria	0.95	0.35	0.11	0.16	0.70
Belgium	0.85	0.24	0.10	0.25	0.81
Denmark	0.55	0.34	0.04	0.16	0.53
Germany	0.72	0.51	0.06	0.13	0.73
Spain	1.97	0.81	0.05	0.38	1.09
Finland	1.58	0.36	0.09	0.09	0.86
France	1.12	0.33	0.09	0.29	0.83
Greece	3.82	0.96	0.78	0.39	0.81
Ireland	1.01	0.56	0.13	0.22	0.52
Italy	1.71	0.38	0.07	0.16	1.10
Luxembourg	0.55	0.20	0.05	0.16	0.60
Netherlands	0.63	0.22	0.02	0.24	0.85
Portugal	2.79	1.46	0.45	0.84	1.13
UK	1.06	0.28	0.01	0.26	0.95
EU-14 average	1.24	0.48	0.09	0.24	0.88

variation in the cross-country patterns across the dimensions can be seen. Most strikingly, there is much more differentiation across countries in levels of basic and secondary deprivation than in the environmental problems dimension: the range for basic deprivation is from a low of 0.6 up to a high of 3.8, whereas for environment dimension it is only from 0.5 to 11. There are very low mean levels of deprivation in housing facilities except in Greece and Portugal, while levels of deprivation in terms of housing deterioration are also much higher in Portugal than elsewhere. Country rankings vary somewhat across the dimensions, with the UK, for example, being below average on the basic and secondary dimensions but above average for the housing and environmental ones, while Italy has above-average basic deprivation but below-average levels for the other dimensions.

Table 5.7 shows the corresponding figures for the three dimensions distinguished in EU-SILC across 26 countries. We see that mean scores on the consumption dimension range from 0.7 in Denmark up to 2.5 in Poland and Lithuania and 2.8 in Latvia, while for the neighbourhood/environment dimension mean levels are generally in the range 0.4–0.6. It is striking that means levels of deprivation on the housing facilities dimension are extremely low in most countries, rising above 0.1 in only 6 countries.

These comparisons are based on deprivation indices constructed as the simple sum of the number of items on which a household is deprived, so that deprivation on a given item simply adds 1 to the index in each country, with no differentiation across items or countries in the weight assigned to different item. As noted in previous chapters, an alternative quite widely

Table 5.7. Mean Deprivation Scores by Dimension of Deprivation across Countries with Prevalence-Weighting of Items, EU-SILC 2006

	Consumption	Housing facilities	Neighbourhood environment
Austria	0.8	0.0	0.4
Belgium	0.9	0.1	0.6
Cyprus	1.7	0.1	0.7
Czech Republic	1.4	0.1	0.5
Germany	1.1	0.0	0.7
Denmark	0.7	0.0	0.4
Estonia	1.5	0.5	0.6
Spain	1.0	0.0	0.6
Finland	0.9	0.1	0.5
France	1.0	0.1	0.5
Greece	1.6	0.1	0.5
Hungary	2.2	0.2	0.4
Ireland	1.0	0.0	0.4
Iceland	0.8	0.0	0.2
Italy	1.1	0.0	0.6
Lithuania	2.5	0.7	0.4
Luxembourg	0.4	0.0	0.5
Latvia	2.8	0.6	0.8
Netherlands	0.6	0.0	0.6
Norway	0.6	0.0	0.3
Poland	2.5	0.3	0.4
Portugal	1.6	0.2	0.6
Sweden	0.5	0.0	0.3
Slovenia	1.2	0.1	0.5
Slovakia	2.2	0.1	0.5
UK	0.8	0.0	0.6
EU	1.2	0.1	0.6

employed in the comparative research using deprivation indicators is to assign different weights to different items that reflect, in some fashion, how seriously deprivation on a given item is to be regarded. One may believe, for example, that it is a greater deprivation to be doing without an item that almost everyone else in one's country has than an item that many fellow-citizens are also doing without. The most straightforward way to incorporate this into the deprivation measures is to weight each item by the proportion in the country in question *not* deprived of it. (An alternative is to let such weights vary with the proportion in the population regarding the item in question as a necessity.) This means first that within a particular country some items will be given more weight than others in constructing a deprivation index. Secondly, and crucially in the comparative context, it means that a given item will be given more weight in a country where only a small proportion are deprived of it than in one where such deprivation is more common. When we construct such 'prevalence-weighted' deprivation indices using data from the ECHP, the mean deprivation scores by dimension are as shown in Table 5.8.

Table 5.8. Mean Deprivation Scores by Dimension of Deprivation across Countries with Prevalence-Weighting of Items, ECHP 1996

	Basic deprivation	Secondary deprivation	Housing facilities	Housing deterioration	Environmental problems
Austria	0.70	0.31	0.10	0.15	0.57
Belgium	0.68	0.23	0.10	0.23	0.66
Denmark	0.47	0.31	0.04	0.15	0.46
Germany	0.60	0.44	0.06	0.12	0.57
Spain	1.05	0.63	0.05	0.32	0.83
Finland	1.08	0.33	0.09	0.08	0.69
France	0.83	0.30	0.08	0.26	0.67
Greece	1.37	0.73	0.29	0.34	0.65
Ireland	0.78	0.47	0.12	0.20	0.46
Italy	1.04	0.34	0.06	0.15	0.82
Luxembourg	0.48	0.19	0.05	0.15	0.51
Netherlands	0.54	0.21	0.02	0.22	0.65
Portugal	1.15	0.95	0.38	0.59	0.86
UK	0.82	0.26	0.01	0.23	0.74
EU	0.88	0.43	0.11	0.24	0.69

Comparing these results with those in Table 5.6, we see that moving away from the equal-weights approach to a prevalence-weighted one has substantially narrowed the range of deprivation levels across countries. On the basic deprivation dimension, for example, the range of mean scores is now from 0.5 in Denmark up to 1.4 in Greece, whereas previously it went from 0.6 to 3.8. So the use of prevalence weights has most impact on countries with relatively high levels of deprivation, in effect reducing the level of measured deprivation there because it is considered less of a deprivation to be doing without items that many others are doing without. In the richer countries, by contrast, most people are not deprived so the prevalence-based weight is not very different to the weight of one implicitly applied in the equal weights approach.

In the same vein, Table 5.9 shows the prevalence-weighted mean deprivation levels for the 3 dimensions distinguished in EU-SILC across the 26 countries, with a similar contrast to the figures in Table 5.7. The mean level on the consumption deprivation index, for example, now ranges from 0.6 in Denmark up to 1.4 in Poland, compared with the range from 0.6 up to 2.8 seen with the equal-weights approach. So the impact of using prevalence weights is to narrow very considerably the gap in measured deprivation levels between the richer and poorer countries in terms of average income per head. One cannot say a priori that one of these approaches is better than the other: instead, the most appropriate approach depends on precisely what question one is seeking to answer or what one is trying to achieve in measuring deprivation, as we will bring out in our analysis and discussion in subsequent chapters.

Table 5.9. Mean Deprivation Scores by Dimension of Deprivation across Countries, EU-SILC 2006

	Consumption	Housing facilities	Neighbourhood environment
Austria	0.64	0.04	0.35
Belgium	0.77	0.07	0.46
Cyprus	1.05	0.07	0.52
Czech Republic	1.00	0.07	0.43
Germany	0.78	0.04	0.50
Denmark	0.60	0.04	0.35
Estonia	0.95	0.39	0.50
Spain	0.74	0.02	0.49
Finland	0.72	0.07	0.40
France	0.77	0.05	0.43
Greece	1.11	0.09	0.39
Hungary	1.27	0.21	0.35
Ireland	0.75	0.04	0.34
Iceland	0.62	0.04	0.22
Italy	0.80	0.04	0.48
Lithuania	1.31	0.55	0.35
Luxembourg	0.33	0.02	0.43
Latvia	1.39	0.52	0.57
Netherlands	0.54	0.00	0.48
Norway	0.48	0.02	0.24
Poland	1.41	0.25	0.37
Portugal	0.97	0.20	0.46
Sweden	0.46	0.01	0.30
Slovenia	0.85	0.06	0.41
Slovakia	1.29	0.11	0.39
UK	0.63	0.02	0.48
EU	0.82	0.07	0.45

5.5 The Relationship between Dimensions and the Extent of Multiple Deprivation

As well as analysing different dimensions of deprivation individually, it is of significant interest to look at how they relate to one another, and in particular at the extent to which some people experience more than one type of deprivation. Being able to capture multiple deprivation is important not only because different aspects of deprivation must be taken into account if we are to have a comprehensive picture of a household's situation, but also because these different forms of deprivation may interact with and reinforce one another—their effects may be cumulative in the sense of being more than additive.

The extent to which the different dimensions of deprivation we are distinguishing are to be found together in the same household may be examined first in terms of correlations. The correlation between dimensions is in fact quite low. Table 5.10 shows the correlation between each of the 5

Table 5.10. Correlations between Deprivation Dimensions, ECHP

	Basic	Secondary	housing facilities	Housing deterioration	Environmental problems
Basic	1				
Secondary	0.446	1			
Housing facilities	0.118	0.127	1		
Housing deterioration	0.233	0.167	0.137	1	
Environmental problems	0.195	0.129	0.057	0.241	1

Table 5.11. Correlations Matrix for EU Prevalence Weighted Deprivation Dimensions, EU-SILC

	Consumption	Household	Environment
Consumption	1		
Household	0.349	1	
Environment	0.093	0.005	1

dimensions identified in the ECHP. We see that the highest correlation by far is between the basic and secondary dimensions, at 0.45. The other correlations are strikingly low, on the order of 0.1–0.2.

For the three dimensions distinguished in EU-SILC, Table 5.11 shows that the correlation between consumption deprivation and household facilities deprivation is 0.35, but the correlation of each of these with environment/ neighbourhood problems is very low indeed.

It is not surprising, then, that both national and cross-country studies suggest that the numbers of households combining high levels of deprivation across a number of dimensions together are generally quite modest. If we look at the 5 dimensions distinguished in the ECHP, Figure 5.1 categorizes the sample for each country into those displaying no deprivation versus those deprived on 1, 2, 3, 4, or all 5 dimensions. We see that only in Portugal and Greece is the number reporting deprivation on all 5 dimensions appreciably above 0. Outside Greece, Portugal, and Spain the percentage reporting deprivation on 4 or more dimensions does not exceed 13% and in most cases it is substantially lower.

To explore patterns of multiple deprivation in EU-SILC, we first define a threshold for each dimension. For consumption deprivation a threshold of 3+ is chosen, because there is a sharp differentiation between those above and below this threshold in terms of reported difficulty in making ends meet (Whelan and Maître, 2007b). For both the housing facilities and neighbourhood environment indices, with their limited number of items, we use a lower threshold of 2. Table 5.12 shows the percentage above these thresholds by dimension by country. Across the EU, approximately one-fifth of the

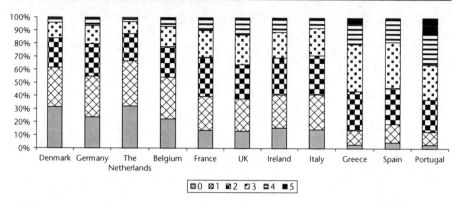

Figure 5.1. Percentage of persons lacking at least 1 item for 5 deprivation dimensions, ECHP 1994.

Table 5.12. Level of Deprivation by Dimension across Countries, EU-SILC 2006: Percentage above Threshold on Consumption, Housing, and Neighbourhood Deprivation

	Consumption 3+ (%)	Housing facilities 2+ (%)	Neighbourhood 2+ (%)
Austria	10.9	0.5	14.0
Belgium	13.6	0.8	21.7
Cyprus	31.9	1.7	33.5
Czech Republic	21.7	0.9	21.8
Germany	14.1	0.4	25.2
Denmark	7.6	0.1	12.9
Estonia	20.6	13.9	27.0
Spain	13.4	0.2	26.1
Finland	10.8	0.9	13.3
France	14.3	0.7	19.4
Greece	26.4	1.6	20.0
Hungary	39.5	5.2	19.6
Ireland	14.1	0.3	16.0
Iceland	7.7	0.1	6.8
Italy	15.1	0.4	26.2
Lithuania	44.7	21.7	22.4
Luxembourg	3.5	0.3	19.6
Latvia	53.2	19.6	38.3
Netherlands	6.9	0.0	22.4
Norway	5.8	0.2	7.6
Poland	47.8	7.0	23.5
Portugal	24.7	4.2	25.5
Sweden	6.3	0.0	9.8
Slovenia	16.3	1.1	20.8
Slovakia	39.8	2.2	17.3
UK	11.5	0.1	23.2
EU-26	19.7	2.6	21.2

Table 5.13. Multiple Deprivation Scores across Countries, EU-SILC 2006: Sum of Consumption, Housing, and Neighbourhood Deprivation

Deprivation score	0 (%)	1 (%)	2 (%)	3 (%)
Austria	78.2	18.3	3.3	0.1
Belgium	69.5	25.1	5.3	0.2
Cyprus	46.3	40.8	12.3	0.5
Czech Republic	64.0	27.8	7.9	0.3
Germany	67.1	27.7	5.2	2.7
Denmark	82.5	14.7	2.7	0.0
Estonia	53.9	32.6	11.4	2.0
Spain	67.5	28.3	4.1	0.0
Finland	78.1	19.2	2.6	0.1
France	71.0	23.8	5.0	0.1
Greece	61.0	30.3	8.3	0.4
Hungary	51.5	35.2	11.2	2.1
Ireland	75.1	19.7	5.1	0.0
Iceland	87.1	11.5	1.4	0.0
Italy	65.2	28.0	6.6	0.2
Lithuania	39.8	35.9	20.0	4.3
Luxembourg	78.2	20.3	1.4	0.1
Latvia	27.8	40.1	25.1	6.9
Netherlands	73.9	23.0	3.1	0.0
Norway	88.4	10.3	1.3	0.0
Poland	42.6	39.1	15.7	2.6
Portugal	57.4	32.0	9.3	1.3
Sweden	85.5	13.1	1.4	0.0
Slovenia	68.2	25.8	5.6	0.4
Slovakia	50.9	39.6	8.9	0.6
UK	69.8	25.8	4.4	0.0
EU-26	65.1	27.1	7.1	0.7

population are above the threshold on the consumption deprivation index and the same number are above the neighbourhood deprivation threshold, but less than 3% are above the threshold on the housing facilities dimension. In the countries with the highest levels of deprivation, such as Latvia, Lithuania, and Poland, these figures are very much higher, with as many as half of all households identified as deprived on the consumption deprivation index, up to one-fifth deprived on the housing facilities index, and up to 40% deprived on the neighbourhood deprivation index.

We can then look at the extent to which households are above the deprivation threshold on more than 1 dimension. We see in Table 5.13 that less than 1% are above the threshold on all 3 dimensions in the EU as a whole, and this is also true in 20 of the 26 countries. The only countries where that level is much higher are Lithuania and Latvia where 4 and 7% are deprived on all 3. This is strongly influenced by the fact that housing facilities deprivation is so low in most countries and so weakly related to the other dimensions: most of those above the threshold for consumption and neighbourhood deprivation are below the housing facilities threshold. Even if we focus on those deprived on 2 or more dimensions, levels of multiple deprivation remain modest: less than 10% in 19 of the 26 countries, and only substantially higher than that in Latvia and Lithuania where it is 18 and 24%, respectively.

The 'cumulatively deprived' are clearly of particular interest from a policy perspective, having distinctive needs and in all likelihood requiring specially designed forms of intervention. The levels of multiple deprivation one identifies will also be dependent on the particular dimensions included in the analysis and the choice of thresholds on the relevant indices. However, the findings presented here about the extent of multiple deprivation are broadly in line with a range of analyses using both national and European data (see Tsakloglou and Papadopoulous, 2002b; Whelan et al., 2002a; Gallie et al., 2003; Whelan and Maître, 2007b; Halleröd and Larsson, 2008).

5.6 Analysing the Different Dimensions of Deprivation

Analysis of the different dimensions of deprivation focusing on the factors associated with each type of deprivation and the manner in which this varies across dimensions and countries has the potential to uncover important features of the causal process underpinning them. Our earlier studies based on the ECHP have shown that deprivation in terms of relation to what we have termed basic and secondary deprivation is quite strongly related to low income, whereas poor housing facilities, housing deterioration, and neighbourhood environmental problems display a rather weak relationship even with persistently low income. When scores on the various indices are regressed on the log of household annual (equivalized income) the results show that the impact of income is consistently strongest for basic deprivation but still substantial for secondary deprivation but much weaker across for the housing and environment dimensions. When the basic and secondary dimensions are combined into an index we have labelled 'current life-style deprivation' (CLSD), the findings reported in the last column of Table 5.14 show that in every case it exhibits the highest correlation with income (see Whelan et al., 2001, for further details). The fact that the relationship with income varies across the deprivation dimensions in a very similar fashion is a striking finding with important implications both for understanding deprivation and for using such measures.

While the broad pattern of variation in the income-deprivation variation is relatively uniform across countries, we also observe striking variation across countries in the strength of the relationship for all dimensions other than the neighbourhood index. For both the basic and secondary deprivation measures and most particularly the CLSD index the magnitude of the effect increases as one moves from the more affluent to the less affluent countries. For Germany and Denmark the value of the coefficient is less than −1.0. For Italy it rises

Table 5.14. Unstandardized Regression Coefficients for Log of Equivalent Household Income and Deprivation Indices

	Basic	Secondary	Housing facilities	Housing deterioration	Environmental problems	Current life-style deprivation
Germany	−0.63	−0.20	−0.07	−0.06	−0.08	−0.83
Denmark	−0.64	−0.34	−0.11	−0.03	−0.13	−0.98
Netherlands	−0.85	−0.34	−0.03	−0.03	−0.18	−1.19
Belgium	−0.65	−0.35	−0.15	−0.04	−0.06	−1.02
Luxembourg	−0.52	−0.30	−0.07	−0.12	−0.16	−0.82
France	−1.02	−0.36	−0.11	−0.15	−0.06	−1.38
UK	−1.04	−0.37	−0.01	−0.11	−0.09	−1.41
Ireland	−1.05	−0.55	−0.13	−0.19	−0.15	−1.61
Italy	−1.06	−0.33	−0.05	−0.11	0.18	−1.41
Greece	−1.62	−0.55	−0.46	−0.28	0.11	−2.17
Spain	−1.25	−0.90	−0.08	−0.21	0.04	−2.15
Portugal	−1.34	−0.95	−0.53	−0.32	0.05	−2.29

to −1.38. Finally, for Portugal it peaks at 2.29. The negative impact of income on both of the housing dimensions, while still considerably weaker than in the case of the CLSD measure, is distinctively high in Spain, Greece, and Portugal.

The deprivation measures available in EU-SILC are of a significantly more restricted form than for the ECHP. However, the more heterogeneous nature of the countries participating means that cross-country variation becomes of increased significance. From Table 5.15 we can see that in every case the income coefficient for consumption is substantially higher than for the remaining two dimensions. For the 7-item consumption index the value of the regression coefficient ranges from −0.533 in Norway to −1.8 in the Czech Republic. For housing facilities the figure goes from −0.008 in Norway to −0.697 in Lithuania. For neighbourhood environment, where the pattern of variation is less systematic, the strongest effect of −0.286 is observed in the Czech Republic and the weakest of −0.052 in Slovakia.

Focusing on cross-country variation, for housing amenities we see that values are highest in the Baltic countries ranging from −0.367 in Estonia to −0.524 in Latvia and −0.697 in Lithuania. For neighbourhood environment cross-country variation appears to be influenced by a variety of somewhat different factors with the highest values of −0.25 being observed in France and Luxembourg where immigration is likely to be an important influence and Poland, the Czech Republic, and Estonia, where the impact of earlier industrial policies on urban areas are the most likely influence. In both cases income plays a modest role and there appears to be little prospect of improving on conventional income poverty measures by focusing on such measures. It is also necessary to keep in mind the limited reliability of these indices, particularly in the more affluent countries. Improved understanding of the factors

95

Table 5.15. Unstandardized Regression Coefficients for Log of Equivalent Income and EU-SILC 2006 Deprivation Indices

	Consumption	Housing facilities	Neighbourhood environment
Norway	−0.531	−0.008	−0.086
Sweden	−0.533	−0.014	−0.094
Spain	−0.663	−0.023	−0.060
UK	−0.664	−0.011	−0.128
Luxembourg	−0.694	−0.039	−0.250
Netherlands	−0.766	−0.008	−0.199
Denmark	−0.820	−0.072	−0.170
Austria	−0.838	−0.047	−0.043
Iceland	−0.892	−0.018	−0.132
Germany	−0.927	−0.037	−0.152
Italy	−0.959	−0.043	−0.127
Portugal	−0.999	−0.168	−0.058
Finland	−1.092	−0.084	−0.093
Ireland	−1.148	−0.037	−0.143
France	−1.169	−0.067	−0.256
Belgium	−1.177	−0.085	−0.180
Slovenia	−1.200	−0.107	−0.131
Estonia	−1.223	−0.367	−0.217
Greece	−1.333	−0.126	−0.068
Latvia	−1.320	−0.524	−0.084
Lithuania	−1.392	−0.697	−0.141
Slovakia	−1.427	−0.161	−0.052
Hungary	−1.458	−0.307	−0.143
Cyprus	−1.475	−0.086	−0.142
Poland	−1.555	−0.246	−0.217
Czech Republic	−1.808	−0.143	−0.285

influencing housing and neighbourhood deprivation and the manner in which they vary cross-nationally requires the development of indices that are substantially superior to those currently available in EU-SILC.

The 7-item consumption deprivation index does provide the possibility of complementing the income poverty measure with an appropriate deprivation index. It is clearly systematically related to income while also providing information that is distinct from that captured by income. The limited overlap between income and deprivation does not simply reflect the limitations of a current income measure: it continues to hold when both deprivation and income are measured over a number of years rather than just at one point in time. Whelan, Layte, and Maître (2003), for example, show that a variety of factors related to household resources—such as education, labour market experience, and social class as well as needs related to marital status and social structure—help to predict persistent deprivation even when one controls for persistently low income.

These results reinforce the consistent finding from more in-depth analysis of the ECHP that deprivation items and dimensions reflecting (more or less

Table 5.16. Ordinary Least Squares Regression on Economic Stress on Consumption, Housing, and Neighbourhood Deprivation Dimensions for EU-SILC-26

	B	B	B
Consumption	0.517	0.510	
Housing facilities		−0.049	0.491
Neighbourhood environment		0.073	0.214
R^2	0.405	0.409	0.066
Constant	3.977	4.022	3.484
N	520,443	520,443	520,443

closely) current consumption are more strongly related to command over economic resources than are items and dimensions capturing aspects of housing facilities and quality and the local neighbourhood environment. This does not make housing and neighbourhood deprivation any less important—and distinguishing them as separate dimensions allows their determinants to be identified and policies directed towards addressing them to be designed more effectively. It does mean, though, that these items/dimensions are less suitable for inclusion in a measure of generalized deprivation arising from a lack of resources. This is the core rationale underpinning our focusing primarily on the CLSD measure from the ECHP and consumption deprivation from EU-SILC: because, however imperfect, we judge them to be the most satisfactory measures tapping latent generalized deprivation available in those datasets.

Further validation of this focus can be provided by examining how levels of deprivation on different dimensions relate to the way households view their own financial situation, notably by reference to their responses to the question already mentioned earlier about how difficult they were finding it to 'make ends meet'. In Table 5.16 we show the impact of the three deprivation dimensions on this outcome, varying the order of entry of dimensions for the EU-SILC sample as a whole. This obviously involves some oversimplification as does the use of ordinary least squares. However, the analysis is sufficient to bring home the point we wish to make regarding the relative value of the deprivation dimensions for our current purposes. Entering the 7-item consumption index first accounts for 40.5% of the variance of the six-category economic stress variable. Entering the housing facilities and neighbourhood environment variable increase the level of variance explanation to 40.9% and reduces the consumption coefficient to 0.510. The net housing coefficient is actually negative while the neighbourhood coefficient reaches 0.073. Entering the latter 2 variables on their own explains 0.066% of the variance. The consumption deprivation dimension accounts uniquely for 34.3% of the variance (40.9–6.6). The remaining dimensions explain 0.04% (40.9–40.5) and 6.2% is shared. The 7-item consumption index is a powerful predictor of subjective economic stress but the housing and environmental deprivation dimensions add very little in the way of explanatory power.

The fact that the income-CLSD and income-7-item consumption deprivation relationship varies systematically across country is likely to reflect the fact that current income provides a less powerful indicator of more generalized command over resources in more affluent countries and in countries where the welfare state is more generous and pervasive. Examining the determinants of the mismatch between income and consumption deprivation at the aggregate EU level is unlikely to be sufficiently informative. For that reason in the chapters that follow we provide a systematic examination of the nature and implications of this mismatch and the factors contributing to it while taking into account the need to address the role of cross-country and welfare regime variation.

5.7 Conclusions

In this chapter we have focused on the dimensional structure of material derivation in the key comparative data sources available to us, that is, the grouping of non-monetary deprivation indicators into sets that reflect distinct aspects of living standards and deprivation. We described the five-dimension structure we identify using the items available in the ECHP, and the less satisfactory set of three dimensions using the narrower set of items currently available in EU-SILC. We teased out how the latter differs in some respects from the structuring put forward in the studies by Guio underpinning the EU's indicators of material deprivation and housing deprivation, and documented the variation across countries in terms of the deprivation dimensions identified, taking into account alternative ways of assigning weights to different items. We examined the extent to which different dimensions of deprivation are experienced together, and found that only a relatively small number of households experience multiple deprivation. Finally we argued that the index we label 'consumption deprivation' is most suitable if one is seeking to capture generalized deprivation. We go on in the following chapters to build on the base established in this and previous chapters to explore in particular how information on particular forms of deprivation can improve the capacity to capture and understand poverty and vulnerability across European countries.

6

Understanding the Mismatch between Income Poverty and Material Deprivation

6.1 Introduction

As Perry (2002) highlighted in a review of the literature, a consistent finding in poverty research is a significant mismatch between poverty measured indirectly using income and direct measures focusing on indicators of material deprivation. In Chapter 4 we looked briefly at the scale of that mismatch and at some preliminary evidence on the relationship one finds between both income poverty and deprivation and subjective economic stress. In this chapter we look at this mismatch in depth, using both comparative and longitudinal perspectives to bring out the various contributing factors and their implications. This underpins our conclusion that the conceptual and measurement problems in relying on income alone to identify the poor suggest that incorporating deprivation into the process could have significant potential.

The chapter opens with a discussion of the reasons why one might expect a household's current equivalized income to have difficulties in fully capturing its command over financial resources in relation to its needs, and thus anticipate a priori that relying simply on income to measure poverty could be problematic. We then investigate in some depth the extent of overlap or mismatch between being below a relative income poverty threshold and above a corresponding consumption-related deprivation threshold, for 26 European countries. We then look at the cross-classification of persons by these income poverty and deprivation standards, distinguishing those who are both income poor and deprived, income poor but not deprived, deprived but not income poor, and neither income poor or deprived. To bring out the nature of the groups identified in this way we focus attention on their social class profile. We proceed to compare the levels of subjective economic stress being reported by these different groups. Finally, we turn from a static cross-sectional perspective to an analysis of the persistence of income poverty and deprivation over time, using the longitudinal data from the ECHP.

6.2 The Limitations of Income as a Measure of Poverty

It is not surprising that current income has serious limitations in capturing poverty. A household's standard of living depends on its command over resources and its needs, and neither would be adequately reflected in current (equivalized) income even if it were measured with perfect accuracy.[1] While disposable cash income is a key element in the resources available to a household, it is by no means the only one. Savings add to the capacity to consume now, and servicing accumulated debt reduces it; past investment in consumer durables influences the extent to which resources must be devoted to such expenditure now; the flow of services from owner-occupied housing—the imputed rent—is often not included; and non-cash income in the form of goods and services provided directly by the State, notably health care, education, and housing, also comprise a major resource for many households. Cash income itself may fluctuate from month to month and year to year, so current income is an imperfect indicator of long-term or 'permanent' income which will influence ability to consume. Needs also differ across households, and in ways that conventional equivalence scales will not capture. These scales are usually based simply on the number of persons or the number of adults and children in the household, and there is little basis for confidence that they accurately reflect even the impact of those differences on living standards. Furthermore, households also vary in a variety of other ways that affect the demands on their income, notably with respect to health status and disability.[2] Work-related expenses such as transport and child-care may also affect the net income actually available to support living standards and avoidance of deprivation. Finally, geographical variation in prices may mean that the purchasing power of a given income varies across households depending on their location.

Some households, even if genuinely on low income for several years, may none the less be able to avoid severe deprivation—for example, by drawing on assets, borrowing from financial institutions, and receiving support from their extended family. Furthermore, some people may be exceptionally good managers of their limited resources, and succeed in obtaining essentials even where most people on that income would not be able to do so. However, another point to note is that some persistently low-income households may

---

[1] See the discussions in, for example, Mayer (1993) and Atkinson et al. (2002).
[2] Ways of incorporating needs associated with disability into equivalence scales have been explored in, for example, Burchardt and Zaidi (2003).

report little or no *enforced* deprivation but still be doing without. As described earlier, some deprivation measures in common use, including here, go beyond whether the person lacks the item or the activity to incorporate a subjective evaluation as to whether they are doing without due to inability to afford. While they may be helpful in trying to capture the impact of financial constraints rather than preferences, there is cause for concern that such responses may be influenced by adaptation to economic circumstances, rather than just tastes (McKay, 2004; Dominy and Kempson, 2006; Halleröd, 2006). There are structured differences across age groups or urban–rural location in the extent to which particular items are seen as necessities—older people may place less value on having a holiday, or urban dwellers on having a car. Where the deprivation measures are constructed that way, one may also have particular concerns about certain types of household becoming habituated to doing without, or having different expectations from the majority (Hallerod, 2006). Where the formulation of the questions allows, it is therefore useful to look both at what people report as enforced deprivation and what they simply lack.

What, conversely, of the households with incomes above the poverty line who are reporting deprivation? This is not difficult to understand when they are close to the poverty line—a few extra euro or pounds over the poverty threshold might not have a dramatic impact on living standards. Those in the top half of the income distribution for some time and still reporting substantial deprivation, on the other hand, may be particularly poor managers of their income, they may have got heavily into debt, or they may have rather different priorities in allocating their spending to the norm. As we emphasized in Chapter 2, deprivation conceptually relates to being denied the opportunity to have or do something; the difficulty is in empirically inferring a constrained opportunity set from what people do not have or do, as opposed to differences in preferences/tastes. As we will argue below, this means that in using deprivation indicators to measure poverty, one may wish to exclude high-income households reporting that they cannot afford things that many lower income households have.

Turning to the measurement of income, one cannot be confident that it has been measured comprehensively and accurately. Household surveys—on which poverty research generally relies—face (intentional or unintentional) mis-reporting of income. They also find it particularly difficult to adequately capture income from self-employment, from home production, from capital, and from the imputed rent attributable to homeowners. One would be particularly concerned about the reliability of very low incomes observed in surveys—particularly in countries with what are thought to be effective social safety-nets—but other incomes may also be mis-measured to an unknown extent. Significant efforts are being made both by national statistics offices together with Eurostat and by researchers to address such issues, for example

101

by measuring stocks of assets and liabilities as well as income flows, by employing different approaches to estimating imputed income from owner-occupation, and by exploring ways of incorporating the value of non-cash benefits into income.[3] There has also been substantial investment in panel surveys to obtain a dynamic rather than static picture of income, so it is particularly important to consider the relationship between income and deprivation over time that these reveal.

In this chapter and subsequently in Chapter 9 we will look in detail at the extent to which taking into account both the persistence of low income and deprivation over time and measurement error in relation to both income and deprivation helps in understanding the mismatch between income poverty and deprivation routinely observed at the cross-sectional level. In this and the following chapters it is not our intention to present a comprehensive multivariate analysis of the determinants of poverty and social exclusion. Instead we will focus on the key socio-economic factors such as principal economic status and social class that enable us to clarify the advantages and limitations of different approaches to the conceptualization and measurement of social exclusion.

The analysis that follows first makes use of EU-SILC data to document the extent of the mismatch between relative income poverty and deprivation across the countries of the enlarged EU.[4] We will then construct a 4-fold poverty typology that incorporates low income and material deprivation and explore the relationship between the distribution of individuals across these categories and their social class position, in order to locate the income poverty–material deprivation mismatch in the context of a broader consideration of the accumulation and erosion of resources. That analysis focuses on cross-sectional relationships while seeking to interpret these in the context of longer term processes.

This approach, as we will see, provides a useful contribution to developing our understanding of the limited overlap between low income and material deprivation. However, it has been increasingly suggested that the key to resolving the mismatch issue lies in longitudinal data and analysis. In light of this, we will extend our analysis to consider dynamic profiles of income poverty and deprivation persistence and the extent to which analysis of their inter-relationship contributes to resolving apparent paradoxes at the cross-sectional level. Our objective is to address the specific issue of the value of longitudinal analysis for the particular purpose of comparing income and deprivation measures, rather than to provide an assessment of contemporary

---

[3] See, for example, Frick and Grabcka (2003, 2009); OECD (2008), chapter 9; Callan, Smeeding, and Tsakloglou (2008); Callan and Keane (2009); and the reports of the AIM-AP project listed on http://www.iser.essex.ac.uk/research/euromod/research-and-policy-analysis-using-euromod/aim-ap/deliverables-publications

[4] On the relationship between relative income poverty and material deprivation using data from EU-SILC, see also Fusco, Guio, and Marlier (2010).

European poverty dynamics. Consequently, we have conducted our analysis employing ECHP data because of their significant superiority to the EU-SILC data in relation to both the number of available panel observations and the duration for which data are available.

6.3 A Comparative Cross-Sectional Analysis of the Mismatch between Income Poverty and Deprivation

In this section we explore the extent of overlap between being below the 60% (equivalized) income poverty threshold and being above a corresponding consumption deprivation threshold based on the 7-item deprivation index identified in Chapter 5. We use a weighted version of this measure in which enforced deprivation on each individual item is weighted inversely to the proportion possessing the item in each country. This deprivation index thus differs from the material deprivation indicator included in the EU's social inclusion set, described in detail in Chapter 3, in 2 respects: the items included overlap substantially but not fully, as teased out in Chapter 5, and country-specific prevalence weighting is used here to 'relativize' the index whereas the EU indicator is more 'absolute' in employing the same weight of 1 for each item irrespective of country. This allows us to examine the extent of overlap between income poverty and deprivation where each is framed vis-à-vis country-specific benchmarks (rather than a common EU standard). We do so by deriving a deprivation threshold for each country which distinguishes as 'deprived' a proportion of the population as close as possible to the number below the 60% income threshold. In principle, this allows for the overlap between the income and deprivation measures to range between 0 and 1.

Our analysis is based on data from EU-SILC 2006 covering 26 countries. While we report results for all 26 countries, in order to facilitate description and interpretation we have grouped the national observations by welfare regime. As Gallie and Paugam (2000, pp. 3–4) describe it, a welfare regime refers to a system of public regulation that is concerned to assure the protection of individuals and to maintain social cohesion by intervening, through both legal measures and the distribution of resources. Their 'employment regime' typology focuses on the degree of benefit coverage and level of financial compensation for the unemployed and the scale of active employment policies. Bukodi and Róbert (2007) add a related concern with the strictness of employment protection legislation comprising a set of rules governing the hiring and firing process that can be provided through labour legislation and collective bargaining arrangements. Combining these criteria with those reflected in the standard Esping-Andersen 'worlds of welfare capitalism'

103

categorization they distinguish six welfare regimes, which we employ in our analysis, as follows:

1) The *social democratic regime* assigns the welfare state a substantial redistributive role. A high level of employment flexibility is combined with high security in the form of generous social welfare and unemployment benefits to guarantee adequate economic resources independently of market or familial reliance. We have included Sweden, Denmark, Iceland, Finland, Norway, and Netherlands in this cluster.[5]

2) The *corporatist regime* involves less emphasis on redistribution and views welfare primarily as a mediator of group-based mutual aid and risk pooling, with rights to benefits depending on being already inserted in the labour market. Relatively strict EPL policies are aimed at protecting established inside workers. This cluster includes Germany, Austria, Belgium, France, and Luxembourg.

3) The *liberal regime* acknowledges the primacy of the market and confines the state to a residual welfare role, social benefits typically being subject to a means test and targeted on those failing in the market. These countries exhibit levels of flexibility coupled with limited measures to actively sustain employment. The UK and Ireland constitute this group.

4) The *southern European regime* is distinguished by the crucial role of family support systems. Labour market policies are poorly developed and selective. The benefit system is uneven and minimalist in nature and lacks a guaranteed minimum income provision. This group comprises Cyprus, Greece, Italy, Portugal, and Spain.

Juhász (2006) and Alber et al. (2007) note the difficulties involved in categorizing the welfare regimes of post-socialist countries, although low levels of spending on social protection and weakness of social rights are common. Bukodi and Róbert (2007) observe that there has been a general increase in employment flexibility with most transition countries displaying a level of labour market flexibility significantly less than the UK but significantly greater than that in southern European countries. They distinguish 2 clusters.

1) The *corporatist post-socialist regime* comprises the central European countries, with mostly transfer oriented labour market measures and a moderate degree of employment protection.The Czech Republic, Hungary, Poland, Slovenia, and Slovakia are included in this cluster.

---

[5] We follow Muffels and Luÿkx (2006) in locating the Netherlands in the social democratic cluster.

Table 6.1. Percentage below the 60% Poverty Threshold and above the Corresponding Consumption Deprivation Threshold by Country

	%
Social democratic	*32.0*
Sweden	31.7
Norway	32.4
Denmark	34.7
Netherlands	27.8
Iceland	24.6
Finland	40.6
Corporatist	*38.1*
Luxembourg	40.2
Austria	33.3
Belgium	44.8
France	38.6
Germany	33.4
Liberal	*47.4*
UK	47.0
Ireland	47.8
Southern European	*39.6*
Spain	33.0
Italy	45.9
Portugal	43.4
Cyprus	32.3
Greece	43.3
Post-socialist corporatist	*38.6*
Slovenia	37.5
Czech Republic	38.7
Hungary	41.3
Slovakia	32.1
Poland	43.4
Post-socialist liberal	*44.5*
Estonia	45.2
Latvia	41.7
Lithuania	46.7

2) The *post-socialist liberal cluster* comprises the Baltic countries, which are characterized by a more flexible labour market, with employers unwilling to abide by legal regulation of the market, and an absence of policies aimed at sustaining employment. Estonia, Latvia, and Lithuania are included in this group.[6]

In Table 6.1, for the 26 countries included in EU-SILC, we show the percentage of individuals in households below the 60% relative income threshold who are also found above the corresponding consumption deprivation threshold.

In no case does the figure rise above 50%. The lowest value of 25% is found for Iceland and the highest of 48% for Ireland. The evidence provides no

---

[6] See also Fenger (2007), who employs hierarchical cluster analysis to arrive at a similar typology.

support for the argument that the limitations of the 'at risk of poverty' derive mainly from the enlargement of the European Union to include substantially less affluent countries. The lowest level of overlap is associated with the most affluent countries. For the social democratic observations, comprising the Scandinavian countries and the Netherlands the average figure is 32%. It rises above 40% only for Finland and in none of the remaining cases does it significantly exceed one-third of the population. For the 5 corporatist countries the mean level is 38% with the figure going from a low of 33% in Austria to a high of 45% in Belgium. The highest level of overlap is observed for the members of the liberal welfare regime with the respective figures for the UK and Ireland being 47 and 49%. The profiles for the southern European and post-socialist cluster do not depart significantly from that observed for the corporatist cluster with averages respectively of 39.6 and 38.6%. For the post-socialist liberal cluster it rises to 45%.

What is of primary interest is not the limited variation in consistency across country but rather the uniformly modest degree of the overlap. Furthermore, as a number of studies have shown, a focus on a lower income threshold, rather than leading to a greater degree of overlap, actually exacerbates the inconsistency due to the lower level of reliability associated with incomes concentrated at the bottom of the distribution (Layte et al., 2001; Whelan et al., 2001; Berthoud et al., 2004). Moving from less to more stringent specifications of the income threshold does not lead, as one would expect, to the identification of correspondingly more deprived groups. If one adopts an entirely national perspective and seeks to use income poverty measures to identify those experiencing high levels of consumption deprivation, the procedure works equally well in 'old' and 'new' member states and in less and more affluent countries. However, in no case does it produce the kind of outcome that we might expect from a valid poverty measure.

In order to explore the consequences of the limited overlap between income poverty and deprivation, we have developed a typology produced by cross-classifying these variables. Consequently we distinguish those individuals who are both income poor and deprived, those who are income poor but not deprived, those who are deprived but not income poor, and finally those who are not experiencing income poverty and are above the deprivation threshold. In Table 6.2 we break down the distribution of individuals across the categories of this typology by country. Focusing first on those who experience neither type of disadvantage we find that the number in this group is close to 80% for the social democratic group and is just below that level for the corporatist cluster. For the liberal and southern European groups it falls to close to 70%. Greater variability is observed within the post-socialist corporatist with the figure for the Czech Republic reaching 85% while for Hungary and Poland it falls to 55 and 74%.

Table 6.2. Combined Income Poverty and Deprivation Typology by Country

	Poverty typology			
	Neither income poor nor deprived (%)	Income poor but not deprived (%)	Deprived but not income poor (%)	Income poor and deprived (%)
Social democratic	*80.9*	*7.3*	*8.6*	*3.3*
Sweden	79.2	8.1	9.0	3.8
Norway	81.5	6.1	9.4	2.9
Denmark	79.6	7.5	8.9	4.0
Netherlands	82.9	7.0	7.3	2.7
Iceland	82.4	7.3	7.9	2.4
Finland	79.6	7.5	8.9	4.0
Corporatist	*78.6*	*8.2*	*8.1*	*5.1*
Luxembourg	79.2	8.4	6.7	5.6
Austria	78.9	8.3	8.6	4.1
Belgium	76.8	8.1	8.5	6.6
France	77.7	8.0	9.3	5.0
Germany	80.5	8.2	7.2	4.1
Liberal	*69.0*	*9.9*	*12.3*	*8.9*
UK	67.0	10.2	13.8	9.0
Ireland	71.0	9.5	10.8	8.7
Southern European	*69.9*	*10.8*	*11.6*	*7.7*
Spain	71.6	10.0	10.1	8.3
Italy	68.5	10.6	11.9	9.0
Portugal	68.9	10.9	12.6	7.6
Cyprus	73.5	10.7	10.7	5.1
Greece	67.0	11.7	12.5	8.8
Post-socialist corporatist	*77.8*	*8.3*	*8.6*	*5.4*
Slovenia	79.5	7.3	8.9	4.4
Czech Republic	84.5	6.0	5.7	3.8
Hungary	74.5	9.4	9.4	6.6
Slovakia	80.4	7.9	8.0	3.7
Poland	70.1	10.8	10.8	8.3
Post-socialist liberal	*67.2*	*12.5*	*11.9*	*8.5*
Estonia	69.3	13.2	11.0	6.5
Latvia	63.3	13.5	13.6	9.6
Lithuania	69.0	10.7	11.0	9.4

For those experiencing only income poverty the rate ranges between 6 and 8% for the social democratic countries. This rises to between 10 to 11% for the post-socialist corporatist cluster. The figure ranges from 6% in the Czech Republic to 11% in Poland. Finally, the highest level is found among the post-socialist liberal cluster where it goes from 11% in Lithuania to 14% in Latvia. Very similar levels are observed in relation to those deprived but not income poor.

Given two relevant pieces of information about a household—income and deprivation—each with limitations from both conceptual and measurement perspectives, incorporating both into the measurement process is one way to seek to improve reliability in identifying the poor. A reasonably straightforward way of doing so is to focus on those who are both on low (relative) income and experiencing high (relative) levels of deprivation. We developed and applied this approach with colleagues in Ireland in the early 1990s to distinguish those 'consistently poor'—that is, poor when assessed both by income and by deprivation. This was subsequently adopted as the official measure of poverty for use in the Irish government's National Anti-Poverty Strategy, and had a major influence on the groups identified as most vulnerable. The focus on those both on low income and manifesting serious deprivation excluded many of those reporting low income from self-employment, and highlighted *inter alia* the relatively disadvantaged situation of families with children in 'working poor' households. This had a considerable influence on the development of policy, including the boosting of child income support levels. Such an approach has also been applied in some other countries (notably Austria) and in making comparisons across EU countries (e.g., Forster, 2005).

The final column of Table 6.2 uses this approach to derive levels of 'consistent poverty' for each of the 26 countries—that is, the percentage both below the 60% of median relative income threshold and above the consumption deprivation threshold described earlier. By far the most favourable position is enjoyed by those living in social democratic regimes with an average of 3%. The figure goes from a low of 2% in Iceland to a high of 4% in Denmark and Sweden. The level rises to 5% for the corporatist cluster with the range going from 4 and 7%. A fairly sharp rise to 9% is then observed for the liberal group. A marginally lower level is found for the southern European cluster, with the exception of Cyprus where it falls to 5%. Within the post-socialist cluster the average level of 5% again conceals a bi-modal pattern. Consistent poverty levels as low as 4% are observed for Slovakia, Slovenia, and the Czech Republic but figure rises to close to twice this level for Hungary and Poland. The level within the post-socialist cluster is very similar to that noted earlier for the liberal group. Overall variation across welfare regimes is a good deal sharper in relation to consistent poverty than with regard to income poverty or deprivation taken alone.

6.4 Income Poverty, Deprivation, and Social Class

Our interest in distinguishing different combinations of income poverty and deprivation goes beyond a descriptive account of their relative magnitude and the nature of their variation across countries and welfare regimes. We are particularly focused on the extent to which the choice of measure or combination of measures affects conclusions regarding the factors influencing poverty levels. It is not our intention to provide here a comprehensive multivariate analysis of the characteristics associated with poverty. While we will refer to such analyses where appropriate, we will focus our attention on social class differentials and the manner in which our conclusions relating to its influence are shaped, to a significant extent, by a shift from a one-dimensional to a multidimensional perspective and from a static to a dynamic viewpoint.

Our concern is to understand how the manner in which we measure poverty affects conclusions relating to socio-economic differentiation. The increased emphasis on de-standardization or individualization of the life-cycle and a related stress on life events, together with a focus on increasing flexibility and precariousness in the labour market and the changing role of the welfare state, has led some to suggest that the impact of factors such as social class are declining (Beck, 1992). A larger proportion of people are thought to experience life-cycle risks and consequent poverty. Poverty is democratized in the sense that it transcends traditional stratification boundaries. Poverty is seen increasingly as both individualized and transitory. Leisering and Liebfried (1999) argue that the 'temporalization and biographization' of poverty are features of the emergence of the 'risk society'.

In what follows we explore the extent to which conclusions relating to the impact of social class are affected by moving from a focus solely on income to an approach that encompasses information relating to material deprivation. In later chapters we will return to the issue of socio-economic differentiation in relation to the impact of choice of geographical unit and the more general consequences of moving from a 1-dimensional and static approach to measuring poverty and social exclusion to one that seeks to take into account their multidimensional and dynamic character.

The analysis that follows is conducted at the level of the individual; however, since income and deprivation are measured at the household level, we assign the social class of the household reference person to all household members. Where more than one person is responsible for the accommodation we use a 'dominance' procedure, taking into account their labour force status and individual class position to decide between them. Through this volume we have chosen to allocate all household reference persons currently unemployed or inactive on the basis of their previous occupation or that of their partner where appropriate. We have done so because, given the outcomes on which we are focusing, to create a separate category for such respondents would obscure rather than clarify underlying relational class processes.

In introducing social class into our analysis, we make use of an aggregated version of the European Socio-economic Classification (ESeC). The schema, following Goldthorpe (2007b), is based on an understanding of forms of employment relationships as viable responses to the weaker or stronger presence of monitoring and asset specificity problems in different work situations. As Goldthorpe (2002, p. 213) observes, one of the primary objectives of ESeC and other social class schemes in the same tradition is to bring out the constraints and opportunities typical of different class positions particularly as they bear 'on individual's *security, stability, and prospects* as a precondition of constructing explanations of empirical regularities'.

In order to capture the main features of class differentiation across countries and regimes we operate with an aggregated version of the ESeC class schema that distinguishes the following four groups.

1) *Professional and managerial*—comprising employers, higher grade professional, administrative and managerial occupations (ESeC Classes 1 and 2);

2) *White collar and technical*—comprising higher grade white collar workers (ESeC Class 3) and lower supervisory and lower technician occupations (ESeC Class 6);

3) *Self-employed*—comprising small employer and self-employed occupations (ESeC Classes 4 and 5); and

4) *Working class*—comprising lower services, sales and clerical occupations, and lower technical occupations (ESeC Classes 7 and 8), routine occupations.

In Table 6.3 we report the results of a multinomial regression analysis in which the dependent variable is the combined income and poverty typology and the independent variable is the set of social class dummies. For social class the reference category is the professional and managerial class and for poverty/deprivation the benchmark is those neither income poor nor deprived. The coefficients reported are log odds or additive coefficients rather than multiplicative coefficients or odds ratios. We have focused on the former because in some cases small cell numbers make comparisons of the latter more difficult to present and interpret.[7] Focusing first on those individuals experiencing income poverty only, we find that rather than observing a clear class gradient, the highest risk of this outcome is associated with self-employment. For 21 of the 26 countries in our analysis the highest log odds is found for the self-employed. This is true for all 6 of the social democratic countries. The log odds are lowest for Norway and Sweden with values of 1.3 and 1.5 before rising to between 2.0 and 2.8 for the remaining countries with Finland at the upper end of the spectrum. Within the corporatist group Luxembourg proves the only exception. For the liberal group the coefficient for the manual class is higher than that for the self-employed. For the southern European countries Cyprus is the only exception, while for the post-socialist countries the exceptions are the Czech Republic and Hungary.

A consistent pattern is also observed whereby the risk of income poverty only is found to be higher for the working class group than for the lower white

---

[7] Log odds of 1, 2, and 3 translate into odds ratios of 2.7, 7.4, and 20.1, respectively.

Table 6.3. Multinomial Regression of Poverty Typology by Social Class by Country: Odds Ratios

	Consistently poor			Deprived only			Income poor only		
	Working class	Self-employed	White collar & technical	Working class	Self-employed	White collar & technical	Working class	Self-employed	White collar & technical
Social democratic	*1.874*	*1.915*	*1.054*	*1.301*	*0.028*	*0.075*	*0.900*	*2.038*	*0.180*
Sweden	1.932	1.558	0.781	1.408	-0.009	0.684	0.406	1.481	0.028
Norway	3.805	3.781	2.257	0.954	0.125	0.573	0.888	1.315	0.018
Denmark	1.037	0.378	0.676	1.037	0.378	0.676	-0.045	1.991	-0.038
Finland	1.578	2.462	0.510	1.859	0.902	1.313	1.071	2.824	0.229
Iceland	0.881	2.549	1.420	1.351	0.240	1.134	1.551	2.361	0.092
Netherlands	2.008	0.764	0.742	1.227	0.029	0.666	0.631	2.256	0.754
Corporatist	*2.915*	*1.754*	*1.218*	*1.752*	*0.629*	*0.805*	*1.669*	*1.843*	*0.700*
Luxembourg	3.189	0.358	1.673	2.032	0.274	0.872	2.452	1.625	1.451
Austria	2.817	1.026	0.502	1.516	0.268	0.440	1.378	0.913	0.550
Belgium	3.770	2.843	1.840	1.891	1.082	1.021	1.629	2.482	0.689
Germany	1.907	1.771	0.821	1.457	0.937	0.849	1.310	1.895	0.325
France	2.893	2.733	1.252	1.912	0.583	0.845	1.574	2.299	0.484
Liberal	*2.745*	*1.017*	*1.399*	*1.813*	*0.874*	*0.863*	*1.472*	*1.614*	*0.922*
UK	3.157	2.179	1.772	1.727	0.906	0.881	1.430	1.906	0.734
Ireland	2.334	-0.146	1.026	1.899	-0.229	0.866	1.514	1.332	1.111
Southern European	*2.957*	*2.698*	*1.267*	*2.207*	*1.544*	*1.340*	*1.892*	*2.411*	*0.844*
Italy	2.727	2.361	1.178	1.326	0.848	0.582	1.646	2.093	0.678
Spain	2.617	2.287	1.145	1.893	1.204	1.265	1.488	2.307	0.609
Cyprus	3.718	2.925	1.766	2.023	1.641	1.129	2.758	2.387	1.749
Greece	2.618	2.984	0.723	2.868	2.195	1.795	1.556	2.442	0.116
Portugal	3.107	2.934	1.524	2.926	1.834	1.927	2.012	2.824	0.921
Post-socialist corporatist	*3.059*	*1.782*	*1.404*	*1.538*	*0.062*	*0.722*	*1.650*	*1.840*	*0.762*
Slovenia	3.043	1.665	1.826	1.769	0.667	0.934	1.415	1.755	0.551
Czech Republic	3.071	2.072	1.223	1.953	1.117	0.957	1.879	1.276	0.995
Slovakia	2.398	0.661	0.815	0.950	0.029	0.329	1.088	1.842	0.555
Poland	3.074	2.735	1.668	1.640	0.558	0.890	1.863	2.657	1.136
Hungary	3.710	1.780	1.487	1.330	0.633	0.500	2.007	1.671	0.572
Post-socialist liberal	*2.269*	*1.768*	*1.170*	*1.167*	*0.052*	*0.816*	*1.363*	*2.088*	*0.871*
Estonia	2.187	2.022	1.322	1.004	-0.304	0.773	1.157	2.308	0.789
Latvia	1.891	0.926	0.635	1.159	0.313	0.811	1.023	1.723	0.569
Lithuania	2.730	2.610	1.362	1.338	0.736	0.863	1.909	2.234	1.254

Note: Consistently non-poor and professional managerial class as the reference categories: logged odds.

collar and technical group. This is true for 24 out of 26 countries in the analysis with the log odds for these countries ranging from 0.406 for Sweden to 2.8 for Greece. For only 2 of the 78 results reported in Table 6.3 do we find an outcome that suggests that the likelihood of being found in the income poor only category is higher for the professional and managerial class than for any of the other groups. A clear ranking emerges, across all welfare regimes, in which the risk of being in this category increases as one moves, in turn, from the professional and managerial class to the lower white collar and technical group to the working class and finally the self-employed.

The outcome relating to experience of deprivation only is somewhat different. On this occasion the highest relative risk of being found in this category is in every case associated with the working class. Among the social democratic countries the log odds value goes from a low of 1.0 in Norway to a high of 1.9 in Finland. On average, the values are slightly higher in the corporatist countries with the minimum value of 1.5 being found for Austria and the maximum of 2.0 associated with Luxembourg. For the UK and Ireland the values are, respectively, 1.7 and 1.9. Within the southern European cluster the value of 1.3 for Italy is the lowest. The log odds for Spain and Cyprus are slightly higher than those for the liberal countries and a sharp increase to 2.9 is observed for Greece and Portugal. The outcomes for the post-socialist corporatist are similar to those for the corporatist group but somewhat more variable. Finally, the values for the post-socialist cluster are towards the lower end of the continuum. When we compare the outcomes for the lower white collar and technical class with those for the self-employed, we find that log odds values are higher in the former case for 19 of the 26 countries. In only 3 cases is the likelihood of being found in this category higher for those in the professional and managerial class in comparison with any other class. Once again a uniform pattern emerges across welfare regimes in which the risk of being in the deprived only category declines as one proceeds from the managerial class to the self-employed, the lower white collar and technical group, and finally the working class.

Finally, turning our attention to the consistently poor group we find that in 25 of the 26 cases the highest log odds is observed for the manual class. The sole exception is Iceland where the highest risk of consistent poverty is found for the self-employed. These higher values, to a significant extent, reflect the extremely low risk of experiencing consistent poverty among the professional and managerial classes with the level exceeding 2% in only two cases. The log odds value is greater than 3 in 9 of the 26 cases. For 7 cases it lies between 2 and 3 and for 5 between 1 and 2. Unlike the case for experience of deprivation only, in 21 of 26 countries the relative risk of being in the consistently poor group is greater for the self-employed than for the lower white collar and technical group. Across welfare regimes, the only deviation from a pattern in which risk declines as one goes from the professional and managerial class to the lower white collar and technical to the self-employed to the working class arises because of the distinctively low level of consistently poverty among the self-employed in Ireland.

Our findings show that the self-employed are particularly likely to be income poor but not deprived but are rather unlikely to be deprived but not income poor. This is entirely consistent with the fact that current income is a significantly poorer indicator of longer term command over resources than in the case of employees. Of course the self-employed are a heterogeneous group and this is reflected in the fact that their risk of consistent poverty is higher than for the white collar and technical group. Once the self-employed are removed from the equation, a clear hierarchy of class effects emerges. These are most pronounced in relation to consistent poverty followed by deprivation only and finally income poverty only. It is clear that an adequate understanding of class effects requires that we take into account the distinction between current and long-term income and the extent to which the significance of this distinction varies across class groups.

6.5 Economic Stress and Forms of Poverty

In order to understand the consequences of the choice of indicator for our understanding of the nature of poverty, we proceed to examine the relation between the combined income and deprivation typology and subjective economic stress. The latter is defined as being in a household that experiences 'difficulty' or 'great difficulty' in making ends meet. In Table 6.4 we show the results from a set of logistic regressions with economic stress as the dependent variable and the class dummies as the independent variables. The coefficients are again log odds. From Table 6.4 we can see that the relative risk of economic stress increases as one goes from the consistently non-poor group to those income poor only, deprived only, and finally consistently poor. However, the pattern we observe is not one of a steady increase but rather involves a sharp contrast between those experiencing deprivation and all others. If we focus first on the relative risk of economic stress for those income poor only in comparison with those consistently non-poor, we can see that in every case the risk is higher for the latter. The impact is weakest in Norway and Sweden with log odds values of 0.1 and 0.3 in Norway and Sweden. For the remaining countries the log odds varies from 0.8 to 1.6 with relatively little additional systematic variation across welfare regimes.

Shifting our attention to the group experiencing deprivation only, we observe a generally sharp increase in the log odds. The value of the coefficients ranges from a low of 1.8 in Latvia and Lithuania to a

Table 6.4. Relative Risk of Experiencing Economic Stress by Poverty Typology by Country: Odds Ratios

	Odds ratio		
	Income poor only	Deprivation only	Consistently poor
Social democratic	*1.013*	*2.917*	*3.310*
SE	0.261	3.284	3.572
NO	0.088	3.194	3.564
DK	1.399	3.001	3.579
FI	1.255	3.036	3.165
IS	0.813	2.302	2.784
NL	1.262	2.682	3.198
Corporatist	*0.924*	*2.794*	*3.110*
LU	0.972	2.493	3.077
AT	1.151	2.621	3.381
BE	1.325	2.755	3.432
DE	0.993	3.143	3.235
FR	1.105	2.957	3.425
Liberal	*0.990*	*2.317*	*3.159*
UK	0.924	2.421	3.093
IE	1.056	2.212	3.225
Southern European	*0.942*	*2.221*	*2.700*
IT	0.952	2.449	3.002
ES	0.804	1.884	2.661
CY	0.955	2.063	2.530
GR	1.112	2.513	2.643
PT	0.887	2.197	2.668
Post-socialist corporatist	*1.114*	*2.399*	*3.371*
SI	1.087	2.353	2.941
CZ	1.559	3.164	3.867
SK	0.815	1.774	2.906
PL	1.119	2.458	3.747
HU	0.992	2.245	3.394
Post-socialist liberal	*1.183*	*2.045*	*3.149*
EE	1.435	2.529	3.584
LV	0.875	1.768	2.907
LT	1.241	1.837	2.957

Note: 'Non-poor and deprived' as reference category: log odds ratios.

high of 3.3 in Sweden. Finally, for all 26 countries we observe an increase in the value of log odds for the consistent poverty group. In this case the lowest value of 2.6 is found for Greece and Portugal while the highest of 3.9 is associated with the Czech Republic. In 14 of the 26 countries the value of the log odds exceeds 3.

Taking deprivation into account produces patterns of social class variation in outcomes in relation to economic stress that are substantially more in line with the profiles we would expect to be associated with a valid poverty measure than is the case for indicators based solely on income.

Finally, for all 26 countries we observe an increase in the value of log odds for the consistent poverty group. In this case the lowest value of 2.6 is found for Greece while the highest of 3.9 is associated with Slovakia. In 14 of the 26 countries the value of the log odds exceeds 3.

6.6 Persistent Poverty and Deprivation

For many the key to resolving the difficulties presented by the mismatch between income and deprivation indicators has increasingly been seen to lie in using longitudinal measures. Research using panel data has drawn attention to the limitations of a static perspective on poverty. Among those poor at any point, there will be some who have only recently dropped below the threshold and whose living standards have, as yet, been unaffected. In contrast, there will be some who have been poor a good deal longer, whose resources have been depleted over time and whose standard of living has been significantly eroded. Panel research has shown that movements into and out of poverty are a great deal more frequent than had been supposed and that a far greater proportion of the population experience poverty at some point in time than is revealed by cross sectional studies (Breen and Moiso, 2004). It is precisely the distinction between the transitory poor and the persistently poor that has motivated attempts to develop social indicators that go beyond cross-sectional measures and take into account the experience of poverty over a period of time (Atkinson et al., 2002).

In attempting to develop our understanding of these issues, we make use of data from the ECHP. This leads to a restriction of the range of countries we can cover in comparison with EU-SILC. However, since our objectives are analytic rather than descriptive, this consideration is outweighed by the larger samples sizes and longer period of observation provided by the ECHP. By extending our measure of income poverty, the aim is to get a better measure of permanent income or command over resources. The expectation would then be that such a measure would be more strongly related to deprivation and would contribute to a reduction in the income poverty–deprivation mismatch. Implicit in this approach is the assumption that deprivation measures are much more stable than income measures and thus that current level of deprivation is a significantly better indicator of persistent deprivation than current income is of its corresponding longitudinal component. Given this, the mismatch problem, evident at the cross-sectional level, would be largely resolved by taking poverty experience over time into account. Further, we would expect that the predictors of income poverty persistence and deprivation persistence would be a great deal more similar than in the case of their cross-sectional counterparts.

In addressing these issues, Whelan et al. (2004) extend the period over which poverty is observed by using the first 5 waves of the ECHP. We have restricted our attention to this 5-year period to avoid difficulties associated with sparse cells. Employing a typology developed by Fourage (2002) and following Fourage and Layte (2005) we characterize the time-dependent nature in terms of four dimensions:

- The length of the observation period;
- The extent of recurrent poverty;
- The length of the poverty spell; and
- The volatility and stability of poverty statuses over time.

Together these 4 dimensions determine the poverty profile for each individual over time. In the analysis that follows we make use of a typology of poverty profiles that will allow us to examine both the persistence and recurrence of poverty by distinguishing between:

a) The persistent non-poor (never poor during the accounting period);

b) The transient poor (poor only once during the accounting period);

c) The recurrent poor (poor more than once but never longer than 2 consecutive years); and

d) The persistent poor (poor for a consecutive period of at least 3 consecutive years).

At both a conceptual and a policy level many would wish to reserve the term poverty for low income relative to a particular level of need and view other forms of deprivation as a consequence of such poverty (Berthoud et al., 2004). From this perspective, the main value of deprivation measures is to assist in calibration income thresholds (Gordon, 2002). In principle, we have considerable sympathy with such an approach and the clear distinction between resources and outcomes that is involved. However, it is necessary to consider how successful the approach is in practice. For the purposes of our present analysis, rather than assuming a priori that income and deprivation are tapping different phenomena, we seek to establish how far we can go in resolving the income–deprivation mismatch through appropriate measurement and analysis.

Our analysis proceeds as follows, employing ECHP panel data, having identified median income poverty lines relating to annual equivalent disposable income for 1993–7, we then calculate the proportion of respondents below such thresholds. We then establish the corresponding deprivation threshold for the years from 1994 to 1998. The deprivation measure is based on a 13-item index of enforced current life-style deprivation (CLSD) weighted inversely to the proportion possessing each item in a particular country. This combines two dimensions identified by Whelan et al. (2001), as discussed earlier: *basic life-style deprivation* comprises items such as food and clothing, a

Table 6.5. Poverty Profiles at 70% of Median Equivalized Income, ECHP 1994–8 (Percentage by Row)

	Persistent non-poor (%)	Transient poor (%)	Recurrent poor (%)	Persistent poor (%)
Denmark	66.8	14.3	10.5	8.3
Netherlands	65.0	11.2	9.7	14.1
Belgium	54.4	13.9	13.5	18.2
France	59.7	10.0	9.7	20.0
Ireland	53.7	9.6	11.3	25.4
Italy	50.7	13.8	13.5	22.0
Greece	50.0	13.0	15.6	21.4
Spain	51.0	12.9	17.5	18.9
Portugal	50.6	11.3	13.9	24.2

Table 6.6. Deprivation Profiles Corresponding to 70% of Median Equivalized Income, ECHP 1994–8 (Percentage by Row)

	Persistent non-deprived (%)	Transient deprived (%)	Recurrent deprived (%)	Persistent deprived (%)
Denmark	67.0	11.6	11.1	10.4
Netherlands	65.2	11.3	9.7	13.9
Belgium	54.1	16.9	11.3	17.7
France	57.8	12.3	12.4	17.5
Ireland	49.1	11.6	15.5	23.7
Italy	46.9	16.6	16.6	19.9
Greece	42.5	17.2	20.2	20.0
Spain	51.9	13.6	16.4	18.1
Portugal	50.3	11.9	14.4	23.5

holiday at least once a year, replacing worn-out furniture, and the experience of arrears for scheduled payments, while secondary life-style deprivation is made up of items less likely to be considered essential such as a car, a phone, a colour television, a video recorder, a microwave, and a dishwasher.

In Tables 6.5 and 6.6 we set out the poverty and deprivation profiles for eight countries in the ECHP for whom appropriate data were available.[8] The 70% median income line has been chosen as a cut-off point, thus avoiding problems arising from sparse numbers in the longitudinal 5-way tables. The distribution of respondents across both the income poverty and deprivation profiles is remarkably similar. The level of persistent poverty ranges from 14% in the Netherlands to 25% in Ireland. The corresponding figures for deprivation are 14% in the Netherlands and 24% in Ireland and Portugal. The number entirely avoiding poverty goes from 65% in the Netherlands to 43% in Greece.

[8] We have excluded Denmark from this analysis because it constitutes an exception whose peculiarities we do not seek to address. As well as displaying distinctively low levels of income poverty and deprivation persistence, it also exhibits a much weaker pattern of association between both forms of persistence.

Table 6.7. Percentage Persistently Deprived by Persistent Income Poverty Profile

	Persistent non-poor (%)	Transient poor (%)	Recurrent poor (%)	Persistent poor (%)
Netherlands	5	15	23	48
Belgium	7	11	28	49
France	6	17	36	44
Ireland	6	28	34	55
Italy	7	13	28	49
Greece	17	19	23	47
Spain	4	17	25	51
Portugal	8	21	34	50
All Countries	6	17	29	49

For deprivation the corresponding figures are 65 and 43%. The transient income poor figure goes from 10 to 14% and the corresponding deprivation figure from 12 to 17%. Finally between 10 and 18% are found in the recurrent income poverty category and between 10 and 20% in the corresponding deprivation category.

In Table 6.7 we set out the relationship between persistent deprivation and persistent income poverty. The results confirm the value of longitudinal income information in identifying those who are persistently deprived. The patterns of association across countries are strikingly similar, such that the overall distribution for the 8 countries combined does not seriously misrepresent that pattern in any of the individual countries. Thus the percentage persistently deprived increases gradually from 6% among the persistently non-poor to 49% for the persistently poor. On the basis of an ordinal logit analysis of the relationship between the two forms of persistence where we consider the cumulative odds comparisons that can be made involving the four categories of the deprivation profile, we find that, in comparison with the persistently non-income poor the odds on the transiently poor being in a group with greater exposure to persistent deprivation is 2.4 times higher. For the recurrent poor this rises to 5.0 and for the persistently poor to 13.3.

We observe a strong relatively uniform relationship between the different forms of persistence for 8 of the 9 countries in our analysis. The longitudinal income measures constitute a significant improvement on its cross-sectional counterpart. However, contrary to expectations, the overlap between the forms of persistence is no greater than that observed at the cross-sectional level. If we exclude Denmark, the overlap for the persistence measure ranges from 44 to 55%. Focusing on the fifth wave, we find that the cross-sectional estimate goes from 48 to 62%. Thus the levels of overlap are remarkably similar.

Table 6.8. Employment Status and Social Class Composition 1998 by Combined Income Poverty and Deprivation Profile

	Employment status		Social class	
	Unemployed > 6 months (%)	Employee and no unemployment in the past 5 years (%)	Manual (%)	Non-manual (%)
Neither income-poor nor deprived	1.6	58.4	40.5	42.1
Persistently income poor only	4.2	41.3	48.1	20.5
Persistently deprived only	6.3	36.1	65.7	19.6
Both income-poor and deprived	11.8	25.3	68.2	9.1

To what extent are conclusions concerning the role of socio-economic factors such as social class influenced by whether one focuses on income poverty or deprivation or persistence or their overlap? Whelan et al.'s (2004) analysis of the factors influencing persistent income poverty and persistent deprivation shows that, consistent with the findings of our earlier cross-sectional analysis, the most striking contrast related to the fact that the impact of being a small holder or being self-employed on income poverty persistence is substantially greater than for persistent deprivation. Thus, even in relation to longitudinal analysis, self-employment generally appears to be a much poorer indicator of command over resources than its relation to income would suggest, because such income estimates are substantially influenced by short-term factors affecting income streams and by the greater options available to the self-employed regarding the manner in which they can take occupational rewards.

One of the problems with the analysis reported above is that it relates to 2 substantially overlapping groups. Focusing on the combined persistent income poverty and deprivation typology allows us to overcome this difficulty. Pursuing such an analysis, Whelan et al. (2004) demonstrated the value of differentiating between different forms of persistence and their overlap in terms of our understanding of the impact of factors such as social class. The scale of the effects can be illustrated by shifting from a risk perspective to an incidence perspective. In Table 6.8 above, we show the composition for each of the categories of the combined income and deprivation persistence profile in relation a manual–non-manual contrast using an aggregated version of the EGP schema. We find the category containing those neither persistently poor nor deprived contains equal numbers of manual and non-manual workers. Manual workers constitute almost half of those persistently income poor only but in this instance they outnumber non-manual workers by a ratio of 2 to 1. For those persistently deprived but not persistently income poor, the share of manual workers rises to two-thirds while non-manual respondents make up only one-fifth. Finally, among those exposed to both types of persistence, over two-thirds are drawn from the manual class while less than one-tenth come from the non-manual class. Thus, as we move across the categories of the combined income and deprivation persistence profile, we go gradually from a position of parity between numbers coming from the manual and non-manual categories in the most privileged group to one of overwhelming manual dominance among those who are doubly disadvantaged.

6.7 Conclusions

In this chapter we have sought to shed light on the mismatch between income poverty and deprivation through a comparative and dynamic analysis of both forms of disadvantage stemming not only from a desire to have confidence in our conclusions relating to levels of poverty, but from the need to develop a secure understanding of socio-economic factors associated with exclusion from a minimally acceptable standard of living due to a lack of resources. Unless we are able to understand the nature of the relationship between income poverty and life-style deprivation, our confidence in both types of measures will be undermined. The rationale underlying the development of measures of persistent income poverty is that such measures of consistent income poverty will provide better indicators of command over resources, and as a consequence will be more strongly associated with material deprivation. Given this, the mismatch evident at the cross-sectional level could be resolved through longitudinal analysis.

Our initial analysis, employing the EU-SILC data set, focused on a comparison of the level of mismatch across the 26 countries included that data set. Our analysis revealed a relatively uniform pattern of overlap between low income and high deprivation across countries. For none of the 6 welfare regimes we identified did it reach one-half. Cross-classifying the income poverty and deprivation measures produced a combined income poverty and deprivation typology. Employing this typology revealed a much sharper variation across welfare regimes in terms of consistent poverty than income poverty. Furthermore, focusing on relative risk, we found that the pattern of differentiation in terms of social class varied systematically across the categories of the typology. The highest risk of being in the income poor only group was associated with self-employment while for deprivation only this group experienced by far the lowest risk. In contrast, a clear hierarchy of class effects emerges for consistent poverty that goes from the professional–managerial class to lower white collar and technical group to the self-employed and finally the working class. Finally, in terms of economic stress, the major contrast is between those groups experiencing deprivation and others although the highest level is exhibited by the consistently poor. These finding appear to reflect the manner in which the different categories capture longer accumulation and erosion of resources.

In order to further our understanding of the operation of such processes, we extended our analysis, employing data from the ECHP involving a more restricted set of countries but allowing us to take a longitudinal perspective. By extending our analysis over 5 waves of the ECHP we were able to take into account the key dimensions characterizing poverty profiles over time. Our conclusions turn out to be remarkably stable across countries and it is on these uniformities that we focus. Persistent income poverty measures offer significant advantages over their cross-sectional counterparts. The income poverty profile turns out to be systematically related to both cross-sectional and longitudinal deprivation. However, contrary to expectations, the level of mismatch at the longitudinal level is no less than that for point-in-time measures.

Cross-classifying the forms of persistence revealed systematic variation across categories in the relative proportions drawn respectively from the working class and the manual classes with the balance shifting towards working class domination as one moves from the consistently non-poor to the consistently poor group. In Chapters 7 and 8 we will extend our analysis of the relationship between income poverty and material deprivation through a more systematic use of multidimensional and dynamic approaches.

7

Comparing Poverty Indicators in an Enlarged EU

7.1 Introduction

In this chapter we extend our analysis in order to assess the extent to which a consideration of welfare regime and socio-economic variation in poverty levels and patterns and the consequences of poverty for subjectively experienced economic stress can inform our understanding of the strengths and weaknesses of alternative poverty indicators in an enlarged EU.

Poverty in the EU is normally defined in terms of income thresholds established at the level of each member state. The 'at-risk-of-poverty' indicator identifies those individuals falling below 60% of the national median disposable equivalent income appropriately adjusted for household composition. The conceptual foundations of this approach can be found in Townsend's (1979) definition of poverty as 'exclusion from ordinary living patterns and activities due to lack of resources'. Those falling more than a certain 'distance' below a nationally defined income level are understood to be excluded from a minimally acceptable way of life.

The current set of common EU indicators of poverty relies heavily on such measures. The emphasis on a purely relative perspective has been justified by the European Commission in the following terms:

An absolute notion is considered less relevant for the EU for two basic reasons. First the challenge for Europe is to make the whole population share the benefits of high average prosperity and not to reach basic standards of living as in less developed parts of the world. Secondly, what is regarded as minimal acceptable living standards depends largely on the general level of social and economic development, which tends to vary considerably across countries. (European Commission, 2004)

However, as Guio (2005) observes, enlargement of the EU and the consequent widening of the gap in living standards between the richest and the poorest member states have provoked concern about the ability of the current portfolio of indicators to satisfactorily reflect the situation of the new member states and facilitate meaningful comparison between them and the 'old' member states. Förster (2005, p. 32) notes that the labelling of the relative income measure as 'at risk of poverty' reflects the tendency of governments to interpret it as an indicator of inequality in income distribution rather than as a measure of poverty as such.

The apparent paradox presented by the results deriving from the 'at-risk-of-poverty' methodology has encouraged a number of responses. The first, which has been evolving for some time, involves a shift from a 1-dimensional perspective, focusing solely on relative income, to a multidimensional perspective that incorporates both income and material deprivation. The second involves teasing out the implications of indices constructed at an EU level. Critics of the 'at-risk-of-poverty' measure have focused on the fact that middle income households in poorer European states have incomes that are lower than the relative income poverty threshold in richer countries and that a larger share of the population in a richer country, such as Ireland, is considered poor than in less affluent countries, such as Estonia. Confronted with such outcomes, a number of authors have suggested that the use of a 'state bounded approach', i.e., employing measures defined entirely in terms of national relativities, can be challenged both on the grounds of differences in absolute deprivation and in the way people feel about their material living standards.

These paradoxical findings have therefore produced a number of inter-related responses. The first focuses on the limitations imposed by the entirely national frame of reference. Fahey (2007) argues for the development of an EU-wide measure alongside a nationally relative measure and recent exercises of this sort include Brandolini (2007) and Kangas and Ritakallio (2007). An alternative critique focuses on the fact that low income fails to identify those experiencing the forms of deprivation that one would expect to characterize those excluded from customary living patterns (Nolan and Whelan, 2007).

In this chapter we explore both multidimensional and Europe-wide approaches in order to compare the consequence of choice with regard to uni-dimensionality versus multidimensionality and geographical unit. The strength of both critiques is assessed by comparing the outcomes associated with being 'at risk of poverty' and in 'consistent poverty' at both national and EU levels. By the latter we mean being both below a relevant income threshold, such as 60% of equivalized income, and above a specified material deprivation threshold. Five alternative poverty and exclusion measures are constructed and compared: being 'at risk of poverty' vis-à-vis a national and an EU-wide benchmark, being in consistent poverty vis-à-vis a national and EU benchmark, and combining a national income benchmark with an EU-wide deprivation measure.

The chapter compares these alternative indicators of poverty and exclusion in terms of variation across welfare regimes and in socio-economic profile, and discusses which are most closely aligned with expectations of how a satisfactory measure would behave as we discuss at the outset in Section 7.2. Section 7.3 describes how the alternative measures of poverty and exclusion are constructed, and Section 7.4 sets out the variation they lead to across welfare regimes. Section 7.5 looks at the extent and nature of variation in these measures when one combines welfare regime with principal economic status. Section 7.6–7.10 look in more detail at each of the indicators in turn and the patterns they produce. Section 7.11 considers the relationship between subjectively experienced economic stress and these poverty measures across welfare regimes, while Section 7.12 summarizes the conclusions.

7.2 Expectations about Variation in Poverty across and within Countries

This chapter is focused centrally on the variation in poverty rates across countries categorized by welfare regime and across persons categorized by the principal economic status (PES) of the household reference person (HRP).[1] Our aim is to assess the construct validity of alternative indicators of poverty and exclusion by comparing these patterns of variation, in light of prior theoretical expectations of how a satisfactory measure would behave. We therefore start by considering in this section what those expectations might be and the basis for them.

The set of welfare regimes we employ in our analysis are as set out in Chapter 6 and comprises:

- The social democratic regime;
- The corporatist regime;
- The liberal regime;
- The southern European regime;
- The post-socialist corporatist regime; and
- The post-socialist liberal regime.

There is clearly a significant overlap here between the welfare regimes we identify and typologies that would emerge on the basis of GDP or levels of welfare spending.

With our current data it is not possible to disentangle their respective casual influences. Since comparison of patterns of socio-economic differentiation is

---

[1] The household reference person is defined as the individual responsible for the accommodation. Where such responsibility is shared, the older of the two individuals is chosen.

central to our analysis we believe our focus on welfare regimes rather than differentiation in terms of levels of GDP is justified. Esping-Andersen and Myles (2009, pp. 643–4) conclude that the available evidence provides little support for any straightforward link between GDP or higher levels of social spending and reduced inequality and rather suggests that the most important effects derive from the institutional design of welfare states. This provides the basis for a comparison of such regime effects with estimates based on alternative indicators. However, it should be kept in mind that the Esping-Andersen and Myles (2009) conclusion is based on studies using national relative income measures. Alternative measures, such as those based on European income levels, may reveal much stronger affluence effects with associated consequences for the measurement of socio-economic differentiation. An evaluation of the relative merits of alternative poverty measures requires the exercise of judgement in regard to the relative importance of uncovering patterns of socio-economic differentiation as compared with capturing welfare regime variation. It also requires an assessment of the degree to which patterns of variation within and between welfare regimes are consistent with our theoretical understanding of the meaning of poverty.

Below we set out our understanding of how an indicator of poverty should vary across welfare regimes and categories of HRP PES of the household. A satisfactory measure of poverty should identify a minority in each society experiencing 'exclusion from customary living standards due to lack of resources who are excluded from customary living patterns'. Where a proposed measure actually identifies a majority as 'poor' it is clearly unsatisfactory. Where the number of poor is not a great deal lower than that relating to non-poor it should clearly give us cause for concern. However, final judgements on the adequacy of poverty measures requires that we interpret such outcomes together with information relating to patterns of socio-economic differentiation.

As Esping-Andersen and Myles (2009, p. 640) observe, welfare state effects will reflect the effectiveness of insurance against life-cycle and class risks. The social democratic regime offers a comprehensive coverage on the basis of individualization of rights at a higher level of compensation than its counterparts. Maître et al. (2005, p. 168) show that the percentage of households lifted out of poverty by transfers is greatest for the social democratic regime. In line with our assessment of the available evidence, we expect social democratic regime to be most effective in terms of redistribution and consequently to have the lowest poverty rate. Corporatist regimes can be expected to exhibit the next most favourable poverty rate. Given the fact that, as Esping-Andersen and Myles (2009, p. 653) note, its tax-transfer system is far more focused pensioner than others, this outcome is likely to be significantly influenced by the situation of older people. The social democratic regime is substantially more redistributive than the liberal regime despite the role of targeting in the latter. The latter is distinctive in the extent to which households towards the bottom of the income distribution rely on transfers; it is not particularly effective in removing households from income poverty through welfare state. We therefore expect the liberal regime to be associated with a higher rate of poverty than the foregoing regimes. This outcome is consistent with Korpi and Palme's (1998) 'paradox of redistribution' thesis whereby such targeted transfers are typically ungenerous and stigmatizing while universal benefits are more generous and avoid take-up problems. For the southern European welfare regime the extent of reliance of disadvantaged households is much lower and only a relatively small proportion is lifted out of poverty by transfers. We therefore anticipate that the poverty rates for this regime will be higher than for the liberal regime. The low levels of welfare in the post-socialist regimes will limit the impact of welfare transfers and we expect that the highest rates of poverty will be observed for these regimes with the rate being higher for the liberal variant for reasons similar to those discussed above for the western European regimes.

Expected levels of poverty by welfare regime are derived from associated expectations relating to patterns of socio-economic differentiation in poverty rates within regimes. Given our objective in this chapter to compare poverty measures across welfare regimes, a poverty measure which produces the expected ranking of welfare regimes in terms of poverty levels but fails to produce the hypothesized patterns of socio-economic differentiation within regimes could not be considered satisfactory. It is therefore necessary to take into account the manner in which welfare regime and socio-economic differentiation interact. Specifically we expect to observe a significant impact of each of the forms of economic exclusion within welfare regimes but that the pattern of such variation will differ from one welfare regime to another. We take relativities within the social democratic regime as the reference point. Our key distinction is between the economically excluded and the full-time employed. The former comprises those in households where the household reference person is unemployed, ill/disabled, or inactive. Our analysis reports specific coefficients for each of these forms of economic exclusion. However, for the purposes of this chapter, our focus is not on explaining differences in outcomes between these forms of economic exclusion and we have not sought to develop hypotheses regarding such differentiation. Our principal interest lies rather in demonstrating the similarity in the manner in which their impact varies across regimes and the implications of this finding for an assessment of alternative measures of poverty.[2]

---

[2] Both our subsequent analysis and further analysis we have undertaken shows that collapsing the different forms of economic exclusion into 1 category and conducting the analysis on the

Our primary focus therefore is on economic exclusion. However, our analysis also distinguishes the retired and part-time employees from full-time employees. For our present purposes, this is done primarily to allow us to develop appropriate assessments of the impact of economic exclusion against the reference category of full-time employees. Failing to do so would lead to an underestimation of the effects of economic exclusion since the vast majority of those HRPs who are found in the social excluded categories would seem to be most sensibly thought of as excluded from full-time employment. We have deliberately not included the retired in the economically excluded category because, while for some retirement may mask such exclusion, it would be quite unreasonable to assume a priori that this applies to retirees in general. In case of retirement, in order to achieve appropriate assessments of the economic exclusion effects and the manner in which they vary across welfare regimes, we also allow cross regime variation in the impact of retirement. However, our expectations in relation to such variation are rather different to those relating to forms of economic exclusion. They derive primarily from the contrast between corporatist and liberal regimes. Such variation is not central to our assessment of alternative poverty measures but rather is taken into account in order to refine our estimates of variability in the impact of economic exclusion.

Similarly, the inclusion of a term for part-time employees, which is constrained to be uniform across regimes, contributes to our ability to estimate the impact of social exclusion in relation to the benchmark set by full-time employees.

Overall, while we anticipate that an appropriate measure of poverty will be associated with broadly similar patterns of interaction for each form of economic exclusion across welfare regimes, in every case we expect that the impact of unemployment will be more substantial than for inactivity or illness/disability.

Our expectations in relation to variation in the impact of economic exclusion across regimes are as follows. We anticipate that the weakest effect of economic exclusion will be found in the social democratic regime. Against that benchmark we anticipate that the next weakest impact of economic exclusion on relative 'at risk of poverty' will be observed for the corporatist regime. We also expect as a consequence of the advantages enjoyed by insiders in the labour market, that the impact of unemployment will be particularly

basis of a dichotomous economic exclusion variable has very little effect on our key substantive conclusions. However, we have chosen to present our results in a more differentiated form in order that readers can see that our results are not in any way an artefact of such aggregation. It also allows us to document differences in the average level of impact of different forms of social exclusion.

weak in this case. Our expectations are that the consequences of each of the forms of social exclusion—unemployment, illness/disability, and inactivity—will be greatest in the liberal regime. In the southern European case the limited extent of and level of coverage of welfare combined with a very modest social structuring of welfare dependency is likely to be reflected in comparatively high levels of poverty but an intermediate level of socio-economic differentiation in such levels.[3] For the post-socialist regimes similar reasoning leads us to expect a weaker pattern of differentials than for the liberal regime.

As we noted earlier, terms relating to part-time employees and the retired are included in our analysis in order to refine our estimate of the impact of economic exclusion.[4] In relation to retirement, it is necessary to allow for variation across welfare regime but of rather different kind to that relating to economic exclusion.[5] Expectations based on income-based poverty measures would lead us to anticipate that the impact of retirement would be weak not only in the social democratic regime but also in both forms of corporatist regime while being a good deal stronger in the liberal regimes. However, were we to focus on permanent income rather than current income our expectations would be rather different. In that case our findings are likely to be influenced by the long-term accumulation of resources by older people in terms of housing and other assets. The impact of such factors appears to be reflected in the fact that, as a variety of studies have demonstrated, the overlap between low income and high levels of deprivation is weakest for older people.[6] As a consequence any comparison between the retired and others employed using an indicator with a deprivation component is likely to show smaller difference than when a purely income-based measure is employed. This in turn is likely to lead to more muted variation across welfare regimes.

Earlier work has shown that the experience of subjective economic stress is influenced not only by current poverty and deprivation but also by level of persistence (Whelan et al., 2004). Consequently in evaluating the discriminatory capacity of different poverty indicators we will consider their relationship to a measure of economic stress that has been widely used in the literature and is described below.

---

[3] For further discussion of the analysis on which this hypothesis is based, see Maître et al. (2005).

[4] An alternative to controlling for retirement and part-time employment would be to exclude these groups from the analysis. While once again this would have little effect on your central conclusions it is clearly preferable to base our estimates on the sample as a whole. Doing so also reveals patterns of interaction relating to retirement, which while different from those relating to economic exclusion that are our central concern, are interesting in themselves.

[5] Exploratory analysis revealed no substantively interesting patterns of interaction involving part-time work.

[6] See, for example, McKay (2004), Dominy and Kempson (2006), Halleröd (2006).

7.3 Constructing Alternative Measures of Poverty and Exclusion

Our analysis in this chapter is based on the EU-SILC 2006 dataset, and concentrates on equivalized total household disposable income and the 7-item index of 'consumption deprivation' described in earlier chapters. Our analysis proceeds as follows. Focusing first on 'at risk of poverty', we produce measures at national level (NARP) and for the 24 EU countries (EUARP) included in the EU-SILC 2006 dataset. We then produce a number of consistent poverty measures across geographic units. These indicators are constructed by combining information on 'at risk of poverty' and consumption deprivation. The three indicators are as follows:

1) The first measure is a *national consistent poverty* (NCP) indicator. This is constructed by choosing a deprivation threshold at the national level that identifies a fraction of the population that corresponds as closely as possible to the number below the 60% of the national median equivalized income. This approach will affect national rankings only to the extent that the income and deprivation measures overlap more closely in some countries rather than others.

2) The second measure is an *EU consistent poverty* (EUCP) indicator. In this case those defined as consistently poor are both 'at risk of poverty' using the EU threshold and above the deprivation threshold that identifies a fraction of the population as close as possible to that found below the corresponding income threshold.

3) The final measure constructed is a *mixed level consistent poverty* (MCP) indicator combining income information at the national level with information relating to consumption deprivation at the EU level. The procedure involves identifying a fraction of the EU population as a whole that corresponds as closely as possible to the number below the EU 'at-risk-of-poverty' line relating to 60% of the median of the equivalent income. In order to be defined as poor, an individual must be located below the national 'at-risk-of-poverty' threshold and above the corresponding EU consumption deprivation threshold. In applying a national threshold in relation to income and a European one in relation to deprivation we are not assuming that different reference groups are operating.[7] The income threshold is imposed to fulfil the EU criterion relating to exclusion from minimally acceptable level of living in individual countries while the deprivation stipulation seeks to capture the extent to which individuals in the EU are sharing in the benefits of high average prosperity.

---

[7] For a discussion of related reference group issues, see chapter 9.

Table 7.1. Alternative Poverty Concepts and Measures

Concept	Measurement
National 'at risk of poverty' (NARP)	Percentage of households below 60% of **national** median income
EU 'at risk of poverty'	Percentage of households below 60% of **EU** median income
National consistent poverty	Percentage below 60% of **national** median income and above a deprivation threshold that identifies a proportion of individuals identical to that captured by national income measure
EU consistent poverty	Percentage below 60% of **EU** median income and above a deprivation threshold that identifies a proportion of individuals identical to that captured by corresponding EU income measure
Mixed consistent poverty	Percentage below 60% of **national** median income and above a deprivation threshold that identifies a proportion of individuals identical to that captured by the corresponding EU income measure

The set of measures is summarized in Table 7.1.

Setting deprivation thresholds in terms of the numbers being 'at risk of poverty' has the advantage that it allows for the range of agreement between the measures to ranges from 0 to 1. The measure for which this does not hold is the mixed consistent poverty measure, which combines a national relative threshold in relation to income and a European relative threshold for deprivation derived from the corresponding income threshold. This may appear to combine an absolute approach to material deprivation with a relative approach to income. At a particular point in time this is true. Thus for the EU-SILC 2006 dataset, an individual will be defined as experiencing mixed consistent poverty if they fall below 60% of national relative income and have a raw mean score of 2.8 or above on the 7-item index. However, given the manner in which we have defined the deprivation threshold it will change as the number below the EU 'at-risk-of-poverty' line declines or rises.

The measure of subjective economic stress is once again based on responses of the household reference person to a question about difficulty in make ends meet, with those reporting 'great difficult' or 'difficulty' categorized as experiencing economic stress.

7.4 Poverty Outcomes by Type of Indicator and Welfare Regime

In Table 7.2 we set out the distribution of poverty levels by type of indicator and welfare regime. Population estimates are derived by applying the grossing weight, but where our focus is on relationships we refrain from doing so and our analysis assumes uniformity within regimes. In this latter case we exclude Luxembourg. Focusing first on the NARP rate, we can see that the lowest rate of 11.1% is observed for the social democratic regime. This rises to 13% for the

Table 7.2. National and EU 'At-Risk-of-Poverty' (ARP) and Consistent Poverty (CP) Rates by Welfare Regime

	NARP (%)	NCP (%)	EUARP (%)	EUCP (%)	MCP (%)
Social democratic	11.1	3.4	6.1	1.8	3.2
Liberal	19.2	9.0	9.8	3.4	6.2
Corporatist	13.0	4.6	9.0	4.0	5.7
Southern European	19.7	8.1	22.9	9.0	7.9
Post-socialist corporatist	16.3	7.1	65.2	38.4	12.4
Post-socialist liberal	20.7	9.2	74.1	42.1	15.6

corporatist regime. It then rises to 19.2 and 19.7% respectively for the liberal and southern European regimes. The post-socialist corporatist rate is somewhat lower at 16.3% while the highest level of 20.7% is observed for the post-socialist liberal cluster.

The foregoing pattern of results does not conform to the expectations we outlined earlier. This is particularly true in relation to the comparison between the liberal and southern European regimes and the post-socialist clusters where societies that we know to be significantly less affluent display poverty rates that are lower, or at least not particularly higher, than those we know to be much more favourably placed. Does shifting from a one-dimensional to a multidimensional perspective produce a more plausible ranking of regimes? The results relating to the NCP indicator shows this is not to be the case. This measure takes into account the overlap within countries between low income and high levels of material deprivation. Implementing this approach produces a substantial reduction in poverty rates ranging from a halving to a reduction to less than one-third of their original level. However, there is no evidence that variation in the strength of the relationship between income and deprivation across regime helps to account for the corresponding distribution of NARP. The overlap is weakest at 32 and 36% for the social democratic and corporatist regimes, it is higher at 47% for the liberal regime than for the remaining regimes where the level ranges between 41 and 44%. Contrary to the argument that the 'at-risk-of-poverty' measure proves to be less effective in identifying those excluded from customary living patterns in the new member states, it is precisely in those societies where they prove to be most effective.

Employing the NCP indicator, the social democratic and corporatist regimes continue to display the lowest poverty rates with figures of 3.4 and 4.6%. They are again followed by the post-socialist corporatist group with a rate of 7.1 and the southern European with one of 8.1%. The highest rates of 9.0 and 9.2% respectively are observed for the liberal and post-socialist liberal regimes.

Can the desired profile be achieved by shifting from a national to an EU perspective? We consider the outcomes associated with such a shift initially in relation to 'at risk of poverty'. The EUARP indicator does produce a much sharper pattern of differentiation between regimes in line with levels of societal affluence. The lowest rates of 6.1 and 9.0% are again observed for the social democratic and corporatist regimes with that for the liberal cluster being marginally higher at 9.8%. We then observe a sharp increase to 22.9% for the southern European regime. A sharp escalation occurs for the corporatist and liberal post-socialist clusters with rates of respectively 65.2 and 74.1%. The desired differentiation between more and less affluent regimes is achieved but at the price of this contrast entirely dominating the results and the need to accept as valid a poverty indicator that identifies between two-thirds to three-quarters of individuals in the post-socialist clusters as poor.

Shifting to the EUCP indicator brings an improvement. Unlike the situation at the national level, the overlap is actually greatest for the post-socialist regimes, intermediate for the corporatist and southern European clusters, and lowest for the liberal and social democratic regimes. The poverty rate falls to 1.8% for the social democratic cluster, followed by the liberal and corporatist groups with levels of 3.4 and 4.0% respectively. It then rises to 9.0% for the southern European regime before climbing sharply to 38.4 and 42.1% respectively for the corporatist and post-socialist liberal clusters. While we observe a significant reduction in poverty levels, we are required to accept an outcome in which approximately 4 out of 10 individuals in those societies are defined as poor.

Our final indicator the MCP measure combines a relative income approach with an EU deprivation threshold. The pattern of overlap in relation to low income and deprivation is rather different in this case. The lowest level of overlap of 23.4% is observed in relation to the social democratic regime. This rises to 29.5% for the liberal regime before increasing to 37 and 39% respectively for the southern European and corporatist clusters. In contrast for the post-socialist regimes three out of four of those falling below the NARP threshold are also found above the EU deprivation threshold. The outcome, in terms of poverty rates, is that the lowest rate of 3.2% is observed for the social democratic regime. Slightly higher rates of 5.7 and 6.2% are observed respectively for the corporatist and liberal clusters. We then observe a gradual increase to 7.9% for the southern European group, 12.4% for the post-socialist corporatist cluster, and 15.6 for the post-socialist liberal regime. The MCP measure therefore provides a pattern of regime differentiation consistent with our expectations.

In Table 7.3 the results deriving from a set of logistic regression summarize the welfare regime relativities for the 5 poverty indicators that we have

Table 7.3. Logistic Regression Effect for Welfare Regimes for National and European 'At Risk of Poverty' (ARP) and Consistent Poverty (CP)

	Odds ratios*				
	NARP	NCP	EUARP	EUCP	MCP
Social democratic (ref)	1.000	1.000	1.000	1.000	1.000
Corporatist	1.326	1.589	1.632	2.281	1.885
Liberal	2.084	3.151	1.983	2.594	2.416
Southern European	2.188	2.786	5.463	6.302	2.935
Post-socialist corporatist	1.561	2.052	21.345	27.005	3.735
Post-socialist liberal	2.306	3.225	48.085	37.193	5.372
Nagelkerke R^2	0.019	0.021	0.332	0.240	0.036
N	516,534	504,120	516,534	504,120	504,120

* All significant at $p < 0.001$.

employed. In each case the social democratic regime serves as the benchmark and is assigned an odds ratio of 1. All other outcomes are then expressed as multiples of the risk of being poor in the social democratic group. For the NARP group we see that variation is extremely modest with the liberal, southern European, and post-socialist clusters all located in a narrow range running from 2.1 to 2.3. Switching to the NCP measure serves to differentiate the social democratic regime more sharply from the remaining clusters. However, it has little effect on the pattern of differentials between the latter groups with the odds ratios ranging between 2.8 and 3.2. Switching to the EU level in relation to 'at risk of poverty' leads the post-socialist corporatist cluster odds ratio to increase to 21.3 and the post-socialist liberal regime one to 48.1. For the southern European regime a much more modest disparity of 5.5 is observed and the respective figures for the liberal and corporatist regimes are 2.0 and 1.6.

Moving to the consistent poverty indicator at the European level, a relatively similar pattern is observed. However, the odds ratio for the post-socialist liberal regime falls to 37.1 while those for the remaining regimes increase modestly. It remains true that the major contrast is between the post-socialist regimes and all others. Finally, the MCP measure, which combines both national and EU perspectives, produces the kind of graduated pattern of differentiation across welfare regimes that we would expect to be associated with a valid poverty indicator. The odds on individuals in the corporatist cluster experiencing this form of poverty are 1.9 times higher than for their counterparts in the social democratic regime. This rises to 2.4 for the liberal regime and to 2.9 for the southern European one. It then rises to 3.7 and 5.4 for the corporatist and liberal post-socialist regimes.

7.5 The Combined Effect of Welfare Regime and Principal Economic Status on Poverty Outcomes

In this section we extend our analysis by incorporating consideration of the impact of the principal employment status of the HRP and the manner in which it interacts with welfare regime.[8] We have chosen to focus on the HRP PES both because it is likely to be the most powerful socio-economic predictor of poverty and because its impact is likely to be significantly mediated by welfare regime. In what follows we report key findings from a set of logistic regression relating to the 5 indicators. The independent variables comprise a set of dummy variables relating to welfare regimes with the social democratic category taken as the reference category and a set of dummies referring to HRP PES with full-time employees as the benchmark.[9] In order to allow for the clustering of individuals within households the equations have been estimated using robust standard errors.

While the full range of HPR PES effects are reported, our primary focus is on the impact of the different forms of economic exclusion and the manner in which they vary with welfare regime.

Exploratory analysis revealed little in the way of systematic variation across welfare regimes for part-time employment and its effect has been constrained to be uniform.[10] The impact of all other categories is allowed to vary across welfare regime. In each case the set of interaction proves to be highly significant. In what follows we focus on the patterns of relativities arising from the interaction of welfare regimes and economic exclusion.

7.6 National 'at Risk of Poverty' (NARP)

In Figure 7.1 for the NARP measure and with full-time employees as the reference category, we illustrate the pattern of odds ratios relating to each of the forms of social exclusion across welfare regimes. The results are broadly

---

[8] The issue has been raised as to whether variation in the impact of the HRP PES variable may be affected by corresponding differences in the division of labour within the household and in the manner in which the HRP has been chosen. However, in light of the fact that our concern is with the manner in which welfare regime effects vary across different measures of poverty it seems unlikely to us that our key findings will be influenced by such factors. This view is supported by the fact that the additional analysis using the Eurostat variable relating to household work intensity produces similar conclusions regarding the manner in which the importance of welfare regime effects and socio-economic differentiation varies across alternative poverty indicators. Details of this analysis are available from the authors.

[9] In the latter case we have excluded individuals in households where the reference person is in full-time education and training.

[10] Variation across poverty indicators in the impact of retirement is also modest in comparison with the different forms of social exclusion.

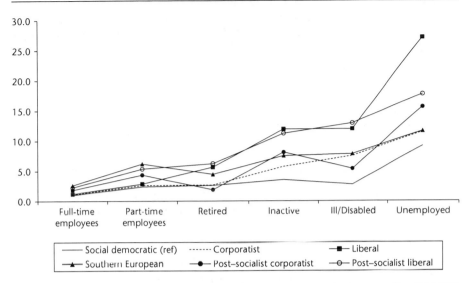

Figure 7.1. Welfare regime variation in levels of national 'at risk of poverty' by HRP PES (odds ratios relative to full-time employed HRPs in the social democratic regime).

consistent with our expectations with the weakest pattern of differentiation in terms of social exclusion being found for the social democratic regime. This involves an odds ratio of 9:1 for the comparison of unemployed and employees while for the ill/disabled and the inactive the odds ratios are respectively 2.8 and 3.5. It is followed by the corporatist, southern European, and post-socialist corporatist regimes, while the sharpest differentials are associated with the post-socialist liberal and liberal regimes. All groups excluded from the labour market are particularly disadvantage in the liberal regime while for the post-socialist liberal regime this is true for the inactive and ill-disabled although the differentials are more modest. The relative position of the retired is particularly favourable in the post-socialist corporatist and southern European clusters while they are particularly disadvantaged in the liberal regime.

While alternative indicators reveal sharper patterns of differentiation by economic exclusion, the broad pattern of results are in line with our expectations. However, taking such differentiation into consideration does not enable us to offer a more plausible interpretation of welfare regime results associated with using this indicator.

Variation in poverty levels across welfare regimes using the NARP indicator continues to be counterintuitive when we look within categories of HRP PES. By far the highest level of poverty among the unemployed is observed for the liberal regimes while the rates for the other economically excluded groups and the retired in this regime are matched only in the post-socialist cluster. Variation across welfare regimes for the NARP deviates from what we would expect from a valid poverty indicator. Comparable levels of poverty for the liberal and

135

post-socialist regimes arise, despite the less favourable position of employees in the latter, because of the substantially higher relative penalties associated with exclusion from the labour market in the former. However, variation by economic exclusion within welfare regimes is broadly in line with our expectations with the strongest contrasts in terms of economic exclusion effects being associated with the liberal regime and the weakest with the post-socialist clusters and the southern European regime.

7.7 National Consistent Poverty (NCP)

Shifting our focus to NCP defined in purely relative terms we find that the impact of economic exclusion is substantially greater than for the NARP indicator for the social democratic regime reference category. The odds ratio relating to the comparison of employees and the unemployed rises to 24.6:1. For the inactive and the ill/disabled the respective figures are 6.4 and 7.7. However, this scaling upwards of the effects of economic exclusion occurs in a relatively uniform manner within regimes. As a consequence, as is illustrated in Figure 7.2, the pattern of between welfare regime differentials in relation to economic exclusion is remarkably similar to that in Figure 7.1.[11]

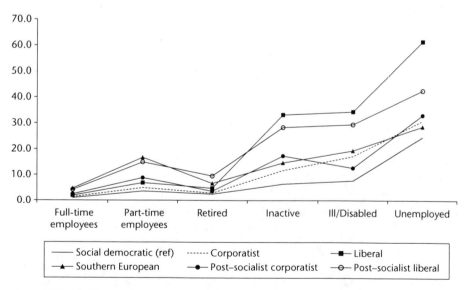

Figure 7.2. Welfare regime variation in levels of national consistent poverty by HRP PES (odds ratios relative to full-time employed HRPs in the social democratic regime).

---

[11] The relative disadvantage enjoyed by the retired in the liberal regime is considerably less in this case.

Overall, the NCP, while superior to the NARP in terms of its ability to reveal socio-economic differentiation, produces welfare regime difference within economically excluded categories that remain counterintuitive.

7.8 EU 'at Risk of Poverty' (EUARP)

Switching from a national to an EU 'at risk of poverty' perspective leads to a situation, as illustrated in Figure 7.3, where between regime differentials, particularly those involving comparison of the post-socialist regimes with the remaining clusters, entirely overshadow within regime relativities. The odds ratio summarizing the comparison between full-time employees in the social democratic and those located in the post-socialist liberal regimes is 46:1 while that involving the post-socialist corporatist group is 23.1:1. For the southern European it falls to 5.8:1. The remaining values do not exceed 1.2:1. Within regime variation appears remarkably modest when placed in the context of the between regime disparities.

With one exception, EUARP rates are higher for all categories of HRP PES in the southern European and post-socialist regimes than for all categories in the remaining regimes. Employing this indicator, it is necessary to accept that poverty rates for full-time employees in the post-socialist clusters are between 1.5 to 3 times higher than for the unemployed in the corporatist and social democratic regimes. Within every category of economic exclusion, the post-socialist liberal group exhibits distinctively high odds of being poor, followed at some distance by the post-socialist corporatist cluster and then even further

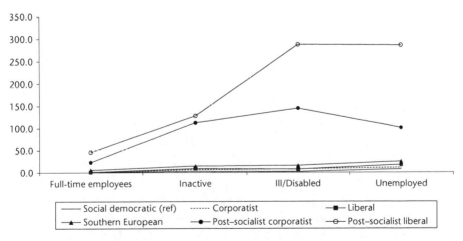

Figure 7.3. Between welfare regime variation in levels of EU 'at risk of poverty' by HRP PES (odds ratios relative to full-time employed HRPs in the social democratic regime).

by the southern European cluster. Variation between the remaining regimes is extremely modest. For the ill/disabled category the odds on experiencing EUARP are 150 times higher in the post-socialist liberal cluster than in the social democratic regimes; for the remaining categories the figure ranges between the high thirties and high forties. For the post-socialist corporatist group the highest disparities of 76 and 43 relate to illness/disability and being inactive. For the remaining categories the inequalities run from 23:1 for employees to 13:1 for the unemployed.

7.9 EU Consistent Poverty

Each time we shift from a national to an EU perspective, the average welfare regime effects are much higher, reflecting as we noted earlier that such measures are likely to lead to welfare regime effects being more highly correlated with affluence effects. For the EUCP indicator they are even sharper than for the EUARP. The odds ratios for the comparison of full-time employees in the social democratic regime with their counterparts in the southern European and post-socialist corporatist and liberal regimes reach 9.6, 39.4, and 54.9. For the remaining comparison they do not rise above 1.8.

From Figure 7.4 we can see that, as with the EUARP indicator, the overriding contrast is between the post-socialist regimes and all others with 11 of the 12 highest odds ratios being associated with these clusters. Poverty rates for full-time employees in the post-socialist clusters are comparable to those for the unemployed in the more affluent regimes. On this occasion there is much less

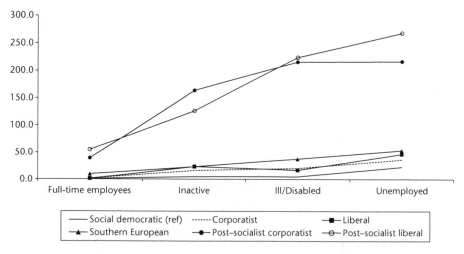

Figure 7.4. Between welfare regime variation in levels of EU consistent poverty by HRP PES (odds ratios relative to full-time employed HRPs in the social democratic regime).

divergence between the two post-socialist clusters. In relation to the relative risk of the HRP being unemployed or ill/inactive in comparison with full-time employees in the social democratic regimes they each experience a similar level of relative disadvantage reflected in odds ratios exceeding 200. For the ill/disabled a comparable level of disadvantage is observed for the post-socialist regime while a somewhat lower disparity is found for the post-corporatist cluster.

The within country relativities for the liberal, social democratic, and corporatist regimes are very similar to those associated with the national consistent poverty indicator and consequently more substantial than in the case of the EUARP measure. For the post-socialist and southern European regimes the odds ratio relating to the within group comparison of the unemployed with full-time employees is approximately 5 in each case. It rises to 20 for the corporatist group, to 23 for the social democratic, and to 37 for the liberal regime. While such effects are a good deal more substantial than for the EUARP measure, between regime effects are of such a magnitude as to make them appear extremely modest.

7.10 Mixed Consistent Poverty (MCP)

In this section we focus on the mixed consistent poverty measure where individuals are defined as poor when they are both 'at risk of poverty' and above the EU deprivation threshold that corresponds to the EUARP line. As seen in Table 7.2, this indicator produces an overall pattern of between regime differentiation consistent with our expectations. From Figure 7.5 we can see that the MCP indicator produces a pattern of variation in terms of the impact of economic exclusion within each welfare regime and a profile by welfare regime within each category of exclusion that is consistent with our expectations of how a valid poverty indicator should behave.

Focusing on the latter, we see that variation in the odds ratio for full-time employees relative to those in the social democratic regimes rises from 1.3 and 1.7 for the liberal and corporatist regimes to 4.9 for the southern European cluster and finally to 5.5 and 7.0 respectively for the corporatist and liberal post-socialist clusters. For the inactive group the odds ratio goes from 6.4 in the social democratic regime to 12.5 in the corporatist cluster. As with the remaining categories relating to labour market exclusion, the odds ratio for the southern European regime at 13.4 is relatively close to that for the corporatist regime. The figure for the liberal regime is substantially higher at 25.6 and close to that of 28.9 for the post-socialist corporatist regime. The level peaks at 34.6 for the post-socialist liberal regime.

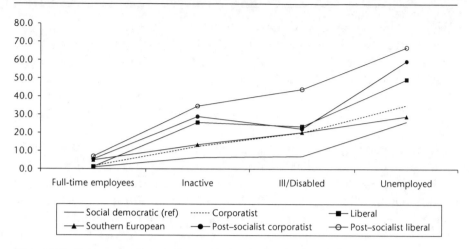

Figure 7.5. Between welfare regime variation in levels of mixed consistent poverty by HRP PES (odds ratios relative to full-time employed HRPs in the social democratic regime).

For illness and disability the major contrast is between the social democratic regime and the post-socialist liberal group with odds ratios of respectively 7.1 and 43.9. For the remaining regimes the relevant odds ratio varies between 20.1 for the corporatist regime and 23.4 for the liberal cluster. The lowest odds ratio for the unemployed group of 26.1 again relates to the social democratic regime. It is followed, somewhat unexpectedly, by the southern European regime with a value of 29.1. It rises to 35.2 for the corporatist cluster before increasing to 49.3 for the liberal regime. Further increases to 59.4 and 67.0 are then observed respectively for the corporatist and liberal post-socialist clusters.

The pattern of between regime relativities is broadly consistent with our expectations with the social democratic regime enjoying the most favourable position in every case and the post-liberal occupying the least favourable. The post-corporatist group is closest to the latter in 4 of the 6 cases while, as we anticipated, it enjoys a relatively favourable position in relation to the retired. The corporatist and liberal regimes display similar patterns of risk for the employee and retired categories but the former enjoys substantial advantages in relation to all categories of economic exclusion but most particularly with regard to unemployment and inactivity. Unlike the cases for the national 'at-risk-of-poverty' measure no significant difference is observed for the retired. The major deviation from our prior expectations relates to the odds on such MCP in the southern European regime associated with being excluded from the labour market. One possible explanation for this outcome is that effects of labour market segmentation for the HRP and household structure combined with the significant role of the 'grey' labour market is influencing both the income and deprivation components of the MCP indicator.

The pattern of within welfare regime relativities relating to economic exclusion is very similar to that found for the NCP measure with the sharpest pattern of variation relating to economic exclusions being observed for the liberal regime, followed by the social democratic and corporatist regime. Differentials are a good deal more modest for the post-socialist clusters and are minimized for the southern European regime.

The MCP measure, as well as identifying a minority as poor in each welfare regime and producing overall welfare regime variation along the hypothesized lines, also reveals patterns of socio-economic differentiation within and between welfare regimes that are broadly consistent with our prior expectations.

7.11 Economic Stress Levels by Welfare Regime and Principal Economic Status

In this section we consider the relationships between subjectively experienced economic stress and welfare regime and poverty outcomes. We set out the results for a set of regression in which welfare regime, poverty outcomes, and their interactions are regressed on each of the 5 indicators. The impact of the consistent poverty indicators is in every case substantially higher than for the 'at-risk-of-poverty' measures. In Figure 7.6 we illustrate variation by welfare regime for each of the 5 indicators. For the NARP measure the odds ratio for poor versus non-poor is lowest for the corporatist regime at 1.7 and for the remaining clusters it varies between 3.3 for the southern European regime and 4.7 for the post-socialist corporatist. The figures for the EUARP indicator

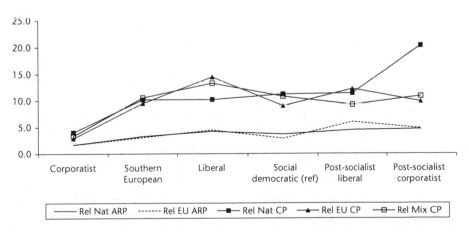

Figure 7.6. The impact of poverty on subjective economic stress by type of indicator within welfare regime (odds ratios relative to reference category of non-poor within each regime).

are extremely similar but rise to 6.0 for the post-socialist liberal group. For the NCP indicator the odds ratio for the corporatist regime is 4.0. The post-socialist corporatist cluster constitutes an outlier of a quite different sort in displaying an odds ratio of 20.3. The remaining values are found in the range running from 10.2 to 11.4. For the EU CP measure the corporatist values is 2.9 and for the remaining regimes the figure goes from 9.0 to 14.4. Finally for the MCP the corporatist value is 3.4 and the remaining observation are located in the range running from 9.2 to 13.3. In both of the previous cases the highest values is associated with the liberal regime.

The relativities in subjective economic stress associated with the consistent poverty indicators are on an order of magnitude three times greater than those observed in relation to the 'at-risk-of-poverty' measure. There is very little to choose between the three consistent poverty measures in terms of discriminatory power.

7.12 Conclusions

In this chapter we have sought to assess the relative merits of different poverty indicators in relation to their capacity to capture variation in poverty across countries and patterns of socio-economic differentiation in who is affected within countries.

For the national 'at-risk-of-poverty' measure we observe the counterintuitive pattern of variation in relation to level of prosperity of the welfare regimes that underpins widespread reluctance to accept it as an appropriate social indicator. Patterns of association for forms of economic exclusion and economic stress take the expected form but the strength of the associations is weaker than in the case of the consistent poverty indicators. The impact of economic exclusion is strongest for the liberal regime and weakest for the southern European while the retired enjoy particular advantages in the corporatist regimes. Crucially between regimes variation continues to display a counterintuitive pattern within categories of principal economic status.

Switching to a consistent poverty perspective at national level reduces the level of poverty but contributes nothing to producing a set of welfare regime differences more consistent with our prior expectations. The limited ability of the NARP to capture exclusion from customary living patterns and activities is reflected in the consistently modest overlap between falling below the national income threshold and being found above the corresponding deprivation benchmark. However, contrary to the argument that the limitations of the NARP are directly related to EU enlargement, it is actually least effective in capturing the most deprived in the social democratic and corporatist regimes. The impact of all forms of economic exclusion, but most particularly unemployment, is much sharper than in the case of NARP and the relationship to economic stress is substantially stronger. The NCP measure is clearly preferable to the NARRP in important respects but neither produces the kind of between regime variation that we might expect of a valid measure of poverty.

Shifting to an EU 'at-risk-of-poverty' perspective produces the desired differentiation between welfare regimes. However, this progress comes at the price of this contrast entirely dominating results. It becomes necessary to accept that between two-thirds to three-quarters of those in the post-socialist regimes are to be counted as poor and that full-time employees in these clusters are more likely to experience such poverty than the unemployed in the more affluent regimes. These outcomes are somewhat less stark when one focuses on the EUCP indicator with substantially greater variation being observed in relation to both economic exclusion and economic stress. Earlier we argued that a satisfactory measure of poverty should identify a minority in each society experiencing 'exclusion' from customary living standards due to a lack of resources. For the EU consistent poverty measure for the post-socialist regimes this figure reaches approximately 40%. While this is still a minority of the population such a larger number being defined as poor is a cause for concern. In addition when employing the EU consistent poverty measure, between regime variation dominates within regime socio-economic variation to the extent that poverty rates for full-times employees in the post-socialist regimes are comparable to those for unemployed in the more affluent regimes. In our judgement, if one of our objectives is to identify within each regime 'a minority experiencing exclusion', this is a highly undesirable outcome. It does not, however, rule out the use of such a measure in combination with other indicators in enhancing our understanding of poverty patterns and processes.

Our analysis provides further support for the conclusion of Marlier et al. (2007, pp. 154–5) that a EU-wide approach by failing to take into account differences in 'the significance of goods in social functioning' would miss people in richer countries who are experiencing genuine exclusion from their own society while counting substantial numbers in the poorer societies who are not experiencing such exclusion.

The MCP indicator produces a significant pattern of differentiation between welfare regimes in line with our prior expectations. Clear patterns of variation are also observed in relation to economic exclusion categories. In addition, welfare regime relativities are broadly maintained with principal economic status categories. As with the other consistent poverty measures, economic exclusion effects are strongest in the liberal regime and its distinctive character of the regime is seen to lie not in high levels of poverty as such but in the scale of disadvantage associated with labour market exclusion and, in particular, unemployment. In contrast, in the southern European and post-socialist regimes higher overall levels of MCP are accompanied by weaker within regime principal economic status differentials with the consequence that between regime differentials are sharper for full-time employees that for those excluded from the labour market. Finally those exposed to MCP are substantially more likely to experience economic stress and this is particularly true for both liberal regimes.

Our findings lead us to agree with Fahey (2007) that in understanding poverty in an enlarged EU it is necessary to consider indicators other than the 'at-risk-of-poverty' measure. We also accept his argument that in attempting to grasp the complexity of patterns of poverty in an enlarged EU it is sensible to employ a variety of indicators. However, our analysis suggests that if one needs to choose a preferred indicator the EU-wide 'at-risk-of-poverty' measure based on 60% of median equivalent income in the EU as a whole proposed by Fahey (2007, p. 45) would prove to be a less than ideal choice. Instead we would propose opting for a measure such as the MCP measure developed here which produces a set of results largely in line with our expectations of how a valid poverty measure should behave. Such an approach would allow us to achieve the stated EU objective of assessing the scale of exclusion from minimally acceptable level of standards of living in individual countries while also assessing the extent to which the whole population of Europe is sharing in the benefits of high average prosperity.

8

Economic Vulnerability and Multiple Deprivation: Welfare State and Social Class Variation

8.1 Introduction

In Chapter 7 we focused on the increasing concern that the enlargement of the European Union has exacerbated the limitations of focusing on relative income poverty measures framed in purely national terms. That approach was seen to produce results that are counterintuitive and at odds with our knowledge of variation across the EU in terms of objective living conditions and subjective feelings of deprivation (Fahey, 2007). We proceeded to consider the case for the development of an EU-wide poverty line alongside national measures. However, we concluded that, while the latter may fail to capture cross-national or welfare regimes differences, the former has correspondingly difficulty in appropriately assessing socio-economic differences within countries.

The resolution of this dilemma we suggested required transcending the limitations of purely income based relative poverty measures. Exploration of the development of a consistent poverty measure that combined a national income threshold with an EU consumption deprivation cut-off point produced a number of fruitful comparisons in terms of patterns of welfare regime and differentials relating to exclusion from the labour market. This, however, involves a fairly restricted extension of the one-dimensional approach. In this chapter we wish to explore further the possibilities afforded by the EU-SILC data set to implement a multidimensional approach to the measurement of social exclusion. We do so by employing multidimensional techniques to identify an 'economically vulnerable' cluster of individuals who are exposed to a set of interrelated risks. We then extend our analysis to deal with restricted and more encompassing forms of multiple deprivation.

In relation to issues concerning EU enlargement, the availability of data from EU-SILC allows us to go significantly beyond earlier efforts. Whelan and Maître's (2005a) analysis, employing the ECHP, covered thirteen EU countries but included no representatives of the new member states (NMS). Whelan and Maître's (2008) analysis extended the measurement to cover a period of 5 years but at the cost of reducing the number of countries covered to 9 of which only 5 were located outside southern Europe. Whelan and Maître (2005b) covered 28 countries using the European Quality of Life Survey (EQLS). However, in order to overcome difficulties associated with small sample sizes and variable response rates, they operated at a high level of aggregation that involved identifying 4 clusters adapted from a classification used by DG REGIO. Furthermore, because of the rather crude nature of the income measurement procedures, it was not possible to calculate income poverty lines and analysis was conducted at the level of within cluster income quartiles.

The EU-SILC dataset offers the first opportunity to conduct an analysis covering the full range of EU counties that allows us to compare multidimensional outcomes with those deriving from the conventional relative income poverty approach. On the basis of previous work, we hypothesize that the successful implementation of a strategy that captures both multidimensionality and dynamic risk will reveal a picture of variation across welfare regimes and socio-economic groups considerably more in line with our expectations relating to valid measures of poverty and social exclusion than is the case with income poverty. In relation to socio-economic variation, we will concentrate on the impact of social class because of our conviction that the ongoing dispute relating to its importance[1] can be further clarified by comparative analysis that combines a relational conceptualization of social class with an appropriate multidimensional analysis of social exclusion.[2]

To move beyond the accumulation of a mass of descriptive detail one needs both conceptual clarity and appropriate measurement models, and in the next section we discuss the concept of social exclusion and how it relates to the notion of 'vulnerability', conceptualized as insecurity and exposure to risk and shocks. The chapter then proceeds to explore vulnerability empirically, applying the statistical techniques of latent class analysis to indicators of household low income, life-style deprivation, and subjective economic stress in a manner described in Section 8.3. The patterning of vulnerability at national, welfare regime, and European levels is examined in Sections 8.4 and 8.5. Section 8.6 examines how vulnerability, captured this way, is associated with wider patterns of multidimensional deprivation, and Section 8.7 summarizes key conclusions.

---

[1] See Atkinson (2007a), Beck (2007), and Goldthorpe (2007a, 2010).
[2] See Goldthorpe (2010) for a discussion of the contrast between 'attributional' and 'relational' approaches to social class.

8.2 Multidimensional Approaches to Social Exclusion and the Concept of Vulnerability

In Chapter 2 we noted that while the value of a multidimensional approach to understanding poverty is now becoming widely recognized, it is generally pursued in an ad hoc manner. The underlying rationale for such an approach is often not spelled out and followed through. In circumstances where a wide range of dimensions was strongly associated with income the poor would be accurately identified by income alone. However, as knowledge of the limitations of relying solely on income to measure poverty and social exclusion has become more widespread, attention has been increasingly focused on multidimensional approaches. Non-monetary indicators are increasingly used, either separately or in combination with income, in individual European countries as well as at the EU level in measuring poverty and social exclusion (Förster, 2005; Nolan and Whelan, 2007). Kakawani and Silber (2008, p. xv) identify the most important recent development in poverty research as the shift from a one-dimensional to a multidimensional approach.

At the level of conceptualization, the case for a multidimensional approach to understanding what it means to be socially excluded is compelling. However, as Nolan and Whelan (2007) argue, the value of a multidimensional approach needs to be empirically established rather than being something that can be read off the multidimensional nature of the concept. Approaches that produce higher rather than lower dimensional profiles are not intrinsically superior. At this point, it seems to be generally agreed that many unresolved conceptual and measurement issues remain in the path of seriously implementing multidimensional measures in any truly operational sense (Thorbecke, 2007). Grusky and Weeden (2007, p. 33) set out the need to develop 'a methodological platform' for analysing the shape and form of social exclusion. In this chapter we seek to contribute to this enterprise specifically in relation to forms of material deprivation.

In recent years general agreement has emerged that, despite the continuing vagueness of the term 'social exclusion', its main value lies in drawing attention to issues of dynamics and multidimensionality (Berghman, 1995; Atkinson, 1998; Room, 1999; Sen, 2000). Kronauer (1998) notes that the emergence of the concept of social exclusion was directly related to the renewed emergence of the threat: of high unemployment and the threat it posed to national modes of integration. Such concerns are reflected in Berghman's (1995) understanding of social exclusion as involving a social process in which the creation and reinforcement of inequalities leads to a state of deprivation and hardship from which it is difficult to escape. Paugam's (1996) focus on spirals of precariousness leading to cumulative disadvantage and a progressive rupturing of social relation also involves this joint emphasis. However, there is a tension in the social exclusion literature between an emphasis on a heterogeneity of trajectories and, on the other hand, an accumulation of disadvantages involving a 'spiral of precariousness' (Paugam, 1996). This tendency is also stressed in Room's (1999, p. 171) discussion of notions of continuity and catastrophe in the social exclusion literature.

Atkinson and Davoudi (2000, p. 434) observe that the pursuit of these issues can lead to a focus on the sense of solidarity within groups involving reciprocity and mutual aid or alternative to concern with issues of 'societal solidarity'.[3] One of the difficulties with the former emphasis and with a focus on social cohesion, involving social connectedness and communal identification (Friedkin, 2004), is that the evidence relating to the impact of factors such as unemployment and material deprivation on such outcomes is extremely modest (Whelan et al., 2002a; Gallie et al., 2003).

An alternative conception of social exclusion, such as that proposed by Levitas et al. (2007), focuses on multidimensional deprivation involving a wider restriction of access to commodities and services necessary for full participation in the society.[4] Adopting this broader focus on multiple deprivation, problems arise from the fact that correlations between deprivation dimensions tend to be a good deal more modest that is often imagined. This is true even in relation to income and consumption deprivation. However, as we documented in Chapter 4, the correlations between such dimensions and factors such as housing, health, and neighbourhood environment are a good deal more modest. Consequently if concern with multidimensionality encompasses such dimensions the observed overlap becomes considerably lower. If concern is extended to social and political participation this conclusion is likely to hold with even greater force. This difficulty is recognized in the Levitas et al. (2007) distinction between social exclusion and 'deep exclusion'. The latter refers to exclusion across more than one dimension of disadvantage, resulting in severe negative consequences for quality of life, well being, and future life chances. However, unless such negative consequences are demonstrated, labelling as 'social exclusion' deprivation in relation to any one or, indeed, combination of a wide range of dimensions is problematic. On the

---

[3] Difficulties arise from the fact that the term 'social cohesion' has partly assimilated older terms such as social solidarity and social integration (Lockwood, 1964) while frequently lacking clarity on the relationship between societal patterns of inequality and forms of such cohesion. See Wilkinson and Pickett (2009).

[4] Levitas et al. (2007) see such multidimensional deprivation as affecting both the quality of life of individuals and the equity and cohesion of society as a whole. However, we would prefer to see such relationships between individual outcomes and societal characteristics as matters for empirical enquiry rather than definition.

other hand, an emphasis on 'deep exclusion' runs the risk of being interpreted in an 'underclass' terms.[5]

At this point, it seems to be generally agreed that many unresolved conceptual and measurement issues remain in the path of seriously implementing multidimensional measures in any truly operational sense (Thorbecke, 2007). At the national level where the data available tend to be considerably more comprehensive that at the EU level, a variety of sophisticated analytic strategies have been employed to explore such issues. These include latent class analysis (De Wilde, 2004; Moisio, 2004; Whelan and Maître, 2005a; Grusky and Weeden, 2007), structural equation modelling (Tomlinson et al., 2008; Carle et al., 2009), item response theory (Cappellari and Jenkins, 2007), and self-organizing maps (Pisati et al., 2010). However, the data currently available at the EU level are considerably less comprehensive and, as our discussion in Chapter 4 made clear, it is considerably more restricted for EU-SILC than for the ECHP.

As Whelan and Whelan (1996, p. 29) argue, while no one would wish to deny that social exclusion arises from of a variety of processes or that it is experienced as involving a good deal more than an income deficit, an uncritical insistence on multidimensionality could paradoxically have the effect of obscuring the processes involved in generating social exclusion. In an effort to distinguish some of the rather different processes that have included under the umbrella term 'social exclusion', we will proceed as follows. Our initial focus will be on the notion of as set of interrelated risks. Initially we will limit our attention to a small number of dimensions but ones whose interrelationships we consider to be crucial to understand. These comprise income poverty, consumption deprivation, and economic stress. Although the analysis reported in this chapter is based on cross-sectional data, a temporal dimension is implicit in such analysis. Not all respondents identified as vulnerable to economic exclusion experience the deprivation that make up its risk profile at a particular point in time. However, by identifying individuals as vulnerable we clearly wish to convey that their prior or subsequent risk of such exposure is significantly greater than that of those allocated to the non-vulnerable class. This approach is consistent with the picture painted by Heath (1981) of 'deprivation as a vicissitude (sometimes transitory) which strikes broadly and unpredictably across the working class (and indeed white collar groups) in response to the vagaries of economic and social policy and life-circumstances'.

Given our desire to distinguish between social exclusion involving as a set of interrelated risks and, on the hand, as involving multiple deprivation at a

---

[5] This tendency is also stressed in Room's (1999, p. 171) discussion of notions of continuity and catastrophe in the social exclusion literature.

particular point in time and bearing in mind the need to take into account the tension between the power of sophisticated methods and the transparency required to serve the needs of policy makers and inform public debate, we will proceed as follows. Our initial analysis will focus on a restricted form of multidimensionality. Having established groups with distinctive risk profiles in relation to income, consumption deprivation, and economic stress, we will consider the relationship between economic vulnerability and multiple deprivation in relation to its constituent elements. We will consider to what extent the movement from a focus solely on income poverty to this restricted multidimensional approach enhances our understanding of welfare regime and social class variation in economic exclusions.

In the final section of this chapter we will then extend our analysis to take a broader perspective on multidimensional deprivation that incorporates health, housing, and neighbourhood deprivation. Our approach avoids trying to provide a single index of multidimensional deprivation. We believe this is appropriate given the unevenness in quality and quantity of the data available to us and given the need to explore underlying processes of exclusion. It is also consistent with the Laeken indicators approach which at the macro level very deliberately presented individually with no attempt to produce an overall 'score' across the dimensions—indeed, Atkinson et al. (2002) argue that this should be avoided precisely because the whole thrust of the European social agenda is to emphasize the multidimensionality of social disadvantage.

This notion of 'economic exclusion' that we employ involves a more restricted focus than for many of the variants of social exclusion that appear in the literature. This is to some extent influenced by the range of data relating to material deprivation available in EU-SILC and our assessment of the quality of various aspects of that information. However, as Sen (2000, p. 9) observes, one of the difficulties of extending the notion of social exclusion to encompass multiple deprivation is that there may be 'a temptation to dress up every type of deprivation as social exclusion'. For our present purposes it is crucial to clarify the distinctions between the notions of social exclusion as multiple deprivation and alternatively as a set of interrelated risks.

Our initial objective is to operationalize the concept of individual 'economic vulnerability' understood as 'heightened risk of multidimensional deprivation'. Our analysis will then be extended to address the relationship between this more limited kind of multiple deprivation and more embracing forms. In doing so we seek to address some of the difficulties associated with the fact that the term 'social exclusion' is frequently simultaneously employed to refer to both economic insecurity and notions of overlapping multiple deprivation.

As De Haan (1998, p. 15) observes, notions of vulnerability are closely associated with the social exclusion perspective. Following Chambers (1989,

p. 1), we can define vulnerability as not necessarily involving current deprivation in either income or other terms but rather insecurity and exposure to risk and shock. In developing measures of vulnerability we are seeking to develop point-in-time proxies for the kind of risk of exposure to persistent disadvantage that is captured in panel surveys. This objective is combined with a concern to develop a genuinely multidimensional perspective. The IMF (2003), the UN (2003), and the World Bank (2000) have developed a range of approaches for measuring vulnerability at the macro level. Consistent with the approach developed here, the World Bank sees vulnerability as reflecting both the risk of experiencing an episode of poverty over time but also a heightened probability of being exposed to a range of risks. However, they note the difficulty of operationalizing this understanding (World Bank, 2000). Bradshaw and Finch (2003) suggest that it is useful to distinguish between *risk factors*, which signal the greater vulnerability of a category of individuals, and *triggers*, which have a direct causal impact. It is on the former that we focus.

Here, following Whelan and Maître (2005a, b), we implement an approach to the measurement of economic vulnerability that involves the use of a statistical technique known as latent class analysis. Our objective is to identify groups vulnerable to economic exclusion in the sense of being distinctive in their risk of falling below a critical resource level, being exposed to life style deprivation and experiencing subjective economic stress. Usually the groups into which researchers classify their observations are known in advance and correspond to the values taken by particular variables or combination of variables. In some cases, however, the groups of interest are not known a priori and must be discovered using suitable classification techniques. Latent class analysis assumes that each individual is a member of 1 and only 1 of N underlying classes and that, conditional on membership of an unobserved class, the observed variables are mutually independent of each others. Conditional independence is a version of the familiar idea that the correlation between 2 variables may be a result of their common dependence on a third variable.

The basic notion is that there are underling processes that result in distinct clusters of individuals. Within those groups indicator outcomes are independent of each other because the factors that lead to individuals being located there are those that accounted for the original correlations. The question is then whether such simplifying assumptions allow us to identify clusters of individuals in a manner that leads to the predicted outcomes from this model closely matching the observed profiles. The contrast between clusters is in terms of risk profiles rather than existing patterns of deprivation. In the analysis that follows we specify that individuals are allocated to 1 of 2 classes. However, neither the size of the underlying clusters nor the risk profiles are specified a priori but are determined by the objective of finding the closest possible fit to the observed data consistent with the simplifying assumptions of our model.

A dichotomization of the population into vulnerable and non-vulnerable clusters is inevitably an oversimplification. However, in light of the prominence that such concepts have achieved in the literature, it remains an important question as to what extent such characterizations of key aspects of social differentiation provide a reasonable representation of the observed empirical regularities.

8.3 Capturing Vulnerability Empirically

Our analysis makes use of the EU-SILC 2006 dataset. Our analysis is conducted at the level of the individual. Where it is appropriate household attributes and characteristics of the household reference person (HRP) have been allocated to the individual. Significance levels have been adjusted for the clustering of individuals within households. The initial outcomes on which we focus comprises income poverty, consumption deprivation, and subjective economic stress.

The income measure we employ is the annual total household disposable income adjusted for household size using the OECD modified equivalence scale. The reference period is the 12 months prior to date of interview. Poverty is defined in terms of levels of median equivalent income. In our subsequent latent class analysis we distinguish 4 categories of income:

1) Those below national 70% of equivalent median income lines;
2) Those between the 60 and 70% lines;
3) Those between the 50 and 60% lines; and
4) Those below the 50% line.

Our analysis focuses on the 7-item index of 'consumption deprivation' that comprises items ranging from enforced absence relating to current requirement such as food and heat to more general consumption items such as being able to afford a holiday, a car, or a PC, as well as experiencing arrears on regular bills such as rent or utilities. As our analysis in Chapter 4 showed, confirmatory factor analysis reveals that this dimension emerges as a distinct factor and reliability analysis confirms that it can be employed for comparative purposes.[6] The version of this measure that we use in our subsequent analysis is a dichotomous one in which the threshold is chosen so the proportion of

---

[6] See Whelan et al. (2008) for further details.

individuals above it corresponds as closely as possible to that below the EU income poverty measure based on 60% of median equivalent income.

The measure of subjective economic stress we employ is based on the following question asked to all household reference persons:

Thinking now of your household's total income, from all sources and from all household members, would you say that your household is able to make ends meet?

Respondents were offered 6 response categories ranging from 'with great difficulty' to 'very easily'. Our analysis focuses on a comparison between those in households experiencing 'great difficulty' and 'difficulty' and all others.

In what follows we consider levels and patterns of variation in economic vulnerability by welfare regime where the categorization of such regimes is as in the earlier chapters. Since our focus is on the impact of welfare regimes, we do not employ population weighting in estimating such effects because countries with large populations would dominate the outcome, obscuring the extent to which countries allocated to the same regime share important features. Similarly, we do not wish our estimates to be influenced by variation in sample sizes across countries. Where we estimate descriptive statistics, such as national poverty rates, at welfare regime level we report *average* rates across countries within regimes. When focusing on *relationships* at the welfare regime level, we assume that the underlying processes are uniform across country. Such an assumption is unlikely to hold in strict statistical terms but the hope is that compensating gains in terms in parsimony will enable us to reveal important patterns of differentiation in relation to poverty and social exclusion. The alternative is not to resort to population weighting or to allow national sample sizes to influence the outcomes but rather to conduct the analysis at a more micro level.

Our analysis focuses on explaining the distribution of individuals across a 4 by 2 by 2 tabulation comprising four categories of income poverty by the dichotomous consumption deprivation by the dichotomous economic stress. Our objective is to find a parsimonious model of the underlying processes producing an allocation of individuals to the 16 cells of this table that generates a set of expected frequencies that comes closes to reproducing the observed frequencies. In Table 8.1 we display the results for model fit, size of the vulnerable class, and conditional probabilities given latent class membership.

Given large sample sizes, ranging from 33,665 in the post-socialist liberal regime to 132,111, any parsimonious model is unlikely to produce a satisfactory fit to the observed data by strict statistical criteria. Nevertheless, the latent class model with 2 classes does remarkably well across all 6 welfare regimes in accounting for patterns of association. The G^2 likelihood ratio chi-square is a

Table 8.1. Economic Vulnerability by Welfare Regime

	Social democratic		Corporatist		Liberal		Southern European		Post-socialist conservative		Post-socialist liberal	
	NV[a]	V	NV	V	NV	V	NV	V	NV	V	NV	V
Class type												
Class size	0.874	0.126	0.850	0.150	0.797	0.203	0.718	0.282	0.654	0.346	0.599	0.401
G^2	22.961		50.112		44.576		165.419		185.898		27.407	
Df.	4		4		4		4		4		4	
Reduction in independence model G^2	99.89		99.80		99.55		99.57		99.60		99.79	
Delta	0.0034		0.0064		0.0104		0.0166		0.0176		0.0135	
< 70%	0.129	0.551	0.138	0.608	0.183	0.636	0.158	0.540	0.115	0.445	0.117	0.495
< 60%	0.071	0.341	0.075	0.430	0.119	0.483	0.102	0.414	0.070	0.324	0.074	0.373
< 50%	0.037	0.168	0.035	0.243	0.065	0.312	0.059	0.278	0.039	0.220	0.041	0.256
Deprivation	0.006	0.644	0.014	0.738	0.014	0.609	0.024	0.634	0.144	0.900	0.167	0.946
Economic stress	0.035	0.578	0.037	0.634	0.058	0.642	0.157	0.846	0.134	0.878	0.058	0.666
N	103,930		90,298		40,643		132,111		119,471		33,665	

[a] V = vulnerable, NV = non-vulnerable.

measure of goodness of fit. The lower its value, the more closely the expected frequencies correspond to the observed. The size of the G^2 for the independence model provides 1 benchmark against which to assess the fit of the latent class model. The latent class model reduces this by a level of from 99.6 to 99.9 for the 6 welfare regimes. Focusing on the criterion of proportion of cases misclassified, this runs from 0.003 for the social democratic to 0.018 for the post-socialist conservative. Thus in each case the latent class model comes close to reproducing the observed data.

A systematic pattern of variation in the size of the vulnerable class is observed across welfare regimes. The lowest level of 12.6% is observed for the social democratic regime. It rises to 15 and 20.3%, respectively, for the corporatist and liberal regimes. It increases to 28.2% for the southern European regime. Finally it rises to 34.6 and to 40.1%, respectively, for the post-socialist corporatist and liberal clusters. This sharp pattern of differentiation can be contrasted with restricted differentiation found in Table 8.2 in relation to national income poverty at 60% of median income averaged across the countries making up the regimes where the mean level ranges between 10.3 and 19.4% and very similar outcomes are observed for the social democratic and post-socialist corporatist clusters on one hand and the liberal regimes on the other.

Drawing on the results set out in Table 8.1, in Figure 8.1 we provide a graphic illustration of the factors differentiating the vulnerable from the non vulnerable. In Table 8.1 findings relating to income poverty are summarized in terms of the proportions falling successively blow the 70, 60, and 50% thresholds. The contrast between vulnerable and non-vulnerable clusters takes a rather similar form across regimes. For the social democratic regime the respective numbers falling below the 60% line for the vulnerable and non-vulnerable classes are 0.071 and 0.341. The outcomes for the corporatist group are relatively similar with the respective figures being 0.075 and 0.430 and main difference being that the figures for the vulnerable cluster is higher and the contrast is therefore sharper. For the liberal and southern European regimes poverty rates are higher for both the vulnerable and non-vulnerable with the figures being 0.119 and 0.483 for the former and 0.102 and 0.414 for

Table 8.2. Mean National Poverty Rates by Welfare Regime

	% Poor
Social democratic	10.3
Corporatist	13.0
Liberal	19.4
Southern Europe	18.7
Post-socialist corporatist	13.7
Post-socialist liberal	19.9

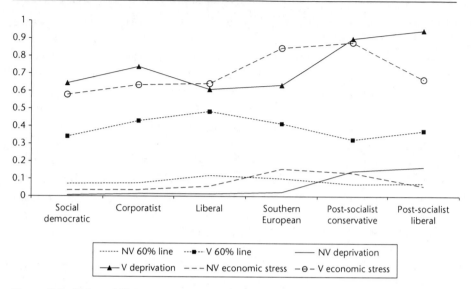

Figure 8.1. Vulnerability to economic exclusion.

the latter. For the post-socialist regimes the extent to which poverty rates are higher than for the southern European regime depends on the line on which one focuses but the differences in each case are rather modest. Overall we observe sharp differentiation between the vulnerable and non-vulnerable clusters with variation across regimes in such differentiation being highly restricted.

Notwithstanding such disparities, differentiation in terms of vulnerability is least on income poverty. When we focus on subjective economic stress, as captured by the indicator relating to difficulty in making ends meet, we find that for the vulnerable cluster the number reporting such difficulties ranges from 58% in the social democratic regime to 95% for the post-socialist liberal cluster; with both liberal regimes being closer to the former and the southern European cluster being close to the latter. For the non-vulnerable clusters, on the other hand, the level of economic stress in the social democratic and corporatist regimes is less than 4%. It rises to just less than 6% in the 2 liberal regimes. It then rises substantially to 13.4% for the post-socialist conservative cluster before peaking at 15.7% for the southern European regime.

However, economic stress is not the main differentiating factor. Instead the variable playing this role is consumption deprivation. For the social democratic regime such deprivation is close to 0 for the non-vulnerable cluster but rises to 64% for the vulnerable class. For the corporatist group the respective figures are 1.4 and 74% and for the liberal regime 1.4 and 61%. For the southern European cluster the figure for the non-vulnerable rises to 2.4%

Table 8.3. Within Regime Relativities for Disadvantage Indicators Derived from the Latent Class Model

	Odds ratios		
	Income poverty at 60% of median income	Economic stress dichotomy	Consumption deprivation dichotomy
Social democratic	6.8	37.7	299.3
Corporatist	9.3	45.1	210.2
Liberal	6.9	29.1	109.5
Southern Europe	6.2	29.5	72.4
Post-socialist corporatist	6.4	47.5	46.9
Post-socialist liberal	7.4	32.2	32.4

compared to one of 63% for the vulnerable class. These four regimes can be contrasted with the post-socialist clusters where deprivation levels are substantially higher for both vulnerable and non-vulnerable groups. For the conservative group the respective figure for vulnerable and non-vulnerable clusters are 90.0 and 14% and for the liberal group the corresponding figures are 17 and 95%.

In order to make clear the scale of disparities between the vulnerable and the non-vulnerable and to facilitate comparison within and between welfare re gimes, in Table 8.3 we set out the relevant odds ratios. Focusing first on income poverty at the 60% line, we can see from column 1 that economic vulnerability raises the odds on such poverty by a factor of 6.8 for the Social Democratic regime. The magnitude of this disparity varies little variation across welfare regimes. It rises to 9.3 for the corporatist regime but ranges between 6.2 and 7.4 for the remaining clusters. For subjective economic stress the scale of differentiation is much sharper with the odds ratio for the social democratic regime reaching 38. However, once again variation in the size of the effect across regime is modest running from a low of 29 to 48 and reveals no systematic pattern. The largest odds ratios are associated with the two corporatist clusters and the lowest with the liberal and southern European regimes.

The contrast with the results relating to consumption deprivation is quite striking. Outside the post-socialist regimes the odds ratios are considerably higher. In addition, a clear pattern of differentiation in the magnitude of the odds ratio is observed across welfare regimes. The largest value of almost 300 is associated with the social democratic regime. It falls to 210 for the corporatist cluster; reflecting a somewhat sharper proportionate increase in level of risk for the vulnerable group rather than the non-vulnerable in comparison with the social democratic regime. A further decline to 110 is observed for the liberal regime; arising from the fact that, while the deprivation risk rates for the vulnerable are identical for the liberal and corporatist clusters, the level for the non-vulnerable is lower in the former, producing a less sharp pattern of

Table 8.4. Levels of Multiple Deprivation (Poverty at 60% line + Consumption Deprivation + Economic Stress) by Economic Vulnerability and Welfare Regime

	Economically vulnerable (%)	Non-vulnerable (%)	Total (%)
Social democratic	12.7	0.0	1.6
Corporatist	20.1	0.0	3.0
Liberal	18.9	0.0	3.8
Southern Europe	22.2	0.0	6.3
Post-socialist corporatist	25.6	0.1	9.0
Post-socialist liberal	23.5	0.1	14.2

polarization. A further fall in the value of the relevant odds ratio to 72 is observed for the southern European cluster, largely reflecting a doubling of the levels for the non-vulnerable group, although the absolute levels remains low. For the post-socialist group we observe a decline in the odds ratio to 47. This occurs even though the risk level for the vulnerable group reaches 0.90 because the proportionate increase for the non-vulnerable is a good deal sharper. The further slight fall to 32 for the post-liberal socialist regime arises for similar reasons.

Overall for economic vulnerability we observe a pattern of differentials between welfare regimes whereby polarization is sharper in the more generous and comprehensive regimes. Thus while the absolute risk of being economically vulnerable and experiencing deprivation if one is in the vulnerable class is least in such regimes the degree of polarization in terms of relative risk of deprivation is sharpest in the more generous and comprehensive regimes.[7]

The conditional probabilities from the latent class model allow us to consider the picture deriving from a focus on interrelated risks compared with an emphasis on point-in-time multiple deprivation. As a consequence of the fact that the risk levels for each of our three indicators are independent within latent classes, the likelihood of simultaneously experiencing income poverty, consumption deprivation, and economic stress can be calculated by multiplying through the conditional probabilities for each outcome. In Table 8.4 we report multiple deprivation levels broken down by welfare regime. For the non-vulnerable groups we can see that for all 6 clusters the rate is effectively 0. For the vulnerable group the lowest level of multiple deprivation of 12.7% is observed for the social democratic regime. This rises to 18.9% for the liberal regime and to 20.1 for the corporatist cluster. It then increases gradually to 22.2, 23.5, and 25.6%, respectively, for the southern European, post-socialist liberal, and corporatist clusters. Thus the economically vulnerable are least exposed to multiple deprivation in the social

---

[7] A similar conclusion is reached by Tomaszewski (2009) based on event history analysis of ECHP data.

democratic regime and most subject to such deprivation in the two post-socialist regimes.

Clearly economic vulnerability does not necessarily imply multiple deprivation. Only one in eight of the vulnerable group in the social democratic regime are so deprived and for the remaining regimes it ranges between just below 1 in 4 and 1 in 5. Given the minimal levels of multiple deprivation among the non-vulnerable groups, calculating overall levels of such exposure reduces to multiplying the rates for the economically vulnerable by the proportion vulnerable. For the social democratic regime the proportion multiply deprived is lowest at 1.6%. It rises to 3.0 and 3.8% for, respectively, the corporatist and liberal regimes. Thus, as for the economically vulnerable, the lowest level of multiple deprivation is observed for the social democratic regime. However, the ranking of the liberal and corporatist regimes is reversed. This occurs because, while the rate of multiple deprivation for the vulnerable is lower in the former, the level of vulnerability is higher. The scale of multiple deprivation rises gradually rises from 6.3 to 9.0 and 14.2% as one moves from the southern European to the post-socialist corporatist and liberal regimes. Once again we see the reversal of the rankings of the liberal and corporatist regimes.

Total levels of multiple deprivation are considerably more sharply differentiated by comprehensiveness and generosity of welfare regimes than are the corresponding rates for the vulnerable. However, only for the post-socialist clusters does the figure rise above 6% of the population. This is true despite the fact that the correlations between the three dimensions we have considered are substantially higher than those involving other dimensions of deprivation. In the final section we explore the implication of adopting a more encompassing definition of multiple deprivation.

8.4 Poverty and Economic Vulnerability by Social Class and Welfare Regime

The increased emphasis on de-standardization or individualization of the life-cycle and a related stress on life events, together with increasing flexibility and precariousness in the labour market and the changing role of the welfare state, have led some to suggest that the impact of factors such as social class and indeed education on poverty and inequality are declining (Beck, 1992). A larger proportion of people are thought to experience life-cycle risks and consequent poverty. Poverty is democratized in the sense that it transcends traditional stratification boundaries. Poverty is seen increasingly as both individualized and transitory. Leisering and Liebfried (1999) argue that the 'temporalization and biographization' of poverty are features of the emergence of the 'risk society'.

The increased focus on the de-institutionalization of the life-course has therefore been associated with the argument that the structuring impact of factors such as social class has weakened. Thus, Beck and Beck-Gernsheim (1996) argue that individuals must structure their biographies through their own actions. However, the circumstances that create the need for such choices are to a significant extent beyond the control of the individual and 'elective biography' may become 'risk biography' as the certainties and predictability provided by the previous forms of social structuring are eroded. The notion that individuals construct their own life-course through choices and actions they take within the constraints of social circumstances is a long-standing one in the life-cycle literature (Elder, 1999). What is at issue is nature and degree of influence of such circumstances.

Recent debates have emphasized the distinction between 'new' and 'old' social risks. Old risks tend to involve mainly horizontal redistribution across the life-cycle from the working age groups to children and older people while new risks tend to affect specific sub-groups at particular life stages most keenly (Taylor-Gooby, 2004, 2008). These distinctions are seen to have increasing salience in a context where globalization and economic integration at the European level are seen to present challenges to long-standing welfare state arrangements. Bovenberg (2007) sets out a particularly explicit version of this argument from a conventional economic perspective. He highlights the changing nature of social risks and the increased importance of human capital, adaptability, and flexibility. Individuals must be provided with the 'discretion' to 'construct' their own biographies and become 'responsible' for their own life-courses. This presentation of the life-cycle perspective involves a very strong emphasis on market mechanisms and individualization of responsibility. However, concern with developing an appropriate recalibration between economic and welfare strategies spans both disciplinary and ideological boundaries (Ferrera and Rhodes, 2000).

The life-cycle and welfare state literature has been driven by 'macro' questions relating to the level and distribution of welfare expenditure. The social exclusion perspective has also developed in the context of the emergence of long-term unemployment and the challenges presented to post-World War II welfare consensus; however, it took a more 'micro' form with a greater focus on the experiences of individuals and households. In consequence, it drew on and developed the literature relating to the dynamics of 'at risk of poverty', longitudinal event history analysis, and the multidimensionality of deprivation.

Closer linkages between the life-cycle and the welfare state literature and the social exclusion literature would, perhaps, have led to a more explicit acceptance that while the notion of 'dynamic interrelated risks' that has recently figured in the life-cycle literature has considerable analytic potential,[8] it is enormously demanding in terms of both the types of analysis required and the quality and type of data required to deliver on that potential.

It is beyond the scope of this volume to provide a detailed account of the substantial literature in poverty and the life-cycle. However, in the rest of this chapter and the one that follows we will seek to assess the manner in which developing an approach to inter-related risks that takes seriously the methodological challenges of capturing both the dynamic and multidimensional aspects of social exclusion shapes our understanding of the extent and nature of social class differentials.

Our analysis makes use of a slightly aggregated version of the European Socio-economic Classification (ESeC).[9] The schema, following Goldthorpe (2007b), is based on an understanding of forms of employment relationship as viable responses to the weaker or stronger presence of monitoring and asset specificity problems in different work situations. Each is seen as a response by employers to certain problems or moral hazards they face in ensuring employees perform as required.[10] As Rose and Harrison (2007, 2009) note, it focuses on the relational as well as the distributive aspects of inequality. Individuals are understood to posses certain resources by virtue of the positions they occupy and consequently face a range of possibilities and constraints. As Goldthorpe (2002, p. 213), observes, one of the primary objectives of schemas such as ESeC is to bring out the constraints and opportunities typical of different class positions particularly as they bear 'on individuals' *security, stability and prospects* as a precondition of constructing explanations of empirical regularities'. The latent profile of economic vulnerability provides a particularly appropriate outcome indicator in examining the impact of social class defined in this manner. A failure to observe systematic variation by social class in exposure to economic vulnerability would seriously undermine claims that social class remains fundamental to the distribution of life chances in industrial and post-industrial societies. Our analysis employs a 7-category aggregated version of the ESeC. As before we assign the class position of the household reference person, apply dominance procedures, and make use of information on previous class position for unemployed or inactive HRPs.

The 7 classes with which we operate are as follows:

- Large employers, higher grade professional, administrative, and managerial occupations: 'the higher salariat' (ESeC Class 1);
- Lower grade professional, administrative, and managerial occupations: 'the lower salariat' (ESeC Class 2);

---

[8] See D'Addio and Whiteford (2007, p. 22). [9] See Rose and Harrison (2007, 2010).
[10] See Goldthorpe (2007b) and McGovern et al. (2007) for further discussion.

- Intermediate occupations and lower supervisory and technician occupations: 'higher grade white & blue collar' (ESeC Classes 3 & 6);
- Small employer and self-employed non-professional occupations: 'petit bourgeoise' (ESeC Class 4);
- Farmers (ESeC Class 5);
- Lower services, sales, and clerical occupations and lower technical occupations—'lower white collar & skilled manual' (ESeC Classes 7 & 8); and
- Routine occupations—'semi-unskilled manual' (ESeC Class 9).

In Table 8.5 we show the breakdown of average national poverty levels within welfare regime by social class. It is apparent that across regimes the major aspect of class differentiation arises not from a hierarchical ordering of classes but from the contrast between the property-owning classes and all others. In almost every case the highest level of poverty is observed for the farming class. The figure is lowest at 21% for the social democratic regime. It then rises to 25 and 29%, respectively, for the corporatist and liberal cluster. For the post-socialist groups the figure rises to 34/5% and it peaks at 39% for the southern European cluster. The petit bourgeoisie also display uniformly high poverty rates although, with the exception of the post-socialist group, the figure is in each case somewhat lower than for farmers. Variation across regimes is restricted ranging from 20% in the social democratic cluster to 37% for the post-socialist liberal group. For the property-owning groups we are struck more by the contrast between them and the remaining classes than by variation across welfare regimes.

Between regimes variation in poverty levels for the higher and lower salariat is also extremely limited. For the former the main contrast is between the post-

Table 8.5. Mean Level of National Income Poverty at 60% of Median Income by ESeC Class Schema by Welfare Regime

	Welfare regimes					
	Social democratic (%)	Corporatist (%)	Liberal (%)	Southern European (%)	Post-socialist corporatist (%)	Post-socialist liberal (%)
Higher salariat (1)	3.6	3.4	4.9	4.1	4.0	11.7
Lower salariat (2)	4.0	4.3	8.4	4.3	5.2	11.1
Higher grade white collar & lower supervisory (3 & 6)	5.6	8.7	14.4	9.4	7.9	17.5
Petit bourgeoise (4)	19.6	22.0	23.5	26.4	24.4	36.7
Farmers (5)	21.4	25.4	29.8	39.3	33.5	34.9
Lower services, sales, clerical & technical (7,8)	10.9	24.1	25.8	21.1	17.0	28.7
Semi-unskilled manual (9)	11.5	25.7	27.8	26.3	22.9	35.9

socialist liberal group where the level is 12% and the remaining regimes where it does not rise above 5%. For the lower salariat the main contrast is between the liberal and post-socialist liberal regimes with poverty rates of 8 and 11% and the remaining groups where the figure again does not exceed 5%. On this occasion it is the relatively uniform low levels of poverty that is most striking rather than variation across regimes.

For the remaining classes, we observe a recurring pattern in which the highest poverty rates are observed for the liberal clusters and the lowest for the social democratic while the remaining groups occupy an intermediate position. For the higher grade white and blue collar class the poverty rates for the post-socialist liberal and liberal regimes are 18 and 14%, respectively. The social democratic regime has a distinctively low rate of 6% while for the remaining clusters the figure is 8/9%. For lower white collar and skilled manual classes a similar pattern is observed with the rates for the two liberal regime being 29 and 26% while at the opposite end of the spectrum the social democratic rate is 11%. For the other clusters the figure lies between 17 and 24%. Finally, for the semi-unskilled manual class the poverty rate for the post-socialist liberal group reaches 36% and is followed the liberal group with a rate of 28%. In contrast, the rate for the social democratic group is 12%. For the remaining clusters the figure lies between 23 and 26%.

The major contrast in terms of levels of poverty involves the property classes and most particularly the farmers. For the remaining classes, we observe variation that takes a hierarchical form. The combined impact of the property and hierarchical effects results in relatively restricted welfare regime variation within social classes. It is most systematic for the non-propertied class outside the salariat. The pattern is one that involves fairly sharp contrasts between the social democratic regime and the 2 liberal regimes with the remaining clusters occupying the middle ground.

In Table 8.6 we set out the comparable results in relation to economic vulnerability. The distinctive uniformly high levels observed for propertied classes with regard to poverty are not replicated in the case of vulnerability. Furthermore, variation across welfare regimes is substantially sharper and involves a somewhat different pattern. The major contrast is now between the post-socialist liberal and social democratic regimes. The post-socialist corporatist cluster is located closest to the latter. The remaining clusters occupy an intermediate position but the southern European cluster is fairly sharply differentiated from the corporatist and liberal clusters in relation to the property-owning classes and, in particular, farmers.

In every case the highest level of economic vulnerability is found for the semi-unskilled class but with considerable variation across regimes. The lowest level of vulnerability of 17.9% is found for the social democratic regime. It increases to 31–2% for the corporatist and liberal regimes. It then rises sharply

Table 8.6. Level of Economic Vulnerability by ESeC Class Schema by Welfare Regime

	Welfare regimes					
	Social democratic (%)	Corporatist (%)	Liberal (%)	Southern European (%)	Post-socialist corporatist (%)	Post-socialist liberal (%)
Higher salariat (1)	3.0	3.9	4.7	5.1	11.7	17.3
Lower salariat (2)	4.5	7.0	8.2	9.1	18.9	29.0
Higher white & blue collar (3 & 6)	8.1	13.5	13.9	19.3	28.8	39.0
Petit bourgeoise (4)	8.9	15.4	11.6	25.4	29.7	26.8
Farmers (5)	6.6	12.4	9.4	39.8	50.8	42.2
Lower white collar & skilled manual (7,8)	14.1	24.2	28.9	38.1	45.9	49.7
Semi-unskilled manual (9)	17.9	30.6	32.0	40.6	52.3	59.1

to 41% for the southern European regime and to 52% for the post-socialist corporatist cluster before peaking at 59% for the post-socialist liberal cluster. A similar pattern is observed for the lower white collar and skilled manual class. The lowest level of economic vulnerability of 14% is associated with the social democratic cluster. It increases to 24 and 29% for the corporatist and liberal regimes. It then rises to 38 and 46% for the southern European liberal and post-socialist corporatist clusters before reaching its highest values of 50% for the post-socialist liberal group. This patterning is sustained for the higher white and blue collar group. For the social democratic group the vulnerability level is 8%. It increases to 14% for the corporatist and liberal regimes; it then rises successively to 19, 29, and 39% for the remaining clusters. The distribution for the lower salariat conforms to this recurring pattern with a level of vulnerability for social democratic regime of less than 5% that rises to between 7 and 9% for the intermediate regimes before increasing sharply to 19 and 28%, respectively. for the corporatist and liberal post-socialist regimes. For the higher salariat the major contrast is between the post-socialist clusters and the others. For the latter the level of vulnerability averages 4%. Within the former, it reaches 12 and 17%, respectively, for the corporatist and liberal groups.

For the propertied classes, outside the southern European and post-socialist regimes, vulnerability levels are significantly lower than corresponding poverty rates. For these clusters farmers' levels go from 7% in the social democratic group to 12% in the liberal cluster. For the petit bourgeoisie the level goes from 9% for the social democratic regime to 15% for the corporatist cluster. For the southern European regime the vulnerability level reaches 25% for the petit bourgeoisie and 40% for farmers. For the post-socialist regime the figures for the petit bourgeoisie are, respectively, 27 and 30% for the post-socialist liberal and corporatist regimes. For the farmers the corresponding figures are 42 and

51%. From Table 8.6 we see that the relative outcomes for the latter two regimes are reversed as one moves from the self-employed to the employee classes.

The more substantial differences between social classes within regimes, combined with substantially greater variation across regimes within classes, produces an overall pattern of differentiation that is considerably at variance with that relating to poverty. Taking the difference between the higher salariat in the social democratic cluster and the semi-unskilled manual class in the post-socialist liberal regime as a crude indicator of the cumulative impact of hierarchical class effects and welfare regime we find that for poverty the respective levels are 3.6 and 36% while for economic vulnerability the corresponding figures are 3.0 and 59%.

8.5 Relative Risk of Poverty and Economic Vulnerability by Social Class and Welfare Regime

The analysis set out in Tables 8.5 and 8.6 documents absolute variations in poverty and vulnerability levels across social class classes and welfare regimes. However, in order to undertake a systematic comparison of the relative impact of social class across welfare regimes and outcomes it is necessary to move from an inspection of percentages to a comparison of odds ratios. In Table 8.7 we set out the results from a set of logistic regressions relating to social class to poverty for each of the welfare regimes.[11] With the higher salariat as the benchmark, for every regime the odds on being poor rather than non-poor are most strongly influenced by membership of the farming class. For the social democratic regime it increases the odds by a factor of 7.5. This rises to 10.5 for the corporatist cluster and 11.5 for the two liberal regimes. It increases further to 13.2 for the post-socialist corporatist cluster and finally to 14.4 for the southern European. The next strongest average effect is observed for the petit bourgeoisie. The weakest effect is observed for the post-socialist liberal and liberal cluster with odds ratios of 3.5 and 5.4, respectively. For the remaining clusters, the figure ranges between 7.3 and 8.8.

The differential between the higher and lower salariat is positive in every case, positive but modest. It ranges from a low of 1.1 in the socials democratic and southern European regimes to 1.7 in the liberal regime. The impact increases for the higher white and blue collar and runs from 1.7 for the social democratic cluster to 3.2 for the liberal regimes. A significant strengthening of the class effect is found for the lower white collar and skilled manual. Once again the lowest value of 3.5 is found for the social democratic regime. The

[11] Standard errors in Tables 8.5 and 8.6 have been calculated to take into account the clustering of individuals within households.

Table 8.7. Logistic Regression of Poverty by ESeC Class Schema by Welfare Regime

	Odds ratios					
	Social democratic	Corporatist	Liberal	Southern European	Post-socialist corporatist	Post-socialist liberal
Higher salariat (1)	Ref.	Ref.	Ref.	Ref.	Ref.	Ref.
Lower salariat (2)	1.147	1.323	1.703	1.087	1.265	1.281
Higher white & blue collar (3 & 6)	1.671	2.731	3.209	2.502	2.158	2.312
Petit bourgeoise (4)	7.772	8.068	5.385	8.787	7.294	3.530
Farmers (5)	7.511	10.457	11.478	14.365	13.221	11.559
Lower white collar & skilled manual (7 & 8)	3.452	8.067	6.500	6.205	5.408	4.743
Semi-unskilled manual (9)	3.788	9.639	7.202	8.222	6.477	7.466
Nagelkerke R	0.078	0.130	0.112	0.131	0.119	0.121
Degrees of freedom	6	6	6	6	6	6
N	91,420	85,127	36.195	125.498	109,426	22,058

highest value of 8.1 is associated with the corporatist regime. The remaining values range between 4.7 for the post-socialist liberal regime to 6.5 for the liberal. For the semi-unskilled class a further increase in the odds ratio is observed in each case. Once again the lowest and the highest odds ratios are observed in the social democratic and corporatist regimes with respective values of 3.8 and 9.6. The remaining values run from 6.5 in the post-socialist corporatist cluster to 8.2 for the southern European regime.

In general, we observe strong class effects relating to property with weaker but systematic class hierarchy effects. However, the impact of social class across welfare regimes is generally modest.

In Table 8.8 we report the results from the corresponding set of logistic regressions relating to economic vulnerability.[12] In contrast to the situation for poverty, by far the strongest differential is associated with the semi-unskilled manual class. Two of the 3 lowest odds ratios are observed for the post-socialist regimes with the respective values for the liberal and corporatist variants being 6.9 and 8.3. These values are lower than in a number of other regimes despite the high absolute levels of economic vulnerability in such classes. They occur because the disparities in vulnerability levels within the higher salariat between the post-socialist regimes and the social democratic cluster are sharper than those occurring within the semi-unskilled class. The

[12] The estimates in Table 8.6 are based on employing the LEM modal class procedure for the identification of the dependent variable. Each observation is assigned to that latent class for which, given the manifest scores, the estimated classification probability is largest. Allocation to clusters is on the basis of modal assignment.

Table 8.8. Logistic Regression of Level of Economic Vulnerability by ESeC Class Schema by Welfare Regime

	Odds ratios					
	Social democratic	Corporatist	Liberal	Southern European	Post-socialist corporatist	Post-socialist liberal
Higher salariat (1)	Ref.	Ref.	Ref.	Ref.	Ref.	Ref.
Lower salariat (2)	1.536	1.864	1.816	1.865	1.764	1.952
Higher white & blue collar (3 & 6)	2.868	3.900	3.302	4.453	3.057	3.048
Petit bourgeoise (4)	3.187	4.527	2.678	6.365	3.192	1.741
Farmers (5)	2.268	3.546	2.146	12.346	7.794	3.492
Lower white collar & skilled manual (7,8)	5.330	7.988	8.304	11.478	6.411	4.716
Semi-unskilled manual (9)	7.045	11.005	9.632	12.733	8.287	6.901
Nagelkerke R	0.073	0.109	0.135	0.137	0.137	0.125
Reduction in log likelihood ratio	2,751.0	5,226.6	2,881.8	12,166.4	11,330.6	2.213.1
Degrees of freedom	6	6	6	6	6	6
N	89,149	84,511	35,835	125,105	108.655	22.026

next lowest value of 7.0 is observed for the social democratic regime. It arises for a quite different reason relating to the distinctively low level of vulnerability among those in the semi-unskilled manual class in this regime. The odds ratio rises gradually as one moves from the liberal to the corporatist and finally to the southern European regimes from 9.6 to 11.0 and 12.7.

A similar pattern, although involving slightly weaker effects, is observed for the lower white collar and skilled manual class. For the post-socialist cluster the weakest effect of 4.7 is again observed for the liberal variant while that for the corporatist form reaches 6.4. A similarly relatively low value of 5.3 is associated with the social democratic regime. We again observe a gradual increase from 7.9 to 8.3 to 11.5 as we move from the liberal to the corporatist and the southern European regime. For the higher white and blue collar class an odds ratio of varies between 2.9 and 3.1 for the post-socialist clusters and the social democratic regime. This rises to 3.9 and 3.3, respectively, for the corporatist and liberal regimes and to 4.5 for the southern European cluster. Differentiation relating to the impact of membership of the lower and higher salariat across regimes is relatively slight.

The impact of being a member of either the petit bourgeoisie or the farming class is substantially weaker in the case of economic vulnerability but variation across regimes is considerably greater. For the petit bourgeoisie we see that the weakest effects are observed for the liberal regimes and the highest for the corporatist and southern European clusters. For farming the post-socialist and southern European regime have distinctively high odds ratios of 7.8 and

12.3 while in no other case does the value rise above 3.6. The scale of the observed effects for the self-employed classes is generally substantially weaker than for poverty.

8.6 Multiple Deprivation

Attempts to grapple with the changing nature of social stratification have provoked increased reference to the emergence of multiple disadvantage, which is considered to be qualitatively different from that formerly associated with working-class disadvantage or with the exposure to poverty. Yet, at the same time as the shifts from a 1-dimensional to multidimensional perspective, from static to dynamic analyses, and to an emphasis on relations have become defining characteristics of the social exclusion perspective, the volume of research documenting the nature and extent of multiple disadvantage has been rather modest and has focused largely on the effects of unemployment and employment precarity on social isolation (Paugam, 1996a, b; Paugam and Russell, 2000).

In view of this, it is regrettable that much of the treatment of social exclusion overstates both the novelty of emphasizing multiple disadvantage and the limitations of traditional poverty analysis. As we have emphasized earlier, a variety of studies have shown the danger of assuming rather than establishing multiple disadvantage by demonstrating that the weak relationship between low income and material deprivation. Similarly a range of studies focusing on the dimensionality of deprivation have shown that there is considerable variation in the magnitude of the correlations between different dimensions of deprivation. Such variability reflects the fact that rather different socio-economic factors may be involved in explaining, for example, health problems as opposed to poor housing conditions and both in turn may have somewhat different sources than those associated with an unsatisfactory neighbourhood environment. Halleröd and Larsson (2008), employing Swedish data, concluded that consumption deprivation measures were substantially more likely than low income to be related to other negative welfare problems such as ill-health and psychological distress. However, they conclude that aspects often looked upon as central to the debate on social exclusion—such as exclusion from the political arena and spatial segregation—were only weakly related to each other and consumption deprivation.

While the social exclusion perspective has focused attention on the processes leading to exposure to multiple disadvantage and social isolation, despite the influence the perspective has had on both academic and policy discussions, conceptual analysis has remained imprecise and empirical evidence modest. Furthermore, methodological issues relating to the analysis of multiple disadvantage—which have a long pedigree—have largely been ignored Thus, as Heath (1981) stresses, if we wish to document the existence of multiple deprivation, we must go beyond the degree of association between variables for the population as a whole and demonstrate the scale of overlap at the extremes. Significant inter-correlation among variables does not in itself guarantee that any substantial proportion of the population experiences multiple disadvantage. Consequently, patterns of inter-related risk do not necessarily lead to outcomes characterized by multiple deprivation.

The combination of economic deprivation that we have considered under the heading 'economic vulnerability' is somewhat more restricted than those for which the term 'multiple deprivation' is usually reserved. In this section we extend our analysis to deal more with broadly conceived patterns. By locating our analysis based on a more restricted group of items relating to economic vulnerability in the context of findings arising from the broader set, we can establish the extent to which indices based on the former succeed in capturing more widespread patterns of differentiation. In doing so we establish whether a restricted set of indicators may be sufficient to identify those who experience more broadly based deprivation. As we noted earlier, the degree of multidimensionality required in identifying the poor/excluded is an empirical matter. It is not something one can simply read off from the multidimensional nature of the concepts themselves. The strategy we pursue here is similar to that employed by McKay and Collard (2003) in developing deprivation indicators for the UK Family Resources Survey; in that we seek to demonstrate that it is not necessary to have a large suite of questions if a smaller set exhibit comparable discriminatory power. The additional dimensions that we incorporate in our analysis at this point are as follows:

- Household facilities, comprising 5 items that relate to permanent household facilities such as bath or shower and indoor toilet, and also includes being able to afford a telephone, a colour TV, and a washing machine;
- Neighbourhood environment, comprising 3 items relating to noise, pollution, crime, and violence; and
- Health status of the HRP, comprising 3 items relating to overall evaluation of health status, having a chronic illness or disability and restricted mobility.

A case can be made that indicators relating to health status should not be incorporated in a poverty index or, perhaps, in a definition of material deprivation as such. However, the available evidence shows that, in contrasts with the much weaker associations observed in the case of factors such as social isolation that are often included under the notion of social exclusion, health status is affected by such deprivation. Consequently, we think it is not unreasonable to included health problems as one element of a multidimensional profile. On the other hand, items relating to social networks and social participation which have been relatively weakly associated with material deprivation may be better thought of as involving social cohesion rather than social exclusion with the relationship between them being a matter of empirical enquiry.

In order to reach conclusions concerning multiple deprivations we define a threshold in relation to each dimension. Any such threshold must to some extent be arbitrary. Our preferred option would be to define the thresholds so that there are equal numbers above them for each of the dimensions. Unfortunately, the fact that the indices are comprised of variable numbers of indicators, and have rather differently shaped distributions, means that this is not a feasible option. We have chosen therefore to define our thresholds so that in each case a significant, but variable minority are above the deprivation cut-off point and so to ensure that significant variation. This is consistent with the notion that multiple deprivation arises where excluded minorities overlap substantially. Thus for the housing and neighbourhood environment dimensions the thresholds are, respectively, 1+ and 2+. In each case approximately 1 in 7 are above the threshold. For health the threshold is 2+ and approximately 1 in 5 are above the threshold.

In Table 8.9 we look at the relationship between economic vulnerability and being above each of the deprivation thresholds. Starting with housing, we find that in every case there is a clear relationship between economic vulnerability and experiencing deprivation in relation to at least 1 item. Outside the post-socialist regimes the magnitude of multiple deprivation among the non-vulnerable does not rise above 1%. Among the economically vulnerable the lowest level of 5% is observed for the liberal regime and the highest of 12% is observed for the corporatist group. For the social democratic and southern European regimes it ranges between 8 and 9%. For the post-socialist corporatist group the figures rise to 4 and 19%, respectively, for the non-vulnerable and vulnerable classes. A further sharp increase is observed for the post-socialist liberal groups where the respective figures are 22 and 46%.

Viewing these results in relative terms, we find that the highest odds ratio is observed for the corporatist regime where the odds on the vulnerable class being above the housing deprivation threshold are almost 13 times higher than that for the non-vulnerable. It is followed by the social democratic and southern European regime with an odds ration of 9. For the liberal regimes the figure is a good deal lower, with the modest numbers in the vulnerable class reporting such deprivation contributing to much lower odds ration of 5. For the post-corporatist cluster substantially higher numbers in both vulnerable and non-vulnerable categories produces an odds ratio of 6. Finally, for the post-socialist cluster, despite the large numbers in the vulnerable class

Table 8.9. Percentage Deprived on Housing, Neighbourhood, and Health Deprivation by Economic Vulnerability and Corresponding Odds Ratios

Welfare regime	Housing			Neighbourhood 2+			Health		
	Non-vulnerable (%)	Vulnerable (%)	Odds ratio	Non-vulnerable (%)	Vulnerable (%)	Odds ratio	Non-vulnerable (%)	Vulnerable (%)	Odds ratio
Social democratic	1.2	8.9	9.0	8.8	16.9	2.1	12.5	24.3	2.2
Corporatist	1.0	11.8	13.3	13.5	25.4	2.2	19.8	37.0	2.4
Liberal	1.3	5.0	5.2	13.0	19.6	1.6	14.9	27.8	2.2
Southern European	1.1	8.4	9.1	15.9	19.9	1.3	18.6	29.3	1.8
Post-socialist corporatist	3.9	18.7	5.7	12.6	16.2	1.3	23.1	37.9	2.0
Post-socialist liberal	21.9	46.2	3.1	15.9	18.3	1.2	15.7	33.3	2.7

reporting housing deprivation, the fact that over one-fifth of the non-vulnerable class also do so produces an odds ratio of just above 3.

Focusing on neighbourhood deprivation, we find that in every case the economically vulnerable are more likely to experience such deprivation. For the vulnerable class the level of deprivation runs from just above 18% in the in the post-socialist regime to 25% in the corporatist group. For the non-vulnerable the range runs from 9% for the social democratic regime to 16% in the southern European and post-socialist liberal clusters. In contrast with the case for housing, neighbourhood deprivation levels in the post-socialist regimes are on average no higher than for the other regimes, apart from the social democratic cluster. In relative terms, vulnerability differentials are a great deal more modest in the less affluent regimes. The odds ratios go from 2.2 in the social democratic regime to 1.2 in the post-socialist cluster. Clearly other factors with relatively little association to economic vulnerability, such as urban–rural location, play a major role in relation to neighbourhood deprivation.

The situation for health is reasonably similar to that for neighbourhood environment. Once again in every case the level of deprivation is higher for the vulnerable class. For the vulnerable class the figure is highest in the 2 corporatist regimes, coming close to 40% in both cases. It falls slightly to 33% for the post-socialist liberal cluster. The figures for the remaining clusters range between 29% for southern Europe and 24% for the social democratic regime. Among the non-vulnerable the highest levels are again observed for the corporatist clusters with respective levels of 23 and 20% for the post-socialist and non-socialist cluster. Similarly, the lowest level of 13% is associated with the social democratic regime. These patterns of absolute difference produce almost identical relativities with the odds ratio for the six welfare regimes ranging from 1.9 to 2.3.

Our analysis shows that that over and above the deprivation elements making up the economic vulnerability profile, the members of this group experience higher exposure to deprivation relating to housing, neighbourhood environment, and health. However, even with regard to housing where the differentials are greatest, the relativities between vulnerable and non-vulnerable are of a significantly lesser magnitude than in the case of consumption deprivation and economic stress. In the case of neighbourhood environment and health, the disparities are considerable more modest. The magnitude of these associations will have an impact on the extent to which economic vulnerability results in multiple deprivation; as will the degree of association between the individual deprivation dimensions.

In Table 8.10 we document levels of multiple deprivation broken down by economic vulnerability. The former is defined as being above the deprivation threshold on at least 2 of the housing, health, and neighbourhood

Table 8.10. Percentage Multiply Deprived and Corresponding Odds Ratio by Economic Vulnerability

Welfare regime	Non-vulnerable (%)	Vulnerable (%)	Odds ratio
Social democratic	1.6	8.7	5.6
Corporatist	3.5	16.0	5.3
Liberal	2.8	8.7	3.3
Southern European	4.1	10.3	2.5
Post-socialist corporatist	5.2	15.4	3.3
Post-socialist liberal	8.8	24.0	3.3

dimensions. For every regime the level of multiple deprivation is substantially higher for the economically vulnerable class. The lowest level among the vulnerable class of 9% is observed for the social democratic and liberal regimes. It rises to 10% for the southern European cluster before increasing to 15 and 16% for the 2 corporatist regimes. Finally, the figure peaks at 24% for the post-socialist cluster. Among the non-vulnerable class the lowest level of multiple deprivation of less than 2% is observed for the social democratic regime and the highest of 9% for the post-socialist liberal cluster. For the remaining regimes it ranges between 3 and 5%.

While the lowest levels of multiple deprivation for both vulnerable and non-vulnerable classes are observed for the social democratic regime, the relative disadvantage experienced by the vulnerable class is also greatest there. This is reflected in an odds ratio of 5.6, indicating that the vulnerable class are almost 6 times more likely than the non-vulnerable to experience multiple deprivation. Variation in relative impact across regimes is relatively modest with the magnitude of the odds ratio for the remaining clusters ranging from 2.5 for the southern European group to 5.3 for the corporatist cluster.

Finally, focusing on absolute levels of deprivation in the population we seek to establish what proportion of the population experience such deprivation, as defined above, but also what are the corresponding levels where such deprivation is defined to also include economic vulnerability. In the first column of Table 8.11 we focus on the former type of deprivation. This is lowest in the social democratic regime where the figure is 2.6%. It is followed by the liberal regime with a level of 4%. The figures for the corporatist and southern European regimes rise, respectively, to 5.3 and 5.8%. For the post-socialist corporatist and liberal regimes the figure rises, respectively, to 8.7 and 14.9%.

Where multiple deprivation is defined to encompass economic vulnerability, a broadly similar pattern is observed but the levels of deprivation are substantially reduced. From column 2 in Table 8.11 we can see that the lowest level of this accentuated form of multiple deprivation is observed for the social

Table 8.11. Level Multiple Deprivation and Combined Economic Vulnerability and Multiple Deprivation by Welfare Regime

Welfare regime	Multiple deprivation (%)	Economic vulnerability & multiple deprivation (%)
Social democratic	2.6	1.1
Corporatist	5.3	2.4
Liberal	4.0	1.8
Southern European	5.8	2.9
Post-socialist corporatist	8.7	5.3
Post-socialist liberal	14.9	9.6

democratic regime where the figure is 1.1%. The figure for the liberal regime is marginally higher at 1.8%. The figures for the corporatist and southern European regimes are, respectively, 2.4 and 2.9%. We then observe a significant increase to 5.3% for the post-socialist cluster before almost doubling to 9.6% for the liberal counterpart.

Our analysis reveals that individuals in the economically vulnerable cluster are characterized by higher exposure to a set of interrelated risks and deprivations. However, the level of correlation between the different aspects of the multiple deprivation profile and the variability in the association between economic vulnerability and the remaining forms of deprivation ensures that this results in rather lower levels of multiple deprivation than many might have imagined.

8.7 Conclusions

In this chapter we have addressed a set of interrelated issues. These comprise the relative merits of 1-dimensional versus multidimensional approaches to poverty and social exclusion, increasing concerns about reliance on a nationally based income poverty measures in the context of EU-enlargement, the continuing relevance of class-based explanations of variation in life chances, and the relationship between economic vulnerability and multiple deprivation.

While entirely persuaded by the theoretical arguments relating to the virtues of a multidimensional approach, we have stressed the need for methodological progress that allows us to fruitfully explore key issues relating to poverty and social exclusion.

We have sought to do so by applying latent class analysis to distinguish groups of individual that are distinguished in terms of restricted form of social exclusion that we have labelled social exclusion. This approach is informed by a concern with both multidimensional and dynamic aspects of the social exclusion process.

In contrast to the situation with national income poverty measures, levels of economic vulnerability vary systematically across welfare regimes in a manner consistent with our knowledge of both living standards in those societies and the manner in which such welfare regimes operate. Levels increase as we move from the social democratic to the corporatist to the liberal to the corporatist to the southern European and finally corporatist and liberal post-socialist regimes. Within each regime, the economic vulnerability approach distinguishes a group of individuals that exhibit a multidimensional profile in terms of social exclusion that sharply differentiates them from the reminder of the population.

The latent class approach to economic vulnerability enables us to provide a coherent account of patterns of social exclusion within and across welfare regimes. Despite the scale of variation across welfare regimes, the numbers above the vulnerability threshold in the post-socialist regimes are considerably lower than the corresponding figures employing a European level relative income approach. It shares with an EU level 'at-risk-of-poverty' approach the capacity to reveal the expected differentiation between welfare regimes in terms of levels of prosperity without resulting in a situation where the contrast between the post-socialist regimes and all others comes to entirely dominate the results.

In addition to the advantages that it enjoys in identifying a segment of the population characterized by a distinctive social exclusion profile, the latent class approach also reveals striking patterns of differentiation by social class within welfare regimes.[13] Unlike the national relative income approach the latent class approach produces a pattern of class differentiation that is not dominated by the contrast between the property-owning classes and all others. At the same time, it uncovers important variations in such effects across regimes. In contrast to a European-wide relative income approach it also simultaneously captures the fact that *absolute* levels of vulnerability are distinctively high among the lower social classes in the less affluent regimes while class *relativities* are sharper in a number of the more affluent regimes.[14]

No single indicator is likely to prove adequate in capturing the diversity of experience of poverty and social exclusion in an enlarged European Union. In light of this we have considerable sympathy with those who argue for the need to supplement nationally based indicators with EU-wide indicators.

---

[13] It is clear, however, that efforts at targeting within post-socialist regimes would require supplementary measures.

[14] In Chapter 9, we will demonstrate that the economic vulnerability approach has significant advantages over income and deprivation measures in relation to problems of measurement error that arise in analysis of dynamics. As a consequence it proves considerably more effective in revealing the impact of social class on patterns of persistent disadvantage over time.

However, in this chapter we have sought to demonstrate that a more effective strategy may be to take more seriously the need to invest greater effort to translating the conceptually compelling case for a multidimensional approach to social exclusion into an appropriate set of operational alternatives. It also shows that, where this is done, patterns of differentiation by social class appear a great deal more striking than when the focus is restricted solely to income measures.

Our analysis makes clear that social exclusion in the sense of patterns of inter-related risks of the form associated with economic vulnerability needs to be clearly distinguished from multiple deprivation in the sense of a set of overlapping deprivations that can be observed at a particular point in time. It is true that economic vulnerability is consistently related to higher levels of deprivation relating to housing, health, and neighbourhood environment. However, its discriminatory power in relation to such dimensions is considerably weaker that with regard to its constituent components.

Consequently the fact that economic vulnerability exerts multiple influences does not necessarily result in extremes of multiple disadvantage on any substantial scale. The same finding has been shown to hold in earlier studies relating to the impact of persistent poverty and deprivation (Whelan et al., 2003). The relationships we observe are probabilistic and, as is true in the social sciences as a whole, that even what we consider to be strong relationships often involve modest levels of correlation. It is clear that a great many factors other than economic vulnerability play a role in determining deprivation and these factors vary across dimensions.

9

The Dynamics of Poverty, Deprivation, and Economic Vulnerability

9.1 Introduction

The availability of the European Community Household Panel (ECHP), designed from the outset as a longitudinal survey, made it possible to undertake a comparative analysis of the relationship between income poverty and deprivation measures not only in cross-sectional form but also over time for the same individuals and households. As we have noted earlier, interest in exploring this relationship has been stimulated by the observation that there is a significant mismatch between poverty measured indirectly using an income approach and direct measures focusing on life-style deprivation. This presents a serious challenge to the use of relative income poverty lines to identify those excluded from a minimal acceptable standard of living through a lack of resources. The issue is one of validity i.e., whether it is reasonable to interpret relative income measures as adequately capturing such exclusion.

Our starting point in this chapter is the fact that, as documented in Chapter 6, even where we employ longitudinal measures income poverty and deprivation appear to be tapping rather different phenomena. We now extend that analysis to address issues of reliability in relation to income and deprivation dynamics. In particular, we investigate the extent to which conclusions relating to the mismatch between income and deprivation at the longitudinal level may be affected by the fact these dimensions are differentially affected by measurement error. We outline in Section 9.2 what has been learned from recent studies on measurement error and reliability, and bring out how this might affect the observed 'mismatch' between low income and deprivation. Section 9.3 sets out the variables we focus on in order to investigate this empirically and describes their main features over time. We then build on recent approaches to the statistical modelling of poverty dynamics to analyse mobility in relation to both poverty and deprivation, with Section 9.4

describing the models estimated and Section 9.5 setting out what they show about the extent and nature of observed income poverty and deprivation dynamics.

In the rest of the chapter we extend that analysis by combining features of recent approaches to statistical modelling of poverty dynamics and multidimensional deprivation to analyse the dynamics of economic vulnerability. By integrating these approaches we seek to demonstrate conclusively the importance of taking into account both dynamics and multidimensionality. Section 9.6 describes how latent class models are fitted at the cross-sectional level for each of the 5 years and individuals in each country are allocated between economically vulnerable and non-vulnerable classes. Section 9.7 then proceeds to apply dynamic error-corrected models to the analysis of longitudinal patterns of economic vulnerability. Using the results Section 9.8 assesses the extent to which conclusions regarding the socio-economic distribution of social exclusion are affected by how successfully we take into account its multidimensional and dynamic nature. Earlier chapters have shown that conclusions relating to the impact of labour market exclusion or social class on poverty and exclusion are strikingly different, depending on whether one focuses on income poverty, consistent poverty, or economic vulnerability. Economic vulnerability attempts not only to deal with the multidimensionality of social exclusion but also to provide a proxy for longitudinal exposure to risk; this chapter asks how much taking dynamic patterns of vulnerability into account directly, in a way that corrects for measurement error, affects our understanding of social exclusion, with conclusions summarized in Section 9.9.

9.2 Measurement Error and 'Mismatch' between Low Income and Deprivation

We now wish to reconsider the possibility, raised in Chapter 6, that by paying appropriate attention to the longitudinal aspects of poverty and deprivation we may avoid the need for multidimensional measurement suggested by the mismatch between income poverty and deprivation apparent at the cross-sectional level. A particularly strong version of this hypothesis suggest that the key to resolving these issues lies in using longitudinal measures because different measures tap the same dynamic process but in its different phases (Gordon, 2002). Without going this far, we might expect that by measuring income poverty and deprivation over time we could make significant progress in reducing the mismatch associated with point-in-time measures. Panel research has shown that movements into and out of poverty are a great deal more frequent than had been supposed and that a far greater proportion of the population experience poverty at some point than revealed by cross-sectional studies[1] By extending our measure of income poverty over time, we might hope to get a better measure of command over resources. Our expectation would then be that such a measure would be more strongly related to deprivation and would contribute to a reduction in the income poverty–deprivation mismatch. Implicit in this approach is the assumption that deprivation measures are more stable than income measures with the consequence that current level of deprivation is a significantly better indicator of persistent deprivation than current income is of its longitudinal counterpart. Given this, the mismatch problem, evident at the cross-sectional level, would be largely resolved by taking poverty experience over time into account.

As we have discussed in detail in Chapter 5, analysis by Whelan et al. (2004) of the first 5 waves of the ECHP showed that, for the nine countries included in their analysis, a measure of extent of exposure to income poverty over the 5-year spell offered significant advantages over its cross-sectional counterpart. An income poverty profile schema that differentiated respondents in terms of exposure to poverty over time was shown to be systematically related to both cross-sectional and longitudinal deprivation. However, contrary to expectations, the level of mismatch at the longitudinal level was no less than for point-in-time measures.

Thus, even where we are in a position to observe both income poverty and life-style deprivation over a reasonable period of time, the available evidence points to the conclusion that, while there is a substantial correlation between these dimensions, they are to a significant extent tapping different phenomena. Consequently, if poverty continues to be defined in terms of 'exclusion from a minimally acceptable standard of living through a lack of resources' it is necessary to conclude that even longitudinal measures of income poverty cannot be taken on their own as providing valid measures of the underlying construct and it remains necessary to take into account direct measures of deprivation. However, 1 factor that has not been taken into account in earlier analyses is the role of measurement error. This is not unusual and indeed Breen and Moisio (2004) could find only 1 effort prior to their own by Rendtel et al. (1998) that developed a model to distinguish between true poverty mobility and measurement error. As they note, conclusions about income poverty dynamics drawn on the basis of observed data implicitly assume a saturated structural model, rather than one based on more parsimonious assumptions, and a measurement model that assumes exact correspondence between observed poverty and true poverty. Studies of this kind based on the ECHP have shown generally high levels of mobility into and out of poverty

---

[1] See Jarvis and Jenkins (1999); Layte and Whelan (2003); Breen and Moisio (2004).

with a much larger proportion of the population experiencing poverty at some point during the period of observation than suggested by the cross-sectional figures (Bane and Ellwood, 1986; Duncan et al. 1993; Jarvis and Jenkins, 1999). At the same time the incidence of income poverty is concentrated in the same part of the population (Jarvis and Jenkins, 1999; Leisering and Liebfried, 1999; Layte and Whelan, 2003; Whelan et al., 2004). As Breen and Moisio (2004) note, these 2 aspects of income poverty dynamics seem to surface in 1 form or other in most studies of the phenomenon.

While there is a remarkable consistency in such findings, recent studies that have taken measurement error into account produce a strikingly different picture. Measurement error in relation to income poverty can arise for a variety of reasons. The respondent may report erroneous information relating to either income components or household composition. Surveys request income over a fixed period such as the previous year and respondents may have different perceptions of time in relation to income. The meaning of 'household' may be misunderstood. Finally there may be sources of income that the respondent does not wish to reveal (Moisio, 2004). Measures of lifestyle deprivation frequently ask respondents to indicate not only the presence or absence of an item but, in the case of absence, whether this arises because of inability to afford the item. There are thus 2 distinct sources of error. Moisio (2004) notes that, while with cross-sectional measures we may reasonably assume that measurement errors cancel out each other, so that our estimates are unbiased if random errors are uncorrelated, this convenient attribute does not apply with repeated measures.

Rendtel et al. (1998) sought to correct for measurement error and measure latent rather than manifest poverty. They proceed to analyse such poverty by use of a Markov chain model which assumes that poverty at each point is influenced only by the preceding point in the chain. In other words, poverty at time t is influenced by the outcome at point $t - 1$ but is entirely uninfluenced by the state at time $t - 2$. Employing this approach they reached the striking conclusion that almost half the observed income poverty mobility in the German Socio-Economic Panel could be accounted for by measurement error. Basic and Rendtel (2004) extended such analysis by applying such models to a comparison of the first and fifth wave of the Finnish ECHP survey and corresponding administrative data and concluded that overestimation of income poverty transitions as a consequence of measurement error was a substantially more serious problem than errors in estimation associated with selective attrition.

Breen and Moisio (2004) and Moisio (2004) extended this analysis in a number of important respects. They applied a range of models of graduated complexity to income poverty dynamics in 10 countries using 4 waves of the ECHP. These models range from a simple Markov model to a time-heterogeneous mover-stayer model that allows error in the measurement of the movers' states. The simple Markov chain model, as we have noted, assumes that the state occupied at time t depends only on the state occupied at time $t - 1$. The most parsimonious version restricts the 2-way transition matrices to be stable across time while an alternative version allows for heterogeneity. Such models, which assume a homogeneous population and a uniform underlying process, rarely provide a satisfactory fit. A mixed Markov model allows for more than 1 chain. The best known of such models is a mover-stayer model where the transition probabilities in the second chain relating to the stayers are assumed to be either 1 or 0. The model thus assumes 2 underlying groups—1 stable between successive years and another comprising individuals who move in and out of income poverty according to a simple Markov change process. This model takes no account of measurement error. Such error can be incorporated by combining latent class and Markov chain modelling.

The final model applied by Breen and Moisio (2004), which provides the most satisfactory account of income poverty dynamics across the 10 countries included in their analysis, is a latent mover-stayer model in which the movers' chain is allowed to be heterogeneous over time.[2] Applying this model, they confirm the earlier result of Rendtel et al. (1998) that mobility in income poverty dynamics is overestimated by between 25 and 50% if measurement error is ignored. Whelan and Maître (2006) sought to pursue the implications of these striking findings for earlier work concerning the relationship between income poverty persistence and deprivation persistence. This work has shown that these different forms of persistence display both distinct patterns of socio-economic variation and highly variable consequences for outcomes such as subjective economic stress (Whelan et al., 2001, 2004). These results suggest that these measures are tapping somewhat different underlying dimensions. If, however, it was the case that deprivation persistence was measured with much greater accuracy than was the case for income persistence then a significant part of the observed difference might derive from differential reliability.

9.3 Income Poverty and Deprivation over Time

In the analysis that follows we will seek to explore these issues by applying the heterogeneous latent mover-stayer model to both income poverty and deprivation dynamics for the range of countries for which such information is contained in the User Data Base (UDB) of the ECHP.

---

[2] For an account of the full range of models applied by Breen and Moisio (2004) and the corresponding LEM syntax, see Moisio (2004).

For the purposes of the analyses in this chapter we employ 13 deprivation items serving as indicators of the concept of current life-style deprivation (CLSD) discussed and employed in earlier chapters. These are:

- A car or van;
- A colour TV;
- A video recorder;
- A microwave;
- A dishwasher;
- A telephone;
- Keeping your home adequately warm;
- Paying for a week's annual holiday away from home;
- Replacing any worn-out furniture;
- Buying new, rather than second hand clothes;
- Eating meat, chicken, or fish every second day, if you wanted to;
- Having friends or family for a drink or meal at least once a month; and
- Unable to pay scheduled mortgage payments, utility bills, or hire purchase instalments during the past 12 months.

An index based on a simple addition of these 13 items gives an alpha reliability coefficient of 0.80. Here we use the weighted version of this measure in which each individual item is weighted to the proportion of households not suffering an enforced lack of that item in each country. The weighted CLSD measure makes it possible to identify for each country, and for each income poverty line, a corresponding deprivation threshold where the proportions of persons in income poverty and in deprivation are the same. This procedure has the advantage that comparisons are unaffected by differences in the respective size of the income poor and deprived groups.

Like Whelan and Maître (2006) we focus on an income poverty threshold set at 70% rather than 60% of the median because, given that the analysis covers 5 years, opting for a lower threshold would lead to sparse observations in a number of cells of the 5-way transition table, particularly those involving persistent income poverty. (In Breen and Moisio's (2004) analysis of the 4 waves of the ECHP, the percentage falling below the 60% line in all 4 years exceeded 10% in only 1 country, and exceeded 7% in only 3.)

Before proceeding to estimate models of poverty and deprivation dynamics, we provide an account of the observed patterns for the core variables. In Table 9.1 we set out the cross-sectional poverty rates for the balanced panel for the first 5 waves of the ECHP involving all individuals who are present in all 5 waves. We can see that income poverty dynamics during the first 5 waves took place in the context of relatively modest variation in the cross-sectional rates. In the first wave the rate varied from 15% in Denmark to 29% in Portugal. Between the first and fifth waves the rate increase by 4 percentage

Table 9.1. Observed Income Poverty Rates in Each Wave

	Poverty rates				
	1994	1995	1996	1997	1998
Denmark	14.5	14.7	15.2	16.8	18.5
Netherlands	19.7	18.7	18.3	17.5	16.5
Belgium	23.1	22.8	21.7	21.0	21.9
France	22.1	21.0	21.3	20.7	21.3
Ireland	24.4	27.2	28.9	26.7	27.6
Italy	26.8	25.9	27.0	26.8	24.7
Greece	27.4	27.3	27.0	27.9	27.5
Spain	28.8	26.4	25.2	26.9	25.9
Portugal	29.2	30.2	30.4	29.9	28.1
Average	24.0	23.8	23.9	23.8	23.6

points in Denmark and declined by 3 percentage points in Spain; otherwise, variation was extremely modest and obviously plays a minor role in structuring poverty dynamics.

In Table 9.2 we show the percentage classified as income poor N times out 5 for both income poverty and deprivation. The proportion exposed to poverty at any point during the 5 years ranged from 31% in Denmark to 49% in Portugal. As with earlier work, there is a remarkable uniformity in the ratio of the 'ever-poor' figure to the income poverty rate in the first wave. The observed ratios all lie in the narrow range running from 1.62 in Denmark to 1.83 in Ireland. The proportion exposed to poverty in all 5 waves ranges from 6% in Denmark to 14% in Portugal. The 'always poor' rate ranges between approximately one-third and less than one-half of the cross-sectional rates. The figures for deprivation persistence are very similar to those for income poverty. Thus the percentage exposed to deprivation on at least 1 occasion ranges from 34% in the Netherlands to 47% in Ireland. The average difference between the income poverty and deprivation figures is on the order of 3%. Similarly the proportion experiencing poverty in all 5 years ranges from 4% in Denmark to 15% in Portugal, with average difference between the poverty and deprivation figures being less than 2%.

As in the case of the earlier analysis by Breen and Moisio (2004), while income poverty spells are generally of short duration, the risk of poverty recurring remains persistently high. From Table 9.3 we can see that, given that one is income poor in wave 1, the risk of income poverty recurring declines very modestly across the 5 waves. Thus, on average in wave 2, the conditional probability was 0.69 and by the fifth wave it was still as high as 0.59.[3] Relatively

---

[3] Throughout this chapter when we report averages they are simply the mean of the reported country values. Our objective is not to calculate some weighted European figure but simply to provide a reference point for results relating to individual figures.

Table 9.2. Percentage Classified as Income Poor and above the Current Life-Style Deprivation Threshold N Times out of 5

	Income poverty at 70% of equivalent income					
	0/5 (%)	1/5 (%)	2/5 (%)	3/5 (%)	4/5 (%)	5/5 (%)
Denmark	68.6	11.8	6.5	3.3	4.1	5.7
Netherlands	66.4	10.9	6.3	5.0	4.8	6.6
Belgium	60.3	12.4	7.3	5.6	5.6	8.9
France	62.5	11.8	6.2	4.7	6.0	8.8
Ireland	56.4	9.5	8.0	6.5	8.4	11.2
Italy	53.3	13.5	9.0	7.0	7.5	9.8
Greece	51.5	13.3	9.0	8.7	7.7	9.8
Spain	53.4	11.7	9.7	8.2	7.0	9.8
Portugal	51.4	11.6	9.2	6.8	7.2	13.7
Average	58.2	11.8	7.9	6.2	6.5	9.4

	Current life-style deprivation					
	0/5 (%)	1/5 (%)	2/5 (%)	3/5 (%)	4/5 (%)	5/5 (%)
Denmark	66.4	14.2	8.3	4.6	2.7	3.9
Netherlands	65.9	10.9	5.9	4.8	4.9	7.6
Belgium	54.2	18.9	7.9	5.5	5.2	8.2
France	60.0	13.0	7.1	6.5	5.8	7.7
Ireland	53.0	12.7	8.7	8.6	6.7	10.4
Italy	48.4	17.1	11.4	8.0	8.3	6.8
Greece	44.7	18.0	12.2	9.8	8.4	6.9
Spain	50.9	14.7	9.8	8.9	7.9	7.9
Portugal	50.5	12.8	8.4	6.7	6.9	14.7
Average	54.9	14.7	8.9	7.0	6.3	8.2

modest overall risk of uninterrupted poverty is accompanied by high levels of recurrence. The results for deprivation are remarkably similar. The conditional risk of being above the deprivation threshold in the second wave, having been deprived in the first wave, is 0.64. A modest decline to 0.57 is observed by wave 5. Overall the observed income poverty and deprivation mobility patterns, rather than suggesting greater stability and persistence for the deprivation dimension, reveal remarkably similar patterns for both variables. In the section that follows our focus shifts from the observed to the latent patterns.

9.4 Modelling Income Poverty Deprivation and Dynamics

Whelan and Maître (2006) follow Breen and Moisio (2004), in modelling income poverty and deprivation dynamics by attempting to improve on the goodness of fit of a simple Markov model by taking account of variables underlying processes and measurement error. The former is accommodated through a mixed Markov model that involves 2 chains with the expected frequencies involving a sum over these transition patterns that takes into

Table 9.3. Risk of Poverty and Deprivation in Subsequent Waves after Being Poor/Deprived in Wave 1

	Income poverty at 70% of equivalent income			
	P(2/1)	P(3/1)	P(4/1)	P(5/1)
Denmark	62.0	57.7	54.0	61.7
Netherlands	68.6	61.5	59.0	51.1
Belgium	67.0	62.6	62.1	61.0
France	66.0	63.8	60.2	58.9
Ireland	75.9	72.1	67.4	64.6
Italy	67.2	65.1	62.6	56.0
Greece	66.6	63.9	62.1	58.0
Spain	67.0	59.3	59.5	58.2
Portugal	77.5	68.9	66.9	62.5
Average	68.6	63.9	61.5	59.1

	Current life-style deprivation			
	P(2/1)	P(3/1)	P(4/1)	P(5/1)
Denmark	53.1	49.5	48.4	50.0
Netherlands	68.0	66.0	61.1	55.7
Belgium	64.2	60.4	58.3	55.0
France	65.7	64.6	61.3	61.4
Ireland	70.6	71.6	65.8	64.3
Italy	61.7	56.2	51.1	48.8
Greece	55.7	52.2	51.1	53.5
Spain	65.2	60.5	59.8	63.3
Portugal	72.8	65.4	66.7	61.2
Average	64.1	60.7	58.2	57.0

account the proportions associated with each sequence. Membership of the different chains is specified in terms of latent classes. The chains hypothesized are those capturing the classic mover-stayer mode. This specifies that that there are two underlying or latent stayer or immobile groups, one never in poverty and one always in poverty. In addition, there is a group of movers whose pattern of transitions follows a simple Markov chain in which the state occupied at time one depends only on the state occupied at time $t - 1$. The time-heterogeneous version of this model allows for the poverty transition probabilities of the mover group to vary over time. In others word, the likelihood of change as one goes from time t to $t + 1$ is allowed to differ from that relating to moves from $t + 1$ to $t + 2$, etc.

The equation specification underlying this model allows us to estimate the number of individuals in each of types we have identified, the initial state of each of these types, their transitional probabilities given these states, and finally the number of individuals with a sequential history of being in state i, followed by state j, followed by state k, followed by state l, followed by state m.

Measurement error is captured through a latent class formulation by assuming that to each observation of the states there corresponds a latent variable that measures the true distribution over the state. These latent variables are completely specified by the size of the latent classes and the probabilities of being observed in a given manifest class conditional on being in a given latent class. The final model combines this measurement model with the time-heterogeneous mover-stayer model. This final model thus involves assumptions relating to both the underlying structural processes and the nature of measurement error relating to the states we consider. The stayers are assumed to be measured without error and the reliabilities for the movers are constrained to be time homogeneous, which is a usual prerequisite of being able to estimate such models.

For both income poverty and deprivation our analysis focuses on explaining the distribution of individuals across a 2 by 2 by 2 by 2 tabulation showing dynamic profiles. Our objective is to find a parsimonious model of the underlying processes producing an allocation of individuals to the 32 cells of this table that generates a close fit between observed and expected frequencies. In Table 9.4 we show the fit for final model for both income and deprivation dynamics for the 9 countries included in our analysis. For each country, for both income poverty and deprivation dynamics, we report a number of summary indicators. The G^2 likelihood ratio chi-square is a measure of goodness of fit. The lower its value, the more closely the expected frequencies correspond to the observed. The size of the G^2 for the independence model provides 1 benchmark against which to assess the fit of the latent class model. The index of dissimilarity or the percentage of cases misclassified provides an additional indicator of how well the statistical model reproduces the observed frequencies. As is generally the case with large sample sizes, in most cases the model does not provide a strict statistical fit. However, in the

Table 9.4. Fit statistics for Time-Heterogeneous Latent Mover-Stayer Model and Percentage Reduction in G^2 from the Independence Model

	Income			Deprivation		
	G^2	Index of dissimilarity	Reduction in G^2	G^2	Index of dissimilarity	Reduction in G^2
Denmark	88.2	2.7	98.4	55.9	2.2	98.3
Netherlands	72.7	1.7	99.4	75.6	1.8	99.4
Belgium	137.7	2.5	98.6	81.0	2.5	99.0
France	66.0	1.3	99.7	40.5	1.2	99.8
Ireland	153.2	3.0	99.0	111.1	2.6	99.1
Italy	93.2	1.9	99.6	135.3	2.2	99.2
Greece	84.4	1.9	99.5	83.6	2.1	99.2
Spain	210.4	2.4	99.0	119.9	2.2	99.3
Portugal	214.2	2.4	99.0	360.8	3.8	98.4

case of income poverty we find that the time-heterogeneous latent mover-stayer model accounts for between 98.4 and 99.7% of the independence deviance with the G^2 varying between 66.0 in France and 214.2 in Portugal. The percentage of cases misclassified varies between 1.3% in France and 3% in Ireland. The findings relating to deprivation dynamics are remarkably similar. The model accounts for between 98.3 and 99.8% of the independence model deviance with the G^2 varying between 40.5 in France and 360.8 in Portugal. The percentage of cases misclassified ranges from 1.2% in France to 3.8% in Portugal. Thus consistent with the earlier work of Breen and Moisio (2004) and Moisio (2004), the model provides a generally satisfactory account of both income poverty and deprivation dynamics.

9.5 Observed Income Poverty and Deprivation Dynamics

A full discussion of the similarities and difference between income poverty and deprivation dynamics requires that we simultaneously take into account differences in the size of the latent mover-stayer classes, the initial poverty/deprivation rates, and corrected transition rates for stayers. All of these elements are reflected in the estimates, set out in Table 9.5, of the latent risk of being in poverty/deprivation in subsequent waves given that one is poor/deprived in wave 1. These figures can be compared with the corresponding observed figure in Table 9.3. There we observed that persistence was somewhat stronger for income poverty than for deprivation. Thus the observed conditional poverty rates declined gradually from 0.69 in the second wave to 0.59 in the fifth wave, while for the observed conditional deprivation rate the corresponding figures were 0.64 and 0.57. Having corrected for measurement

Table 9.5. Latent Risk of Poverty/Deprivation after Poverty/Deprivation in Wave 1

	Latent risk of poverty in subsequent waves after wave 1 in poverty				Latent risk of deprivation in subsequent waves after wave 1 in deprivation			
	P(1/2)	P(1/3)	P(1/4)	P(1/5)	P(1/2)	P(1/3)	P(1/4)	P(1/5)
Denmark	0.78	0.70	0.70	0.70	0.76	0.67	0.57	0.58
Netherlands	0.86	0.75	0.66	0.57	0.86	0.82	0.74	0.63
Belgium	0.90	0.77	0.73	0.72	0.92	0.83	0.79	0.69
France	0.78	0.74	0.67	0.65	0.94	0.88	0.83	0.81
Ireland	0.85	0.80	0.71	0.67	0.99	0.97	0.84	0.83
Italy	0.85	0.78	0.72	0.63	0.79	0.71	0.61	0.52
Greece	0.84	0.77	0.72	0.67	0.73	0.64	0.62	0.60
Spain	0.81	0.70	0.69	0.63	0.96	0.90	0.88	0.87
Portugal	0.89	0.80	0.74	0.67	0.82	0.74	0.70	0.65
Average	0.84	0.76	0.70	0.66	0.86	0.80	0.73	0.69

error, however, we find the opposite is true. The successive latent conditional rates of 0.84, 0.76, 0.70, and 0.66 for income poverty are in each case lower than the corresponding deprivation rates of 0.86, 0.80, 0.73, and 0.69. France, Ireland, and Spain are characterized both by very high levels of latent deprivation persistence and by large gaps between the observed and latent values. However, with these exceptions, one is more struck by the level of uniformity across dimensions and countries than by differences.

In Table 9.6 we compare the distribution of observed and latent income poverty and deprivation distributions across time. However, in this case, rather than using a count of the number of years out of 5 in poverty, we have followed Fouarge and Layte (2005) in constructing poverty profiles that allow us to examine both the persistence and recurrence of income poverty by distinguishing between:

- The persistent non-poor—never poor during the accounting period;
- The transient poor—poor only once during the accounting period;
- The recurrent poor—poor more than once but never longer than 2 consecutive years; and
- The persistent poor—poor for a consecutive period of at least 3 consecutive years.

In the vast majority of cases the observed poverty and deprivation profiles are similar. This is also the case for the latent profiles. For both the income poverty and deprivation profiles movement is substantially lower when account is taken of measurement error. The average level of persistent non-poverty is 58% for the observed level and 66% for the latent. The corresponding figures for deprivation are 55 and 67%. Persistent poverty and deprivation on the other hand are much higher at the latent than the observed level, with the respective figures for poverty and deprivation being 18 versus 23% and 17 versus 23%. It is the intermediate states of transient and recurrent poverty that are substantially overestimated. The observed level of transient and recurrent income poverty of 24% is twice that of the corresponding latent figure. For deprivation the gap between the observed and latent figures for these intermediate categories is even wider with the respective figures being 28 and 10%. Turning from average levels to variation across countries, we find that the level of observed non-poverty persistence ranges from 69% in Denmark to 51% for Portugal. The corresponding range for the latent non-poverty estimates is 8% in Denmark to 56% in Greece. The level of observed persistent income poverty ranges from 11% in Denmark to 24% in Portugal compared to 11 and 30% for latent persistence. Combining the transient and recurrent categories we obtain observed figures ranging from 20 to 28% compared to latent figures of 8 to 16%.

Table 9.6. Latent and Observed Income and Deprivation Profiles

	Poverty profiles				Deprivation profiles			
	Persistent non-poor	Transient poor	Recurrent poor	Persistent poor	Persistent non-deprived	Transient deprived	Recurrent deprived	Persistent deprived
Denmark	68.6	11.8	8.6	11.0	66.4	14.1	11.4	8.0
Denmark (latent)	80.7	5.8	2.4	11.0	67.0	9.4	7.6	16.0
Netherlands	66.4	10.9	9.4	13.3	65.9	10.9	8.9	14.3
Netherlands (latent)	75.2	3.8	4.7	16.3	76.1	3.4	2.4	18.1
Belgium	60.3	12.4	11.7	15.7	54.2	18.9	12.1	14.8
Belgium (latent)	68.3	4.4	4.9	22.4	71.6	4.1	4.2	20.1
France	62.5	11.8	9.0	16.8	60.1	12.8	11.8	15.3
France (latent)	70.5	6.3	3.5	19.7	71.4	3.5	3.0	22.1
Ireland	56.4	9.5	11.6	22.5	52.7	12.5	14.9	19.9
Ireland (latent)	61.7	6.5	6.8	25.1	63.6	1.8	3.7	31.0
Italy	53.3	13.5	13.4	19.9	48.4	17.1	16.1	18.3
Italy (latent)	66.7	4.5	5.3	23.6	66.5	6.9	5.7	20.9
Greece	51.5	13.3	14.9	20.2	44.7	18.0	19.1	18.1
Greece (latent)	56.1	7.9	7.2	28.8	59.2	10.5	5.7	24.6
Spain	53.4	11.7	16.2	18.7	50.9	14.7	17.3	17.2
Spain (latent)	58.1	7.1	9.0	25.8	64.9	4.8	4.3	26.0
Portugal	51.4	11.6	13.5	23.5	50.5	12.8	12.8	24.0
Portugal (latent)	56.5	6.11	7.10	30.3	59.9	7.3	5.0	27.7
Average	58.2	11.8	12.0	18.0	54.9	14.6	13.8	16.7
Average (latent)	66.0	5.8	5.7	22.6	66.7	5.7	4.6	22.9

The pattern for deprivation is broadly similar. At the observed level the proportion entirely avoiding deprivation ranges from 66% in Denmark to 45% in Greece. The corresponding figures corrected for error run from 76% in the Netherlands to 59% in Greece. Observed deprivation persistence levels run from 8% in Denmark to 24% in Portugal compared to their latent counterparts of 16% in Denmark and 31% in Ireland. Once again combining the intermediate categories involving movement, we find that the observed range of 20% in the Netherlands to 37% in Greece suggests much higher levels of deprivation dynamics than the corresponding latent figures of 6% for the Netherlands and 16% for Greece.

The overall profiles for both observed and latent estimates are remarkably similar for both income poverty and deprivation. The marginally higher level of persistence for income poverty at the observed level disappears with correction for measurement error. Reflecting the pattern of reliability coefficients, some modest differences are observed between northern and southern countries. For the former the numerical superiority of the persistently income poor over the persistently deprived at the observed level—16 versus 14%—is reversed at the latent level with the relevant figures being 19 versus 21%. In the South, on the other hand, persistent poverty levels are higher than persistent deprivation levels the respective figures being 21 versus 19% and 27 versus 25%. Denmark constitutes something of a deviant case. In the case of income poverty, correcting for measurement error leads to a significant increase in persistence avoidance of poverty but to no change in the level of persistent poverty. For deprivation, however, we observe precisely the opposite. Thus the impact of measurement varies across both countries and indicators.

Earlier work suggested that different forms of persistence are tapping related but distinct dimensions that display somewhat different patterns of socio-economic variation and have significantly different consequences for outcomes such as subjective economic strain. It also appeared that the pattern of relationships involving deprivation conformed much more closely to our prior notions of what we might expect from an indicator that is successfully tapping exclusion from a minimally acceptable standard of living due to lack of resources. Our objective in this chapter has been to establish whether such findings could be accounted for by the fact that deprivation persistence was being measured with a great deal more accuracy than income persistence.

In order to address this question Whelan and Maître (2006) applied a model of dynamics incorporating structural and error components. This model performs equally well in accounting for poverty and deprivation dynamics. Their analysis shows a general similarity between error-corrected poverty and deprivation dynamics. In both cases we substantially overestimate mobility. Where differences do arise between poverty and deprivation patterns, the tendency to overestimate mobility tends to be greater in the case of deprivation rather than poverty. This is related to the fact that the proportion of movers tends to be significantly higher in the case of deprivation. In particular, total avoidance of income poverty is more frequent than the corresponding situation relating to deprivation.

Distinguishing between different types of misclassification, we find that by far the largest component of error is associated with overestimation of probability of exiting from such states. There is some North–South variation with exit rates for the income poor being particularly overestimated in the Southern countries. The opposite holds true for deprivation with the tendency to overestimate exits from deprivation being somewhat higher in the northern countries.

Focusing on poverty and deprivation profiles we observe remarkable similarity across dimensions at both observed and latent levels. In both cases levels of poverty and deprivation persistence are higher at the latent than the observed level. However, while in the South poverty is more persistent than deprivation at both observed and latent levels, in the North this pattern though found for the observed data is reversed at the latent level.

Measurement issues relating to poverty and deprivation dynamics almost certainly contribute to the finding that short-term changes over time in deprivation (at the individual or household level) are very weakly related to corresponding variations in income while in contrast mean deprivation over a period is highly correlated with income averaged over a period (Berthoud et al., 2004; Berthoud and Bryan, 2011). However, there is no evidence that earlier results relating to the differences in the determinants of poverty and deprivation persistence are a consequence of differential patterns of reliability. Taking measurement error into account seems more likely to accentuate, rather than diminish, the contrasts highlighted by earlier research.

Since longitudinal differences relating to income poverty and deprivation cannot be accounted for by measurement error, it seems that we must accept that we are confronted with issues relating to validity rather than reliability. In other words, although income poverty and deprivation are substantially correlated, even where we measure them over reasonable periods of time and allow for measurement error they continue to tap relatively distinct phenomenon.

9.6 The Dynamics of Economic Vulnerability

In the foregoing we have addressed one of the key issues relating to developing an understanding of social conclusion by focusing on dynamics. In so doing we have sought to answer the question of whether a dynamic approach to the measurement of income poverty which took into account measurement error might relieve us of the necessity to move from a 1-dimensional to a multidimensional approach. The analysis showed that this was not the case and in the remaining sections of this chapter we focus on the effort of Whelan and Maître (2008) to combine dynamic and multidimensional perspectives. This involves an analysis of the dynamics of economic vulnerability.

The initial analysis involves fitting latent class models at the cross-sectional level for each of the 9 countries and each of the 5 years included in our analysis. Having then allocated individuals in each country between economically vulnerable and non-vulnerable classes for each of these the 5 years included in the analysis we then proceed to apply dynamic error-corrected models to the analysis of longitudinal patterns of economic vulnerability.

The sample of countries available does not allow us to carry out a systematic statistical analysis in welfare regime terms. However, our discussion can be usefully structured in such terms. Countries have been allocated to regimes as follows:

- Social democratic: Denmark, The Netherlands;
- Corporatist: Belgium, France;
- Liberal: Ireland; and
- Southern: Italy, Spain, Portugal, and Greece.

It was anticipated that variation in levels of inequality between regimes and differences in extent of regulation of the labour market, and the associated insider–outsider divisions, within and between regimes will influence both cross-sectional levels of economic vulnerability and degree of persistence over time. The lowest level is expected to be associated with the social democratic regime where the substantial redistributive role of the state seeks to guarantee adequate economic resources independently of market or family reliance. Vulnerability rates are also expected to be relatively low in the corporatist regime where, as Gallie and Paugam (2000, p. 353) observe, 'high-security' employment-centred systems within the corporatist group were highly successful in providing financial protection. Rates are expected to be higher in the liberal regime, which acknowledges the primacy of the market and confines the state to a residual welfare role with social benefits typically being subject to a means test and targeted on those falling in the market. Generally higher levels of economic vulnerability are anticipated in the southern European regime countries. However, rigid labour markets in Spain and Italy involving sharp insider–outsider divisions which operate particularly to the disadvantage of younger workers, combined with high levels of intergenerational co-residence, are likely to differentiate these countries from Portugal and Greece. Since our key variables are measured at the household level, disadvantaged younger people within such households will not be identified as vulnerable.[4] This is likely to be especially true in Italy where labour market regulation is particularly associated with difficulty in entering employment rather than the Spanish case where insecurity of employment is a stronger feature.[5]

Focusing first on the cross-sectional analysis in Table 9.7 we set out the fit statistics for a 2-class latent class model of economic vulnerability for all 5 waves of the ECHP for each of the 9 countries included in our analysis. Given the large sample sizes ranging from 21,424 in wave 1 in Italy to 5,272 in Denmark in wave 5, any highly parsimonious model is unlikely to fit according to conventional statistical criteria. Nevertheless it does well across all 9 countries and 5 observation points in accounting for the patterns of association between the 3 indicators. The G^2 goodness of fit statistic ranges

---

[4] See Gallie and Paugam (2000, pp. 13–18); Iacovou (2004).
[5] See Tohara and Malo (2000); and Ianelli and Soro-Bonmatí (2003).

Table 9.7. Fit Statistics for Cross-Sectional Economic Vulnerability 2 Class Latent Class Models

	1994		1995		1996		1997		1998	
	G^2	Δ	G^2	Δ	G^2	Δ	G^2	Δ	G^2	Δ
Denmark	7.66	0.004	41.69	0.009	17.2	0.007	13.25	0.006	24.77	0.007
Netherlands	15.73	0.005	19.92	0.006	8.00	0.004	6.13	0.002	9.00	0.003
Belgium	42.11	0.009	5.65	0.005	31.53	0.007	24.95	0.008	12.82	0.005
France	13.89	0.004	24.56	0.007	10.38	0.004	41.08	0.009	31.03	0.007
Ireland	30.18	0.008	23.91	0.008	37.7	0.012	33.05	0.011	73.34	0.019
Italy	41.70	0.010	107.03	0.017	74.43	0.014	51.72	0.011	85.54	0.014
Spain	71.03	0.014	75.96	0.012	64.22	0.014	92.18	0.016	68.23	0.012
Portugal	64.17	0.012	69.89	0.015	94.12	0.018	17.97	0.006	8.95	0.006
Greece	38.16	0.012	12.36	0.005	47.33	0.011	58.56	0.016	42.11	0.015

Table 9.8. Estimated Levels of Economic Vulnerability in ECHP Waves 1 to 5 by Country

	Economic vulnerability rates by wave (%)				
	1994	1995	1996	1997	1998
Denmark	21.1	21.9	26.3	17.4	21.4
Netherlands	17.5	17.4	16.3	15.5	15.2
Belgium	18.7	19.2	22.2	21.6	19.2
France	24.3	24.7	24.6	22.3	21.0
Ireland	31.6	30.8	28.0	26.2	22.6
Italy	24.9	23.7	23.6	21.6	26.0
Spain	29.6	27.8	28.3	29.9	29.4
Portugal	32.5	29.5	31.4	29.2	29.2
Greece	37.8	38.2	40.5	41.7	38.2

from 7.7 in wave 1 in Denmark to 107.0 in wave 2 in Italy with 10 degrees of freedom. Focusing on the index of dissimilarity—the proportion of cases misclassified—we find that the level of misclassification ranges from 0.002 in the Netherlands in wave 4 to 0.019 in Ireland in wave 5. No systematic tendency for goodness of fit to vary across waves is observed. The indices of fit for the independence model provide a benchmark for strength of the association between the indicators that requires explanation. The latent class model, which uses 6 additional degrees of freedom, reduces the independence G^2 by at least 98% in 44 of the 45 cases. While some improvement in statistical fit could be achieved by increasing the number of classes it would be on a very modest scale.

In Table 9.8 we set out details of the size of the economically vulnerable class for each country for all waves. Focusing on the first wave, we find that the lowest levels of economic vulnerability, ranging between 18 and 24%, are observed in the social democratic and corporatist countries. The higher level in Denmark rather than the Netherlands is in line with our knowledge of the degree of labour market flexibility in the former. Similarly, the higher level in France rather than Belgium is consistent with the operation of a 'high-security' employment-centred system in the latter. As we would expect, the Irish level of 32% is substantially higher. The average level of vulnerability in the Southern regime countries is similar to the Irish outcome but there is considerable internal variation with the rate varying from a low of 25% in Italy to 38% in Greece. Thus, the mean level is in line with between regime variations in inequality while the lower levels characterizeng Spain, and Italy, are consistent with the dualistic patterns of labour market regulation in those societies and the interaction of such regulation with of family support systems.

Little systematic variation is observed across time. The one exception relates to Ireland where there is a steady decline in the level of vulnerability from 32% in wave 1 to 23% in wave 5. This finding is entirely consistent with the exceptional economic changes affecting the country during that period with the level of unemployment declining from 15% in 1994 to 8% in 1998. For the remaining countries, the largest percentage difference between the first and the fifth waves is 3% and the overall average involves a reduction of 2%. Such variation clearly plays a minor role in structuring vulnerability dynamics.

The general distribution of level of economic vulnerability across countries is consistent with our expectations. In Table 9.9 we document the manner in which the economically vulnerable class is distinguished from the remainder of the population in terms of the probabilities, conditional on membership or non-membership of the economically vulnerable class, of relative income poverty, being above the deprivation threshold, and reporting subjective economic stress. Variation across waves in such multidimensional differentiation is modest.

In line with our earlier analysis in Chapter 8, the key differentiating variable is the risk of being above the deprivation threshold. The non-vulnerable are largely insulated from such risk with the observed conditional probabilities ranging from 0 to 0.10. For the vulnerable class the risk level does not fall below 0.74 and peaks at 0.94. A distinctive, but somewhat less sharp, pattern of differentiation is observed in relation to subjective economic stress. Membership of the vulnerable class was associated with a probability exceeding 0.60 of reporting such stress in 7 of the 9 countries, being highest in the liberal and Southern welfare regimes. For the non-economically vulnerable the conditional probability did not exceed 0.06 in 5 of the 9 countries or 0.21 in 8 out of 9 of the observations. In every case a substantial differential was observed between the vulnerable and the non-vulnerable classes but a clear tendency towards higher levels of stress among the non-vulnerable in the Southern regime countries was reflected in narrower within country differentials. For income poverty levels, a relatively uniform

Table 9.9. Probabilities of Being Income Poor, Deprived, and Experiencing Economic Stress Conditional on Membership of the Economically Vulnerable (EV) Class and the Non-Economically Vulnerable (NEV) Class

Class type	DK		NL		BE		FR		IE		IT		ES		PT		EL	
	NEV	EV	NEV	EV	NEV	EV	NEV	EV	NEV	EV	NEV	EV	NEV	EV	NEV	EV	NEV	EV
Income																		
<70%	0.14	0.33	0.12	0.61	0.18	0.57	0.13	0.16	0.14	0.14	0.15	0.66	0.13	0.59	0.16	0.57	0.14	0.57
<60%	0.08	0.18	0.04	0.36	0.11	0.42	0.08	0.11	0.09	0.09	0.10	0.52	0.08	0.46	0.11	0.47	0.09	0.46
<50%	0.04	0.07	0.02	0.20	0.06	0.25	0.05	0.08	0.06	0.06	0.06	0.38	0.05	0.31	0.08	0.36	0.06	0.36
Deprivation	0.00	0.87	0.05	0.94	0.10	0.92	0.07	0.06	0.05	0.05	0.10	0.81	0.07	0.75	0.06	0.81	0.05	0.74
Economic stress	0.06	0.43	0.02	0.65	0.03	0.56	0.20	0.21	0.31	0.31	0.05	0.70	0.20	0.81	0.21	0.73	0.31	0.94

but much less sharp pattern of differentiation was observed. For convenience we have reported the conditional probabilities of being below respectively the 70, 60, and 50% relative income poverty lines. Perhaps reflecting the impact of active labour market policies, distinctively low levels of income poverty are observed for the economically vulnerable in Denmark. For the remaining 8 countries the conditional probability of being below the 70% median income poverty line ranges from 0.57 to 0.66. For the non-vulnerable the risk level across all 9 countries runs from 0.12 to 0.18. At the 60% line the corresponding figures for the vulnerable run from 0.36 to 0.52 and for the non-vulnerable from 0.04 to 0.11. Finally at the 50% line the respective ranges go from 0.13 to 0.38 and 0.02 to 0.08. Thus, while economic vulnerability is clearly characterized by heightened probability of income poverty, the primary differentiating factor is material deprivation followed by experience of subjective economic stress.

In order to conduct the dynamic analysis that follows, individuals are allocated to a latent class on the basis of the modal assignment rule with each observation in a cell being assigned to the class with the largest conditional probability.[6] The estimated classification error employing this procedure ranges from 3.2% in Denmark in wave 1 to 12.3% in Greece in wave 5. It exceeds 10% for only 4 of our 45 observations and shows modest variation across waves. The proportionate improvement over an approach that assigns all observations to the largest latent class ranges from 0.85 in Denmark in wave 1 to 0.62 in Spain in wave 5.[7]

9.7 Modelling Economic Vulnerability

In this section we consider the outcomes associated with applying the time-heterogeneous mover-stayer model with correction for measurement error, discussed earlier, to the analysis of longitudinal patterns of economic vulnerability.

---

[6] Thus, suppose there are three observed categorical variables A, B, and C, the conditional probability that someone belongs to latent class t given that this person is at level i of A, level j of B, and level k of C is given by the expression

$$\pi_{tijk}^{X\backslash ABC} = \frac{\pi_t^X \pi_{it}^{A\backslash X} \pi_{jt}^{B\backslash X} \pi_{kt}^{C\backslash X}}{\sum_{t=1}^{T} \pi_t^X \pi_{it}^{A\backslash X} \pi_{jt}^{B\backslash X} \pi_{kt}^{C\backslash X}}.$$

The percentage of cases misclassified is calculated as $100 \times \sum_j [(1 - \hat{\pi}_j) \cdot n_j / N]$, where n_j is the number of respondents giving response pattern j, $\hat{\pi}_j$ is the estimated modal latent class probability given response pattern j, and N is the total sample size. As Chan and Goldthorpe (2007, p. 16) note the percentage of cases misclassified by latent class models should be understood in terms of measurement error and not as a measure of goodness of fit.

[7] See McCutcheon (1987: 36–7) for a discussion of these indices.

Table 9.10. Fit Statistics for the Time-Heterogeneous Mover-Stayer Model and Percentage Reduction in G^2 from the Independence Model

	G^2	Δ	$r\,G^2$
Denmark	75.0	0.022	99.2
Netherlands	164.9	0.022	98.7
Belgium	55.0	0.019	99.2
France	294.2	0.034	98.5
Ireland	178.7	0.031	98.6
Italy	383.5	0.033	98.4
Spain	413.9	0.044	98.1
Portugal	337.2	0.041	98.7
Greece	276.4	0.043	98.6

In Table 9.10 we display the fit statistics for the application of the above model to the 5 waves of data deriving from the modal allocation of individuals to the vulnerable or non-vulnerable classes. While the models do not provide a strict statistical fit, they account for between 98.1 and 99.2% of the independence model deviance with the G^2 ranging between 55.0 for Belgium and 413.9 for Spain. The proportion of cases misclassified varies between 0.019 for Belgium and 0.044 for Spain. The comparable range for earlier analysis by Whelan and Maître (2006, p. 314) was 0.017 to 0.030 for income poverty and 0.012 to 0.038 for deprivation. Thus the preferred model provides a broadly satisfactory account of the dynamics of economic vulnerability.

As in the earlier examples involving income poverty and deprivation, we proceed to consider dynamic profiles that allow us to examine both the persistence and recurrence of latent economic vulnerability by distinguishing between:

- The persistently non-vulnerable—never vulnerable during the transient period;
- The transient vulnerable—vulnerable only once during the accounting period;
- The recurrent vulnerable—vulnerable more than once but never longer than 2 consecutive years; and
- The persistently vulnerable—vulnerable for a consecutive period of at least 3 years.

From Table 9.11 we can see that overall over 60% of individuals are found in the persistently non-vulnerable category, 10% are equally divided between the transient and recurrent categories, and 19% are found in the persistently vulnerable group. Compared to earlier findings relating to income poverty and deprivation, this involves a greater concentration of observations in the intermediate categories with corresponding lower levels of both types of persistence.

Table 9.11. Latent Vulnerability Profiles by Country (% by row)

	Persistently non-vulnerable (%)	Transient (%)	Recurrent (%)	Persistently vulnerable (%)
Denmark	65.9	10.9	11.3	11.9
Netherlands	76.6	6.5	6.1	10.8
Belgium	75.1	6.0	6.7	12.2
France	66.5	9.5	7.2	16.9
Ireland	60.2	9.5	8.7	21.5
Italy	66.2	7.9	9.5	16.3
Spain	56.6	8.2	11.8	23.5
Portugal	50.9	11.3	10.2	27.6
Greece	45.4	13.8	14.7	26.2
Average	62.6	9.3	9.6	18.5

For social democratic and corporatist countries it is the number persistently vulnerable that is lower than in the income poverty case. In contrast, for the southern European countries it is the number persistently non-vulnerable that is lower. The foregoing pattern produces sharper contrasts between countries than in the case of income poverty. The Netherlands and Belgium display by far the highest levels of persistent non-vulnerability with three-quarters of respondents falling into this category; while 11 to 12% are found in the persistently vulnerable category. While Denmark has a lower level of persistent non-vulnerability it differs from the Netherlands and Belgium only in being almost twice as likely to be found in the transient and recurrent categories; a finding that is consistent with its active labour market policies. The social democratic welfare countries and the corporatist case closest to a 'high-security' employment-centred system display the lowest levels of economic vulnerability. In France, Italy, and Ireland approximately two-thirds of the respondents are located in the persistently non-vulnerable category. However, the levels of persistent vulnerability are somewhat higher than for all of the foregoing countries with rates of respectively 17, 16, and 22%. In the Spanish case a lower level of persistent non-vulnerability and a corresponding increase in the level of persistent vulnerability is observed; the respective figures being 57 and 24%. However, a less potent version of the factors operating in the Italian case contributes to maintaining a clear differentiation between it and the Portuguese and Greek cases. For the latter cases, the level of persistent non-vulnerability declines to 51 and 46%, respectively, and the scale of persistent vulnerability increases to 28 and 26% These findings are broadly in line with the expectations we outlined earlier on the basis of the welfare and employment regimes literature.

A summary picture of cross-national variation in economic vulnerability and income poverty is provided in Table 9.12 where we display the odds ratios for persistent non-poverty and persistent non-vulnerability with the Netherlands as the reference category. For income poverty the range of odds ratios runs from

Table 9.12. Cross-National Comparisons of Being Persistently Non-Income Poor and Persistently Non-Economically Vulnerable for Latent Outcomes (Reference Category the Netherlands)

	Odds ratios	
	Income poverty	Economic vulnerability
Netherlands	1.00	1.00
Denmark	0.73	1.69
Belgium	1.41	1.09
France	1.27	1.65
Ireland	1.88	2.16
Italy	1.52	1.67
Spain	2.65	2.51
Portugal	2.33	3.16
Greece	2.37	3.94

0.73 in Denmark to 2.65 in Spain. For economic vulnerability, rather than Denmark being the country most insulated from risk, it is the Netherlands followed by Belgium. The change arises because the numbers in the transient and recurrent categories in Denmark are significantly higher than for income poverty. Thus while Danish active labour market problems are particularly successful in preventing income poverty persistence, they are somewhat less effective in comparison with the Netherlands and Belgium in ensuring that individuals are insulated from more broadly defined economic vulnerability. The contrast between the latter countries and the reminder is sharper than in the case of income poverty with the value of the odds ratio varying from 1.00 in the Netherlands to 3.94 in Greece. Three clusters of values emerge with the Netherlands and Belgium at the low end of the continuum, Denmark (because of the high numbers in transient and recurrent categories), France, Italy, and Ireland occupying an intermediate position with values ranging between 1.65 and 2.16, and Spain, Portugal, and Greece at the opposite end of the continuum with respective values of 2.51, 3.16, and 3.94.

9.8 The Distribution of Economic Vulnerability by Social Class

Globalization has been seen as associated with increased but much more widely diffused levels of risk. This pattern is also thought to arise from the erosion of security deriving from traditional career patterns based on full-time employment over the life-cycle. Intensified global competition and the over-riding significance of competitiveness are thought to undermine the buffering capacity of the welfare state. The threat, if not the reality, of unemployment and resulting poverty are considered to have become more pervasive and to extend substantially beyond the working class (Beck, 1992, 2000a, b;

Castells, 2000). Inequality and poverty rather than being differentially distributed between social classes vary between phases in the average work life. 'Temporalization and biographization' of poverty are seen to be features of the emergence of 'the risk society' in which relationship breakdowns and transitional crises are prevalent. Poverty is seen increasingly as both individualized and transitory and is 'democratized' (Leisering and Liebfried, 1999). The extension of employment insecurity and instability and potential poverty across the socio-economic spectrum involves 'capitalism without classes' (Beck 1992, p. 88), and inequality of income becomes detached from its old moorings in class categories (Beck 2000a).

In responding sceptically to the central claims of the latter thesis, recent critiques by Goldthorpe (2007a) and Atkinson (2007a) address a range of issues relating to the extent and consequences of flexibility and non-standard forms of work and their relationship to class position, the downward spiral of the capacity of welfare states to intervene, the scale and consequences of social mobility, and reliance on caricatured versions of traditional class relationships.[8] We are not in a position to examine trends over time in the impact of social class. However, by using an outcome measure that captures both multidimensional and dynamic aspects an dealing with measurement issues in a manner that allows us to focus on individuals underlying economic position rather than short-term fluctuations[9] we hope to add to the evidence base in an area that, as Goldthorpe (2007b) notes, has been characterized by a discrepancy between the strength of the claims made and the degree of systematic investigation.

Recent analysis of income poverty dynamics applying event history methods to the ECHP by Vandecasteele (2010) has concluded that it is not the case that 'horizontal' life events have replaced 'vertical' social stratification effects. Rather the findings suggest that rather than seeing the former type of effect being displaced by the latter the impact of life-cycle effects is often crucially shaped by the interaction with vertical stratification factors. This conclusion is in line with the mainstream sociological literature on the impact of life-cycle factors which stresses that the manner in which the life-cycle unfolds is shaped by social institutions, in particular, those relating to the welfare state (Mayer, 2003, 2004, 2006).[10] These findings suggest both the 'death of social class' argument is greatly overblown. A more accurate appreciation of the importance of new and old social risks and the extent to which they are both shaped by and, in turn, influence welfare state strategies requires that we systematically investigate the manner in which factors such as social class

---

[8] See also the exchange between Atkinson (2007b) and Beck (2007).
[9] See Berthoud and Bryan (2011).
[10] For a recent discussion of these issues, see Whelan and Maître (2008).

and the life-cycle interact. On the basis of the evidence we have presented in this chapter, we suggest that such an approach, rather than leading us to jettison our concern with social class, is likely, as Atkinson (2007a, p. 360) argues, to leave us more impressed by the degree to which the 'slayers' of class are themselves 'riddled with class processes'.

Notwithstanding the value of such systematic analysis of the dynamics of poverty in correcting the more extreme conclusions relating to changing patterns of social stratification, restricting attention to income poverty and failing to take into account the role of measurement error is likely to affect conclusions relating to both the scale and pattern of social class effects. In what follows we seek to document such effects in relation to an outcome indicator that captures both the multidimensional and dynamic nature of economic exclusion. Clearly a failure to observe systematic variation by social class in exposure to persistent economic vulnerability would seriously undermine claims for the continuing importance of class-based explanations of variation in life chances.

Our analysis employs a six-category aggregated version of the ESeC. For our present purposes, we assign the social class of the household reference person to all household members. Where a couple are jointly responsible for the accommodation we use a dominance procedure to decide between them The analysis is this case distinguishes the following 6 classes:[11]

1) Employers, higher grade professional, administrative, and managerial occupations (ESeC Classe 1 & 2);

2) Intermediate occupations—Higher grade white collar workers (ESeC Class 3);

3) Lower supervisory and lower technician occupations (ESeC Class 6);

4) Small employer and self-employed occupations (ESeC Classes 4 & 5);

5) Lower services, sales and clerical occupations and lower technical occupations (ESeC Classes 7 & 8); and

6) Routine occupations (ESeC Class 9).[12]

From Table 9.13 it is clear that, notwithstanding arguments relating to the diversification of risk, in every country, location in the professional and managerial class proves to be an enormously effective buffer against economic vulnerability. The number persistently non-vulnerable ranges from a high of 89% in the Netherlands and Spain to a low of 77% in Denmark. Variation in

---

[11] Little further is gained on this occasion by distinguishing between farmers and other self-employed.
[12] Those who could not be allocated a class position on the basis of their current or previous occupation of the household reference person were excluded from the analysis.

Table 9.13. Economic Vulnerability Profile by ESeC by Country

	Large emp, Hi prof + lo prof (%)	Intermediate occupations (%)	Small emp & self-emp. (inc. ag) (%)	Lo supervis/ technician (%)	Lo services + Lo technical (%)	Routine occupations (%)
Denmark						
Persistent non-EV	77.2	60.5	60.3	70.2	54.1	44.6
Transient EV	8.5	13.6	12.7	8.1	16.3	11.8
Recurrent EV	8.2	8.3	12.9	10.1	16.8	23.0
Persistent EV	6.1	17.6	14.0	11.6	12.8	20.6
Netherlands						
Persistent non-EV	89.0	81.9	65.0	74.3	66.1	60.7
Transient EV	4.2	6.9	6.8	10.9	7.5	10.0
Recurrent EV	3.5	4.2	6.0	7.3	9.8	10.2
Persistent EV	3.2	7.0	22.1	7.4	16.5	19.0
Belgium						
Persistent non-EV	83.4	74.8	68.6	75.1	70.5	64.2
Transient EV	5.1	4.1	6.8	7.8	7.6	7.8
Recurrent EV	4.8	6.1	10.2	6.6	8.1	8.0
Persistent EV	6.7	15.0	14.4	10.5	13.8	20.0
France						
Persistent non-EV	84.9	69.2	56.5	64.2	48.5	42.7
Transient EV	6.5	11.1	11.1	8.9	11.2	11.2
Recurrent EV	3.7	6.6	9.5	7.4	10.8	11.2
Persistent EV	5.0	13.0	22.9	19.4	29.5	34.8
Ireland						
Persistent non-EV	84.4	71.6	63.6	59.6	46.6	38.6
Transient EV	5.9	8.9	15.1	5.1	11.5	10.7
Recurrent EV	2.9	8.6	9.6	7.5	11.5	13.5
Persistent EV	6.8	10.9	11.8	27.7	30.5	37.2
Italy						
Persistent non-EV	85.8	72.3	63.8	62.9	53.5	51.3
Transient EV	4.8	7.3	9.1	9.2	8.7	10.1
Recurrent EV	5.0	9.0	10.9	10.4	9.9	14.4
Persistent EV	4.4	11.5	16.2	17.6	27.9	24.3
Spain						
Persistent non-EV	89.3	78.0	50.4	57.2	41.4	34.3
Transient EV	4.5	7.7	9.4	10.6	8.1	9.6
Recurrent EV	3.3	8.3	14.2	10.4	15.9	16.5
Persistent EV	2.9	6.0	26.0	21.8	34.5	39.7
Portugal						
Persistent non-EV	86.5	77.8	48.1	55.0	35.6	34.4
Transient EV	5.6	7.2	11.5	13.3	13.6	13.4
Recurrent EV	4.4	4.6	9.9	12.8	11.7	17.1
Persistent EV	3.4	10.4	30.5	18.9	39.0	35.1
Greece						
Persistent non-EV	83.2	61.7	33.2	50.6	32.2	30.0
Transient EV	8.6	17.6	14.7	20.4	15.8	12.9
Recurrent EV	4.3	12.4	17.4	15.2	18.9	18.6
Persistent EV	3.9	8.2	34.8	13.8	33.1	38.5

levels of persistent vulnerability is even more modest with the relevant figure going from 3% in Spain to 7% in Ireland. Thus any decline in the favoured position of the professional and managerial class can only have been from an extremely elevated starting position.

Those in intermediate occupations occupy the next most favourable position with the numbers persistently non-vulnerable ranging from 82% in the Netherlands to 61% in Denmark with the corresponding figures for persistent vulnerability running from 6% in Spain to 18% in Denmark. Levels for the self-employed vary substantially across country while their relative position is in each case inferior to the higher white collar groups and close to that of the lower supervisory/technician/services category. Levels of persistent non-vulnerability vary from 69% in Belgium to 33% in Greece for the self-employed and for the lower supervisory group from 75% in Belgium to 51% in Greece. While a broadly similar pattern of relativities is observed in relation to persistent vulnerability, the relative position of the self-employed is much less favourable in France, Portugal, and Greece while in Ireland the opposite is the case.

Substantial variation across countries is also observed for the lower services/technical class and for routine occupations. For the former the level of persistent non-vulnerability ranges from 71% in Belgium to 32% in Greece and for persistent vulnerability from 13% in Denmark to 39% in Portugal. Unlike the case for the higher social classes, the levels vary fairly systematically across welfare regimes. A similar pattern is observed for the routine occupation where the level of persistent non-vulnerability runs from 64% in Belgium to 30% in Greece and the scale of persistent vulnerability from 19% in the Netherlands to 40% in Spain.

In Figure 9.1 we summarize the patterns of relativities across social classes and countries in terms of the odds on being vulnerable rather than non-vulnerable depending on social class position and country. The results are derived from a set of ordered logistic regressions showing the relationship between economic vulnerability and social class with the professional and managerial class taken as the reference category. The ordered logit allows the intercepts to vary but involves assumption of parallel slopes for the $J - 1$ cumulative logits that can be formed from J categories. The model is a proportional odds model with the odds ratio assumed to be constant for each of the cumulative comparison. The odd ratios summarized in Figure 9.1 show the odds on being a category or categories involving a higher degree of vulnerability persistence compared to the odds of being in any one of a lower set of categories for each social class with the professional and managerial class as the benchmark.

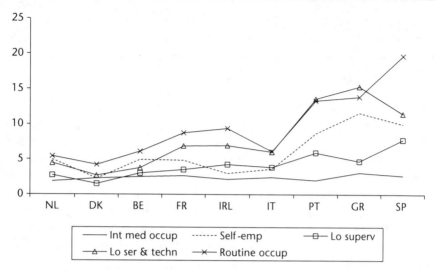

Figure 9.1. Ordered logit for the relationship between relative risk of persistent economic vulnerability and social class.

A clear pattern of class advantage emerges across all 9 countries. The professional and managerial class occupies the most favoured position followed by the intermediate occupations. The self-employed and the lower supervisory/technicians come next in line and the lower services/technical are closest to the routine non-manual.

While the routine occupations class is in every case the most disadvantaged, substantial cross-national variation exist in the scale of such disadvantage. Relative modest disparities between the routine occupations class and the professional and managerial class are observed for the social democratic or strong corporatist welfare regimes, i.e., with the odds ratio varying from 4:1 for Denmark to 6:1 for Belgium. For France, representing a weaker form of corporatist regime, and Ireland the figure rises to 9:1. Italy once again proves to be something of an exception to the Southern European pattern with a relatively modest odds ratio of 6:1. For the remaining southern European countries the odds ratio rises to 13:1 for Portugal, 14:1 for Greece, and 20:1 for Spain.

For the lower services and technical group the absolute value of the coefficients are lower than that for the routine occupations class but the cross-national pattern is similar. For the social democratic and 'high-security' corporatist cases the odds ratio ranges between 3:1 and 4:1. It rises to 7:1 for France and Ireland before reaching 11:1 for Greece, 14:1 for Portugal, and 15:1 for Spain.

For the self-employed the major contrast is between the southern regime countries, excluding Italy, and the remainder. For the former the odds ratio is 10:1 and for the latter 3:1.

Comparing the lower supervisory class with their lower service and technical counterparts, we see a reduction in the values of the odds ratios and the scale of cross-national variation. Thus, the odds ratio relating to the contrast with the professional and managerial class range from less than 2:1 in Denmark to 8:1 in Spain. Finally we observe a further reduction of odds ratio values for the intermediate occupations class accompanied by an extremely modest range of cross-national variation. Thus the level of disadvantage relative to the professional and managerial class runs from 2:1 in the Netherlands to 3:1 in Greece.

Overall a clear hierarchy of class effects emerges across countries. The only qualification to this conclusion is the entirely predictable one that the relative position of the self-employed is worse in the southern regime countries. The sharpness of class differentials varies across welfare regimes in a manner that is broadly in line with our expectations, being greatest in the Southern regime countries and weakest in the social democratic and employment active regimes. Such variation is most pronounced in the classes at the bottom of the class continuum with ability to insulate oneself from economic vulnerability becoming more evenly spread the further one moves up the hierarchy. Thus in all countries patterns of persistent economic vulnerability vary across social classes in a manner largely consistent with the expectations of advocates of the continuing relevance of class analysis.

9.9 Conclusions

Our initial analysis in this chapter sought to address the question of whether adoption of an appropriate dynamic approach to the measurement of income poverty might relieve us of the need to go beyond income and embrace a multidimensional approach to poverty and social and social exclusion. However, applying models that combine appropriate structural and measurement error models suggests that there is no evidence that earlier results relating to the differences in the determinants of poverty and deprivation persistence are a consequence of differential patterns of reliability. Our analysis shows a general similarity between error-corrected poverty and deprivation dynamics. In both cases we substantially overestimate mobility.

Focusing on poverty and deprivation profiles we observe remarkable similarity across dimensions at both observed and latent levels. In both cases levels of poverty and deprivation persistence are higher at the latent than the observed level. However, while in the South poverty is more persistent than deprivation at both observed and latent levels, in the North this pattern though found for the observed data is reversed at the latent level. Taking measurement error into account seems more likely to accentuate, rather than diminish, the contrasts highlighted by earlier research.

Since longitudinal differences relating to income poverty and deprivation cannot be accounted for by measurement error, it seems that we must accept that we are confronted with issues relating to validity rather than reliability. In other words, although income poverty and deprivation are substantially correlated, even where we measure them over reasonable periods of time and allow for measurement error they continue to tap relatively distinct phenomenon. Thus if measures of persistent income poverty are to constitute an important component of EU social indicators, as suggested by Atkinson et al. (2002), a strong case can be made for including parallel measures of deprivation persistence and continuing to explore the relationship between them.

In the second part of this chapter we have sought to implement an approach to social exclusion that captures both multidimensional and dynamics aspects of social exclusion. Such vulnerability varies across welfare regimes in a manner broadly consistent with our expectations. Descriptive accounts of the dynamics of income poverty and deprivation involve significant overestimation of the level of exits from such states. Our analysis of economic vulnerability dynamics shows that problems associated with measurement error are substantially less in this latter case. Levels of persistent vulnerability varied systematically by welfare regime, with a degree of internal variation that was consistent with the influence of insider–outsider labour market arrangements and the mediating role of family support systems.

Sociological interest in vulnerability has been associated with the argument that one of the consequences of globalization has been that exposure to risk has become more pervasive and less structured in class terms. While we are not in a position to examine trends over time in class effects, the fact that in every country the higher social classes enjoy very high levels of protection from persistent economic vulnerability argues against the emergence of a more pervasive distribution of risk. Systematic variation in vulnerability levels was observed across countries and social classes. However, the latter was concentrated among classes at the lower end of the hierarchy; indicating strict limits to cross-national convergence in risk levels associated with globalization.

Our findings suggest that it is possible to accept the importance of the emergence of new forms of social risk and acknowledge the significance of efforts to develop welfare states policies involving a shift of opportunities and decision making on to individuals without accepting the 'death of social class' thesis.[13]

---

[13] For a detailed discussion of the distinction between new and old social risks, see Esping Andersen et al. (2002) and Taylor-Gooby (2004).

10

Europeanization of Inequality and European Reference Groups

10.1 Introduction

In earlier chapters we have addressed the implications for measurement of poverty and social exclusion of focusing on national or European levels. Up to this point we have focused on objective outcomes and have made reference to subjective experience only in relation to the manner in which such outcomes translate into the experience of economic stress. However, arguments for and against focusing at the national and European level are directly related the fact that, in the context of the profound social changes associated with the enlargement of the EU, a debate has developed involving significant disagreement regarding the manner in which individuals evaluate objective inequalities within and across national boundaries. The case for a European-wide perspective has been set out most strongly by Fahey (2007), who argues that a particular sociological approach to understanding relative deprivation has led to a distorted understanding of the role and significance of reference groups. We need to pay more attention to the fact that the impact of objective circumstances depends to a great extent on the reference groups that people adopt that is on the standards and expectations against which they judge their situation.

In this chapter we take advantage of the availability of EU-SILC data for the full range of European countries to address both weak and strong versions of the thesis of Europeanization of reference groups. The former proposes that common standards of evaluation emerge as a consequence of knowledge of conditions in other societies, while the latter argues that people increasingly perceive themselves as part of a larger European stratification system. We begin our investigation in Section 10.2 by reviewing the arguments for a 'Europeanization' of reference groups. The rest of the chapter focuses on how these can be assessed by examining the relationship between material deprivation and subjective economic stress. Section 10.3 looks at how levels of consumption deprivation and subjective economic stress vary across the countries of the enlarged EU. Section 10.4 presents estimates of the impact of consumption deprivation on economic stress and how that varies across countries, and discusses their implications for reference group hypotheses. Finally, Section 10.5 summarizes the conclusions.

10.2 Evaluating the Argument for 'Europeanization' of Reference Groups

The conceptual foundations of the discussion of poverty in the European Union are to be found in Townsend's (1979) definition of poverty as 'exclusion from ordinary living patterns, customs and activities due to lack of resources'. As Fahey et al. (2005, pp. 7–9) stress, Townsend can be seen to have pursued a very different agenda to that motivating those coming from the *American Soldier* tradition.[1] He understood the term 'relative deprivation' in an objective sense and his concern was with the socially relative nature of needs and wants rather than with feelings of satisfaction and injustice.

Townsend's primary focus was on poverty as exclusion from 'ordinary living patterns, customs and activities' as a consequence of inadequate resources. The defining characteristic of poverty for him was the ability to participate in the society to which one belongs. The critical issue involved in evaluating the validity of his position is the relationship between income and the form of rather basic material deprivation with which he was concerned, rather than the correspondence between income and subjective responses. His own efforts at validation were focused on attempting to establish an income threshold beyond which deprivation escalated disproportionately.[2]

Townsend's emphasis on the objective nature of relative deprivation, however, is consistent with Sen's (1983) argument that it is the notion of shame that is the core of poverty; in that the absence of resources puts people in a situation where they cannot live with dignity in their society. His approach implies subjective reactions to such exclusion from both the excluded and the wider population. Focusing on the former, it is with stress arising from exclusion that he is concerned, rather than with satisfaction with material livings standards or with issues of justice evaluation (Jasso, 2000). This is not necessarily a weakness. Failure to take into account the full range of comparisons that people make will undermine the relative income approach only if it obscures the fact that such comparisons may lead individuals to define

---

[1] See Merton and Kitt (1950); Merton (1957).
[2] See the contributions to the debate by Piachaud (1981, 1987) and Desai (1986). More recently, see Gordon et al. (2000).

'acceptable' levels of participation in a different fashion or to construe 'society' in a wider fashion.[3]

For Delhey and Kohler (2006, p. 126) the reference groups to which people orient themselves is the litmus test for the appropriateness of an EU-wide perspective on the distribution of material deprivation. The crucial requirement is that citizens' frames of reference extend beyond the national realm. Whelan and Maître (2009a) suggest that it is possible to think in terms of weak and strong versions of this argument. The former proposes that a common standard relating to an acceptable level of participation in one's own society emerges as a consequence of knowledge of conditions in other societies. Such effects could be observed while the normative framework remained resolutely national; with the obligation for creating the appropriate conditions for participation continuing to be seen to reside with the nation state.[4]

The stronger version requires, as Delhey and Kohler (2006, p. 126) argue, that people perceive themselves as part of a larger European stratification system. Furthermore, the perception of being advantaged or disadvantaged within this system would have to play an important role in individuals' evaluations of their own life circumstances. The stronger case, as Delhey and Kohler (2006, p. 125) note, is linked to the claim that concentration on national societies has led to a distortion of our perceptions of inequalities that will be corrected as a result of Europeanization and the emergence of European-wide distribution conflicts.[5] From this perspective, norms shift from the national to the transnational level, as does the responsibility for meeting the associated claims.[6]

The Europeanization of reference groups is seen to go hand in hand with Europeanization of the economy. However, we should be careful about deducing the former from the latter. Heidenreich and Wunder (2008, p. 25), in their recent analysis of patterns of regional inequality in an enlarged Europe, convincingly demonstrate that there is no necessary relationship between the geographical level at which inequalities are shaped and their consequences for within and between country inequalities. They confirm that supranational regulation of economic affairs and the integration of the national markets mean that the causes of social inequalities are increasingly shaped by the EU. However, they show that such Europeanization has contributed to a situation in which regional inequalities within states in the

---

[3] For a similar line of argument stressing the distinction between 'privately oriented' and 'publicly oriented' reference groups, see Goedemé and Rottiers (2010).

[4] See Ger and Belk (1996) and Keyfitz (1992).

[5] Each of these positions, in turn, can be distinguished from one that sees knowledge of external circumstances having an impact on aspirations but without implications for current notions of entitlement and consequent well being.

[6] See Beck (2000b, 2002).

enlarged Europe have increased by 15% over the past 8 years, while between nation inequalities in Europe have fallen by 45%. Beckfield (2006) also concludes that the remapping of European inequality through regional integration is associated with a decrease in between country inequality and an increase in within country inequality.

Heidenreich and Wunder (2008, pp. 32–3) note that increasing dissatisfaction with Europe may be a consequence of the accentuation of regional and individual inequalities at the national level. In a similar vein, Kangas and Ritakallio (2007, p. 112) suggest that, since the structural funds are aimed at eradicating regional disparities, they also have the potential to intensify internal comparisons. Similarly, as Brandolini (2007, p. 80) observes, while an EU-wide perspective can be seen as a significant step towards viewing the EU as a social entity, it does not necessarily require a strong sense of European identity. Thus, Marlier et al. (2007, p. 154) suggest that the use of EU-wide social indicators could be justified not on the basis of the existence of European-wide reference groups but precisely as a means of *promoting* the adoption of such standards within a social rights perspective.

An evaluation of the changing nature of European reference groups cannot be deduced from a consideration of changes in the geographical level at which inequalities are structured or measured but must be the subject of systematic empirical investigation. Whelan and Maître (2009b) sought to take advantage of the availability of European-wide data in EU-SILC 2006 to provide such an analysis.

What would constitute evidence for the fact that the relative income approach is undermined by the failure to take into account the impact of European reference groups, whether in their weaker or stronger form? Fahey (2007, p. 41) rests his argument on a comparison of absolute material deprivation levels and how people feel about such deprivation. In relation to the former, he notes that economic clusters display a similar ranking in terms of absolute levels of income, material deprivation, and subjective economic stress. He also places particular emphasis on the fact that those at the upper end of the income distribution in the poorer clusters are worse off than those at the lower end of the distribution in the most affluent cluster. However, at no point does he seek to explicitly quantify the scale of within and between cluster variations in material deprivation. Nor does he test the extent to which income allows us to account for such variation. Whelan and Maître (2009a, b) argue that both of these questions must be explicitly addressed before reaching conclusions about the relative value of a national versus an EU-wide frame of reference.

The second strand of Fahey's argument revolves around the claim that the frames of reference people use to evaluate their situation include European-wide as well as national elements. However, as in the case of material deprivation, Fahey (2007, p. 8) does not seek to quantify the extent of within and between cluster variations relating to outcomes such as subjective economic stress. Furthermore, his analysis does not extend to an examination of the *relationships* between income and material and such variation. At no point does he seek to explicitly model the relationships between material deprivation and individuals' subjective evaluations of their economic situation. Consequently, as Delhey and Kohler (2006, p. 126) observe, his conclusions regarding the importance of cross-national reference groups lack an empirical underpinning and remain speculative.

Delhey and Kohler (2006, 2007), using Euromodule and Eurobarometer data relating to satisfaction and ratings of individual, national, and EU-wide social and economic conditions, do succeed in demonstrating that individuals can evaluate living conditions in their own and other countries and that the latter are related to their own levels of satisfaction. However, Whelan and Maître (2009a) conclude that this is not sufficient to establish the stronger version of the reference group argument, which would require the adoption of a more comprehensive justice evaluation methodology involving comparisons of the actual situation with what is considered to be appropriate both for the individual's own situation and a range of reference groups.[7] Even if such relationships were demonstrated, the argument relating to the emergence of a European stratification system would require that one establish to what political level individuals attribute responsibility for the pattern of inequality that exists. The data available to date and the analysis utilizing such data fall a long way short of validating the stronger version of the Europeanization of reference groups thesis.

The weaker version does not require the explicit demonstration of particular patterns of justice evaluation. It assumes only a common standard against which individuals' circumstances are evaluated. The existence of European reference groups of this form can be inferred if we observe a relatively uniform impact of material circumstances across countries. While we lack data over time that would allow us to speak about trends in the Europeanization of reference groups, documenting the extent and pattern of current variation will allow us to make a more informed assessment of the likely scale of such convergence. Whelan and Maître (2007c, 2009a) make use of the EQLS and the first wave of EU-SILC covering 14 countries to test the weaker version and argue that the predominant frame of reference remains national.

Each of the foregoing authors is in agreement that the evidence on which the arguments to date have been based have been far from ideal in terms of providing high quality data for an appropriate range of European countries.

---

[7] For examples of such analyses, see Jasso (1999, 2000).

211

The appropriate database must include information on objective economic circumstances, comparative evaluations and attributions of responsibility for representative samples for a wide range of European countries. EU-SILC is not ideal in this respect but since 2006 in providing information on subjective economic stress and material deprivation for relatively large representative samples for 26 countries it enables us to provide a more comprehensive assessment of some of the key issues than had been possible prior its availability.[8]

10.3 The European Distribution of Consumption Deprivation and Economic Stress

Whelan and Maître (2009a) explored the issue of Europeanization of reference groups using both income and consumption deprivation as independent variables and subjective economic stress. However, they concluded that, given the limited impact of the former on subjective economic stress once one had controlled for the latter and the similarity of key results using both measures, little was gained by the additional analysis involving income. For this reason in what follows we focus on the key finings from the analysis conducted by Whelan and Maître (2009b) making use of EU-SILC 2006 and focusing on the indicators of consumption deprivation and subjective economic stress employed in earlier chapters. The analysis was conducted ate the level of the individual with clustering of individuals being taken into account when assessing significance levels.

The version of this consumption version deprivation employed is the one in which each individual item is weighted by the proportion of households possessing that item across the 24 EU countries. Enforced lack of a widely available item is considered of greater consequence than comparable deprivation in the case of an item whose possession is more strongly concentrated. Since EU levels of possession are taken as the reference point, deprivation of an item such as a PC will be counted equally across all countries included in our analysis. This avoids any arbitrary restriction of between country differences. The consumption deprivation measure is constructed as the sum of the weighted deficits on all 7 items divided by the total proportion of items possessed in the EU. Such standardization produces scores ranging from 0 to 1. The subjective economic stress variable utilized is the dichotomous version distinguishing between those experiencing great difficulty or some difficulty versus all others.

---

[8] It also allows us to explore variation across welfare regimes.

In Table 10.1 we show the breakdown of mean levels of consumption deprivation and subjective economic stress by country. We anticipate that levels of consumption deprivation will vary across countries not only in line with the level of resources available in the society but also in relation to degrees of inequality in their distribution. For this reason and to facilitate interpretation of the detailed patterns of cross-national findings we have also reported the descriptive results relating to variation across welfare regimes. On this occasion we have merged the 2 post-socialist clusters since differentiating between them has no effect on our conclusions.

These results have, where appropriate, been weighted to take into account variation in population size within the clusters.

Table 10.1. Mean Levels of Consumption Deprivation and Economic Stress by Country

	Consumption deprivation (standardized score with range 0–1)	Economic stress (range 0–6)
Social democratic	*0.092*	*2.859*
Sweden	0.072	2.904
Norway	0.087	2.807
Netherlands	0.091	2.944
Denmark	0.096	2.502
Iceland	0.114	3.229
Finland	0.128	2.955
Liberal	*0.108*	*3.218*
United Kingdom	0.108	3.194
Ireland	0.112	3.670
Corporatist	*0.135*	*3.162*
Luxembourg	0.057	2.577
Austria	0.098	3.181
Belgium	0.128	3.327
Germany	0.140	3.415
France	0.135	3.603
Southern European	*0.153*	*4.061*
Spain	0.134	3.802
Italy	0.139	4.139
Cyprus	0.228	4.186
Portugal	0.219	4.225
Greece	0.238	4.403
Post-socialist	*0.333*	*4.317*
Slovenia	0.153	3.953
Czech Republic	0.206	3.948
Estonia	0.254	3.484
Hungary	0.304	4.231
Slovakia	0.328	4.198
Lithuania	0.377	4.129
Poland	0.382	4.520
Latvia	0.431	4.659
EU24	0.160	3.645
Country Eta^2	0.195	0.204
N	193,586	176,831

The pattern of results is largely as we would have expected on the basis of the assumption that individuals have reasonably accurate perceptions of their own and others economic circumstances, with levels of deprivation and economic stress being greatest in the least affluent countries. The correlation between GDP adjusted for purchasing power and mean level of deprivation is 0.84 and with mean level of economic stress it is –0.79. Cross-national variation accounts for close to 20% of the variance of consumption deprivation. The level of deprivation is lowest in the social democratic cluster at 0.092 before rising to 0.108 for the liberal regime, to 0.135 for the corporatist cluster, to 0.153 for the southern European group, and then more than doubling to 0.333 for the post-socialist group.

Within the social democratic group, deprivation ranges from a low of 0.072 in Sweden to 0.128 in Finland. The liberal group members Ireland and UK are almost identical at 0.108 and 0.112. Luxembourg constitutes an outlier within the corporatist group recording the lowest value of all 26 countries of 0.057. The remaining countries are located on a continuum running from 0.098 for Austria to 0.140 for Germany with Belgium and France being closer to the upper rather than the lower end. For the southern European countries a somewhat wider range of variation is observed with Spain and Italy being close to the lower end while for Portugal and Cyprus and Greece the observed values go from 0.228 to 0.238.

As expected, the post-socialist group display the highest levels of deprivation and also the greatest degree of variability. At the lower end of the continuum are Slovenia and the Czech Republic with values of 0.153 and 0.206, respectively. The remaining 6 countries exhibit values higher than all others with the range of values running from 0.254 to 0.431. The consumption deprivation index thus discriminates between countries and within and between welfare regimes in a highly satisfactory manner.

Cross-national variation accounts for 20% of the variance of economic stress. The pattern of variation largely mirrors that for consumption deprivation. The level is lowest for the social democratic cluster at 2.859 before rising to 3.218 and 3.462, respectively, for the liberal and corporatist clusters. It then rises significantly to 4.061 for the southern European group before peaking at 4.317 for the post-socialist cluster.

Within the social Democratic group, Denmark exhibits the lowest level of stress of 2.502 followed by Norway and Sweden, Finland and the Netherlands while Iceland reports the highest levels of stress of 3.229. Among the liberal countries stress levels are somewhat higher in Ireland than in the UK with the respective values being 3.670 and 3.194. Within the corporatist group, Luxembourg is once again the exception with a stress value of 2.577. For the remaining countries the values range between 3.181 and 3.603. All of the southern European countries report higher levels of stress than the countries considered so far with the range running from 3.802 for Spain to 4.403 for Greece. The divide with the post-socialist group is identical to that for consumption deprivation. However, the contrast with the southern European group is less sharp than in the latter case.

The pattern of results suggests that the consumption deprivation measure not only constitutes a highly reliable index but is also a powerful instrument in differentiating between countries and clusters of countries in terms of subjective economic stress. The results confirm Fahey's (2007) finding of a close correspondence, at this level of analysis, between objective levels of deprivation and their subjective counterparts. This is given further confirmation by the fact that a between country regression based on mean levels of deprivation and stress shows that almost 60% of the cross-country variation in economic stress can be accounted for by corresponding variation in consumption deprivation.

Fahey's case for the importance of supranational reference groups was based not just on the strength of the association that we have confirmed above but also on the fact that, viewed in absolute terms, those at the lower end of the income continuum in richer countries experience lower levels of deprivation and stress than those at the top of the income distribution in poorer countries. In order to address this issue, in Figures 10.1A and 10.1B we set out descriptive findings for the 5 welfare regimes that we have identified relating to the breakdown of deprivation and stress by national income quintile. The results confirm Fahey's earlier findings.

The mean deprivation level for the bottom quintile in the social democratic countries is 0.19. This is only marginally higher than that prevailing in the top quintile in the post-socialist cluster and is lower than that in the fourth quintile of the latter. While the contrast between clusters are not as sharp as in Fahey's analysis, the conclusion still holds that the position of the most favoured in the least affluent cluster is not significantly different from that of the least favoured in the most affluent cluster.

The mean level of economic stress for the bottom quintile in the social democratic countries is 3.50. This is equal to the observed level for the top quintile in the post-socialist countries and is only marginally higher than the level for the top quintile in the southern European countries. Similarly, those in the bottom quintile in the liberal countries exhibit lower levels of stress than those in the fourth quintile in the southern European and post-socialist countries. Those in the bottom quintile of the corporatist cluster look similar to those in the third quintile of the 2 least favoured clusters.

Our analysis confirms the 2 key findings on which Fahey based his conclusion relating to the Europeanization of reference groups. The reminder of this chapter is concerned with explaining why, despite the agreement of our analysis with Fahey's on these points, we remain unconvinced by his substantive conclusions.

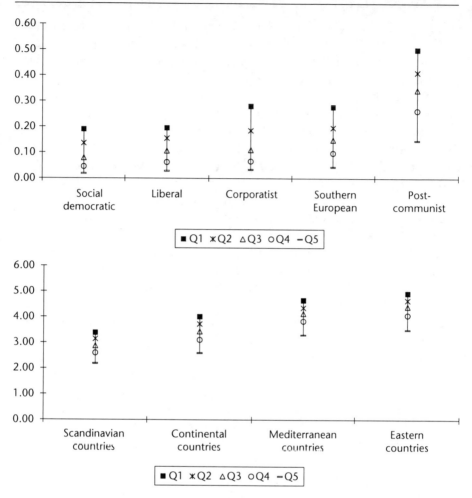

Figure 10.1. (A) Mean consumption deprivation by quintile by welfare regime. (B) Mean level of economic stress by quintile by welfare regime.

10.4 Analysing the Relationship between Consumption Deprivation and Economic Stress

A systematic analysis of the relationship between material deprivation and economic stress across a wide range of countries confronts us with the challenge of interpreting within and between country effects and deciding whether they are tapping the same underlying processes. However, as Snijders and Bosker (1999, p. 26) note, within group relationships can, in principle, derive from completely different principles to those underlying between

group associations. Taken at face value the strong association between consumption deprivation and economic stress at national level is striking. However, the difficulties associated with the interpretation of such between
country relationships are complicated by problems associated with both mul-
ticollinearity and the small number of observations. The countries in our
analysis differ in many other respects than current levels of consumption
deprivation leading to the danger of spurious correlation at a cross-national
level. A range of within country processes with the potential to affect both
economic performance and the manner in which it is evaluated could account
for the association between deprivation and stress at the national level.[9]

In pursuing our analysis, we have opted not to employ a random effects
model because we are interested in specific country effects and do not wish to
consider our 26 observations as randomly selected from a wider population.[10]
It is not possible to validate the strong version of the Europeanization of
reference groups, on this basis of between country correlations. The weaker
version which implies simply that notions of appropriate national thresholds
of what come to be influenced by knowledge of conditions in other societies
suggests that the within country impact of consumption deprivation on
subjective economic stress should be relatively uniform across countries. It is
difficult to see that the strong version of the European reference group
hypothesis can be validated in the absence of support for the weaker version.
Without evidence that notions of what constitutes an unacceptable level of
consumption deprivation have become relatively uniform across countries, it
becomes hard to see that the case for a shift in norms and aspirations from
national to a transnational level and the increasing salience of European-wide
distribution conflicts can be sustained.

The weak versions can be tested by a focus on variation across countries in
the impact of consumption deprivation on economic stress. In Table 10.2 we
set out the analysis appropriate to addressing this issue. In equation (i) we
estimate the simple ordinary least squares equation relating to the impact of
consumption deprivation on economic stress. This estimate combines information on both within and between country variation but makes no adjust-
ment for the multi-level structure of the data in which individuals are
clustered within countries. This provides an estimate of 3.599 for the deprivation coefficient and accounts for 0.385 of the variance. In equation (ii) we
enter the country dummies and obtain a fixed effects estimate of the impact of
consumption deprivation on economic stress that is based solely on within

[9] For a discussion of similar difficulties relating to associations involving GDP, see Frey and
Stutzer (2002) and Inglehart and Klingeman (2000).
[10] In any event, as Snijders and Bosker (1999, p. 44) note, with a small number of second level
units and large sample sizes within clusters the difference between analysis of covariance and
random intercept models will be negligible.

Table 10.2. Regression of Economic Stress by Consumption Deprivation and Country

	(i)		(ii)		(iii)	
	B	SE	B	SE	B	SE
Constant (NL)	3.034		2.639		2.425	0.011
LU			−0.253	0.019	−0.155	0.021
NO			−0.124	0.016	−0.044	0.019
SE			0.023	0.016	0.134	0.018
IS			0.206	0.020	0.261	0.025
DK			−0.462	0.016	−0.366	0.018
FI			−0.113	0.013	0.049	0.016
AT			0.208	0.017	0.359	0.019
BE			0.256	0.016	0.383	0.019
DE			0.302	0.012	0.500	0.015
FR			0.510	0.014	0.725	0.016
UK			0.191	0.016	0.345	0.016
IE			0.654	0.013	0.834	0.018
ES			0.711	0.012	0.813	0.016
IT			1.031	0.012	1.244	0.014
CY			0.779	0.018	1.019	0.025
PT			0.846	0.017	1.088	0.023
GR			0.962	0.016	1.235	0.021
SI			0.797	0.014	1.006	0.018
CZ			0.614	0.017	0.879	0.022
EE			−0.011	0.018	0.405	0.025
HU			0.568	0.015	1.004	0.021
PL			0.596	0.013	1.017	0.017
LT			0.219	0.018	.753	0.027
LV			0.566	0.019	1.108	0.030
SK			0.453	0.017	1.045	0.025
CD	3.599	0.010	3.370	0.011	5.723	0.065
LU* CD					−.320	0.142
NO* CD					−.807	0.105
SE* CD					−.933	0.112
IS* CD					−.961	0.132
DK* CD					−1.125	0.082
FI* CD					−1.952	0.102
AT* CD					−1.705	0.106
BE* CD					−1.678	0.092
DE* CD					−2.242	0.077
FR* CD					−2.361	0.082
UK* CD					−1.810	0.085
IE* CD					−2.058	0.091
ES* CD					−1.525	0.081
IT* CD					−2.347	0.072
CY* CD					−2.468	0.097
PT* CD					−2.481	0.093
GR* CD					−2.606	0.084
SI* CD					−2.325	0.086
CZ* CD					−2.604	0.089
EE* CD					−3.150	0.091
HU* CD					−3.087	0.079
PL* CD					−2.898	0.070
LT* CD					−3.203	0.085
LV* CD					−3.116	0.085
SK* CD					−3.504	0.085
R^2	0.385		0.475		0.489	
N	193,374		193,374		193,374	

country variation. The estimate of the deprivation effect falls to 3.370 while the R^2 increases to 0.475. The assumption underlying equation (ii) is that an absolute increase in consumption deprivation has a uniform effect across countries. In equation (iii) we provide an explicit test of this hypothesis by considering the manner in which consumption deprivation interacts with country. This produces a statistically significant increase in the R^2 to 0.489. A clear pattern of interaction emerges across countries and welfare regime broadly consistent with the interpretation that the impact of consumption deprivation increases as one moves from the least to the most affluent countries/regimes.

The magnitude of the deprivation coefficient ranges from a high of 5.7 for the Netherlands to a low of 2.2 in Slovakia. To facilitate our description of country variation in Table 10.3 we show the regression analysis corresponding to (iii) above for welfare regimes. On this occasion we have not weighted to take population size into account. Instead we operate with the simplifying assumption that the underlying process relating deprivation to stress is uniform within welfare regimes in which case sample size will have no impact on the outcome. In the case of the corporatist regime we have excluded Luxembourg from the analysis because it constitutes such an outlier that its inclusion would obscure an important substantive finding.

Entered on its own, consumption deprivation accounts for 0.383 of the variance. Adding the cluster effects, as in the fixed effects model in equation (ii), increases the level of explanation to 0.427 and entering the interactions between deprivation and welfare regime raises it to 0.462. The pattern of interaction reveals the declining impact of deprivation as one moves from the social democratic regime to the post-socialist cluster with the relevant

Table 10.3. Regression of Economic Stress by Consumption Deprivation and Welfare Regime

	(i)		(ii)		(iii)	
	B	SE	B	SE	B	SE
Constant (social democratic)	3.053		2.545		2.419	
Liberal			0.465	0.009	0.537	0.011
Corporatist			0.441	0.007	0.529	0.009
Southern European			1.003	0.007	1.108	0.008
Post-socialist			0.637	0.007	0.941	0.009
Consumption deprivation (CD)	3.558		3.326		4.583	0.030
Liberal* CD					−0.761	0.052
Corporatist* CD[a]					−0.961	0.041
Southern European* CD					−1.130	0.037
Post-socialist* CD					−1.831	0.034
R^2	0.383		0.427		0.462	
N	189,816		189,816		189,816	

[a] Excluding Luxembourg.

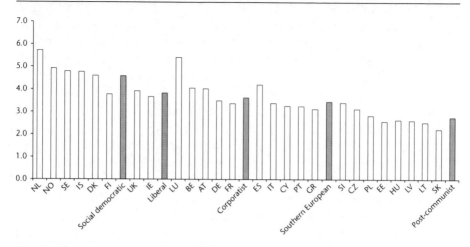

Figure 10.2. Deprivation coefficient by country and by welfare regime.

interaction coefficient decreasing gradually from −0.761 to −0.961 to −1.130 to −1.831. Differences between welfare regimes in their levels of economic stress are conditional on specifying level of consumption deprivation.

In order to illustrate the degree of systematic variation in the impact of consumption deprivation across country and welfare regime, in Figure 10.2 we set out the value of the deprivation effect for all 26 countries and 5 welfare regimes.[11] At the level of welfare regime the largest deprivation coefficient of 4.6 is associated with the social democratic cluster. Within this group the coefficient ranges from 5.7 for the Netherlands to 3.8 for Finland, which constitutes something of an outlier. Sweden, Norway, Iceland, and Denmark are located in the narrow range running from 4.9 to 4.6. For the liberal regime the average value falls to 3.8 with the impact being slightly higher in the UK than in Ireland. A further drop to 3.6 is observed for the corporatist group. The observations in this group are located in the range running from 4.0 to 3.4. The value of the deprivation coefficient for the southern European countries declines to 3.4. The highest value, by some distance, of 4.2 is observed for Spain. It is followed by Italy with a value of 3.4. However, these are the only cases in which there is an overlap with the earlier clusters. Finally, the lowest average value of 2.8 is observed for the post-socialist cluster. The highest values ranging of 3.4 to 3.1 are observed for Slovenia and the Czech Republic. The remaining observations range between 2.8 and 2.2.

Since our data are cross-sectional we cannot rule out the possibility that, despite the striking cross-national differences we have observed, some convergence has occurred over time. However, if so then it was necessarily from a

---

[11] In the latter case Luxembourg is once again excluded.

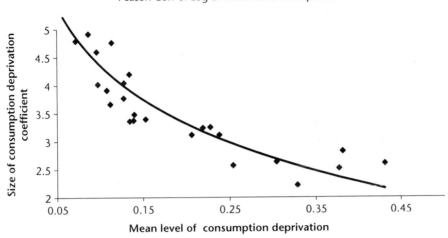

Peason Corr of Log of Mean Level of Deprivation=0.896

Figure 10.3. Magnitude of consumption deprivation by mean level of deprivation by country.

starting point involving very substantial heterogeneity and has some considerable distance to go before one could speak of relative uniformity of reference groups.

The pattern of variation relating to the impact of consumption deprivation on economic stress suggests that it is associated with corresponding cross-national variation in objective living economic circumstances. Taking our measure of consumption deprivation as a proxy for such circumstances, in Figure 10.3 we plot the relationship between national deprivation levels and the magnitude of the deprivation coefficient. A linear specification accounts for 0.663 of the variance. However, a significant improvement is achieved by specifying a natural log form for deprivation that accounts for 0.803 of the variance. The impact of consumption deprivation declines as the average level of deprivation in the society increases. However, this decline takes a proportionate rather than an absolute form.

It remains possible that the observed association is accounted for by a third factor correlated with both consumption deprivation and economic stress. The log specification for GDP is marginally less successful in accounting for variation in the impact of deprivation in producing an R^2 of 0.711 while the log of mean income produces an R^2 of 0.662. One further check relating to the importance of mean level of deprivation versus other closely correlated dimensions such as GDP and average income levels can be derived from varying the order of entry. In both cases entering GDP or income after consumption deprivation produces a negligible increase in the reduction of the variance explained. Reversing this order of entry produces an increase from 0.711 to

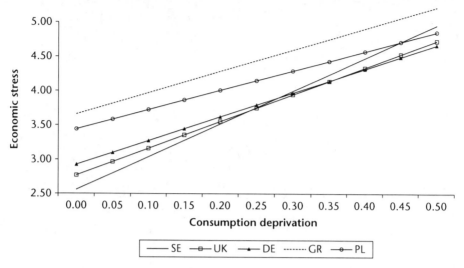

Figure 10.4. Converging economic stress levels with increasing consumption deprivation for a selected set of countries.

0.804 in the case of GDP and from 0.622 to 0.803 in the case of income. This makes it less likely that the observed relationship is spurious.

It is clear that the substantial differences in levels of economic stress observed between countries at low levels of deprivation narrow as mean deprivation increases. In Figure 10.4 we illustrate how cross-national differences vary as the level of deprivation changes. We have done this for 5 countries comprising 1 from each welfare regime. We have restricted our comparison to the range of deprivation running from 0 to 0.45 because beyond this point the numbers found in the more affluent countries become very small. The risk level associated with deprivation and the distribution of individuals across the deprivation continuum both contribute to differences in mean levels of economic stress between countries. While Greece displays higher levels of economic stress than Poland at every point on the deprivation continuum, the mean stress level is higher in the latter. This arises from the fact that the Polish households are more concentrated at the upper end of the deprivation continuum.

From Figure 10.4 we can see that at 0 level of deprivation Sweden enjoys an advantage in terms of economic stress over the 4 remaining countries. Factors other than current cross-national variation in levels of consumption deprivation clearly play a substantial role in producing such differences. Obvious candidates would include comparisons with earlier standards and expectations relating to future economic prospects both personal and national. In the case of Greece the gap at zero level of deprivation amounts to 1.10. This falls to 0.88 for Poland, to 0.36 for Germany, and to 0.21 for the

UK. When deprivation rises to 0.20 the corresponding figures are 0.13 and 0.10, 0.76, and 0.49. At a level of deprivation of 0.45, below which it must be kept in mind that 98% of Swedish households are located, Swedish stress levels are actually slightly higher than those prevailing in the UK and Germany and identical to those in Poland. The process of convergence applies, with varying strength, to each of the 2-way comparisons with the exception of Greece–Poland where, since the starting point for the former involves a higher level of deprivation than the latter, we observe a process of modest divergence.[12]

10.5 Conclusions

Analysis of EU-SILC data relating to material deprivation and subjective economic stress confirms 2 findings that have been key to the claims put forward by advocates of the Europeanization of reference groups thesis. The first concerns a close association at the national level between material deprivation and subjective economic stress. The second involves the confirmation that individuals at the bottom of the household income hierarchy in more affluent countries experience lower levels of deprivation and economic stress than those in the upper levels of the income distribution in the least prosperous countries. However, these descriptive findings are not sufficient to establish a causal relationship between deprivation and stress at the national level.

The observed association may be a consequence of a joint relationship with other variables and the underlying processes may be quite different to those influencing within country variation. The weaker version of the hypothesis of Europeanization of reference groups suggests that a given increase in consumption deprivation, benchmarked in overall EU terms, should have, or should be converging towards, a uniform impact on economic stress across countries. Analysis of the EU-SILC shows that this is clearly not the case. Context matters and systematic variation is observed across countries. The impact of consumption deprivation on economic stress declines progressively as the national level of deprivation increases but in a proportionate rather than an absolute fashion. If a process of convergence is under way it is one that must have started from a point of even more striking cross-country differentials and it is one that has a long way to go before it could be considered to involve a substantively important form of Europeanization of reference groups.

---

[12] Similar differences emerge when we focus on welfare regimes.

The consequence of such variation is that differences in economic stress between countries and regimes are greater for households at the lower rather than the higher end of the deprivation continuum.[13] The evidence thus points decisively in the direction of a rejection of the weaker version of the Europeanization of reference groups hypothesis. It is difficult therefore to see what formulation of the underlying processes could sustain the stronger version relating to a shift in normative reference points from the national to the transnational level.

The evidence we have presented provides further support for the conclusion of Marlier et al. (2007, pp. 154–5) that a EU-wide approach by failing to take into account differences in 'the significance of goods in social functioning' would miss people in richer countries who are experiencing genuine exclusion from their own society while counting substantial numbers in the poorer societies who are not experiencing such exclusion.

As O'Connor (2005, p. 347) notes, the European Social Model is not a reality in the sense in which we think of the national welfare state since the social dimension relates not to direct provision of services but is designed to alleviate the consequences of economic development. For O'Connor (2005, p. 346) the ESM 'reflects a tension between aspirations and values expressed at the EU level and subsidiarity' and for Jespen and Serrano Pascual (2006, p. 5), 'a political project under construction'. In this context, despite the danger of leaving oneself open to being castigated as a 'methodological nationalist',[14] it would seem extremely unwise to attribute an undue degree of policy significance to the relative modest impact of EU-wide reference groups that the previous analysis reveals.

Heidenreich and Wunder (2008) note that, while the causes of social inequality are increasingly shaped at the EU level, this arises through supranational regulation of economic, social, regional, and employment policies and the integration of the national markets rather than through European welfare state processes comparable to national arrangements or, as Diamond (2006, p. 181) expresses it, through negative rather than positive social integration. In a similar fashion Ferrera (2006, pp. 258–9) notes that European integration is based on a logic of economic opening that challenges the spatial demarcations and closure practices that sustain national solidarity.[15]

---

[13] This finding is consistent with the conclusion reached by Whelan and Maître (2007c) based on an analysis of the EQLS data and with Boehnke's (2008) and Whelan and Maître's (2005b) conclusions using the same dataset that adverse conditions are more likely to give rise to marginalization where deprivation is least common.

[14] See Yeates and Irving (2005, p. 43).

[15] For a detailed discussion of the influence of different spheres of EU policy on institutional and substantive social policy outcomes and their impact relative to that of international organizations such as the IMF and the World Bank, see Guillén and Palier (2004).

Heidenreich and Wunder (2008) conclude that, if norms of solidarity refer primarily to a national community, then the pursuit of the European integration process may not be possible without new transnational concepts of solidarity, equality, and justice.[16] If normative claims beyond that national level are to be legitimated, then, as Goedemé and Rottiers (2010) put it, reference group transformation would have to take place the level of public reference groups, in the sense of changed views of appropriate standards at a societal level rather than an individual level. However, it also requires that such claims are accepted as legitimate by the transnational authorities on whom they are made.

Ferrera (2006, p. 274), on the other hand, suggests that it may be necessary to recast the European integration project so that it can be promoted as the best means of safeguarding modernized national social protection systems.[17] The challenge is to achieve an appropriate combination of national and transnational forms of legitimacy. In this context, it is necessary to accept that there is no simple relationship between the Europeanization of inequality and the Europeanization of reference groups.[18]

---

[16] In this context Alber et al. (2007) point to a range of evidence that, in contrast with European elites, ordinary Europeans hesitate to extend notions of solidarity beyond the boundaries of the nation state.

[17] For a more general discussion of the relationship between Europeanization, the welfare state, and issues relating to national identity and self-image, see Cuperus (2006).

[18] Further exploration of these complex issues would be aided by collection of data that combine information on objective inequalities with information of processes of justice evaluation and attribution of responsibility for patterns of inequality.

11

Material Deprivation, the EU 2020 Poverty Target, and the Development of Social Indicators

11.1 Introduction

This final chapter focuses on the use of material deprivation indicators in monitoring progress and setting targets to reduce poverty in Europe. It aims to highlight some key implications of the approaches and analyses presented throughout the book for the understanding of poverty and social exclusion in Europe, and for the best ways to monitor progress in combating them. The ways in which non-monetary indicators have been used in this volume—to identify distinct dimensions of deprivation and explore how they relate to each other, to capture generalized deprivation and 'consistent' poverty, and to identify those vulnerable to poverty and exclusion—have important lessons for the broader monitoring of progress and assessment of strategies as the EU's Social Inclusion Process develops, as well as the way poverty and exclusion are monitored at national level. More specifically, they allow us to unpack the implications of the way the EU has chosen to frame its key headline target for poverty reduction over the next decade adopted in 2010, identifying a target population as anyone either below a specific country-specific relative income poverty threshold, above a material deprivation threshold, or in a 'jobless' household.[1] The chapter thus presents an in-depth analysis and critique of the way that target is formulated, and discusses alternative approaches to combining low income and material deprivation to identify those most in need from a poverty reduction perspective.

---

[1] We do not discuss here the broader implications of moving from poverty and exclusion indicators to targets, but on this see, for example, the discussions in Layte, Nolan, and Whelan (2000), Atkinson et al. (2002), Atkinson, Marlier, and Nolan (2004), Marlier et al. (2007), on the Irish experience with poverty targets; and Walker (2010) on recent French experience.

As we have stressed throughout this book, the value of a multidimensional perspective has to be established both conceptually and empirically and in terms of its capacity to guide and shape policy. It is not enough to have a general awareness that poverty is about more than income, irrespective of whether one's focus is on counting the poor or understanding the experience of poverty or social exclusion. We have consistently argued that measures of poverty and social exclusion must fulfil adequate standards in relation to reliability and construct validity. In particular, we have directed attention to the need to evaluate patterns of differentiation across socio-economic groups and geographical units in terms of a prior conceptual framework directed at facilitating identification and understanding of a minority in each society that experiences exclusion from customary living standards due to lack of re-sources. We have stressed throughout that it is not simply outcomes that matter but the location of such outcomes in the context of a broader pattern of generalized deprivation and the capacity of individual and societal inter-ventions to affect such outcomes in a purposive fashion. As will become transparent, it is not at all clear to us that the approach on which the latest EU poverty target is based can survive such a critical scrutiny.

11.2 The EU's 2020 Poverty Reduction Target: Identifying the Target Population

As described in Chapter 3, at the European Council held in June 2010 the EU member states' Heads of State and Government endorsed a new EU strategy for jobs and smart and sustainable and inclusive growth, known as the Europe 2020 strategy. The Council confirmed 5 headline targets to constitute shared objectives guiding the action of member states and the Union as regards promoting employment, improving the conditions for innovation, research and development, meeting the EU climate change and energy objectives, improving educational levels, and 'promoting social inclusion in particular through the reduction of poverty'. This fifth headline target focuses on lifting at least 20 million people out of risk of poverty and social exclusion. Progress vis-à-vis this target for the Union as a whole will be monitored on the basis of a measure of the target population that incorporates 3 indicators (at risk of poverty; material deprivation; jobless household), using data from EU-SILC, but member states are free to set national targets on the basis of the most appropriate indicators, taking into account their national circumstances and priorities. The population at risk of poverty and exclusion for the purpose of the EU target is defined on the basis of 3 indicators already included in the EU's social inclusion indicator set, but the precise way they are measured in the target differs from the corresponding indicator in the case of material deprivation and low work intensity. More fundamentally, this is the first time these indicators have been combined to identify an overall target group 'at risk of poverty and exclusion'.

Looking at each element in turn, the 'at-risk-of-poverty' indicator distinguishes persons living in households with less than 60% of the national median (equivalized) income—in other words, it is the most widely used of the relative income poverty measures in the Laeken set. The second element, material deprivation, is captured by the 9 items included in the common material deprivation indicator adopted in 2009 (described in detail in Chapter 3), but importantly employs a higher threshold: whereas the common indicator employs a threshold of 3 items to distinguish those to be counted as deprived, this element in the target counts only those reporting at least 4 items out of 9 as deprived. The element relating to household joblessness is based on the pre-existing common indicator of 'work intensity', based on the number of months spent at work over the previous 12-month period by household members aged 18 to 59 (excluding students); for the purpose of the target a threshold of 20% has been adopted to distinguish 'low' work intensity, in other words those in households where (relevant) members were in work for a fifth or less of the available time in aggregate in the year.

The way these 3 indicators are combined to identify the target group is then that meeting *any* of the 3 criteria—being either below the 60% income threshold, or above the material deprivation threshold of 4 items, or in a household with work intensity below the 20% threshold—suffices. In the EU as a whole, using EU-SILC data for 2008, this identifies 24.5% of the total population, or 120 million people, so the agreed target is to lift at least 20 million of these people out of 'the risk of poverty and exclusion'. In terms of the individual elements, 17% of the population are 'at risk of poverty' in terms of the 60% national median threshold, 8% are above that material deprivation threshold, and a similar figure is counted by this low work intensity measure, but since a significant proportion is captured by more than 1 of the 3 indicators (as we will examine in depth below) the aggregated EU figure is a good deal less than the sum of the 3 indicators.

This way of identifying the population 'at risk' has major implications, and it is worth noting that when the idea of a poverty reduction target was first mooted in concrete form by the President of the European Commission earlier in 2010, the focus was on those 'at risk of poverty' as captured simply by the relative income poverty measure. This has been the most prominent measure among the Social Inclusion Process indicators since they were adopted in Laeken, and indeed had been previously used at EU level as a basis for the most widely quoted headline numbers on poverty in the EU. With 80 million people in the Union 'at risk of poverty' on this basis in 2008, the initial proposal was for a target of reducing this by one-fifth, or 20 million persons.

However, various member states were not satisfied with that proposal, and the formulation eventually agreed is significantly different. Most obviously, the size of the target group is 50% greater but the reduction in numbers to be aimed for is still 20 million, so the target is much less ambitious in that sense— for a reduction of one-sixth rather than one-quarter in the number at risk of poverty and exclusion. In addition, though, expanding the indicators beyond the relative income poverty to include material deprivation and household joblessness has a significant impact on which persons and types of person are to be included in the target group.

11.3 The EU's 2020 Poverty Reduction Target: The Implications of the Multidimensional Approach Adopted

Combining these 3 distinct indicators represents a multidimensional approach to identifying the target population, and the move away from a reliance on a single indicator such as low income, for this purpose, is in our view a step forward. However, the expansion of the indicators employed beyond relative income poverty to include material deprivation and household joblessness, and the precise ways in which this has been done, have major implications, some of which we regard as problematic. We now explore these implications in some detail, and consider on that basis, as well as on conceptual grounds, the advantages and limitations of identifying the target population in this way. The elements to be considered in this context are the indicators chosen, the way each is framed, and the way they are then combined to produce what is in effect a single poverty (risk) measure. It is worth noting in that regard that no explicit rationale has been advanced at EU level for either the indicators employed or the way they have been adapted and combined. On specific details, the use of a threshold of 4 rather than 3 on the material deprivation element and the selection of a 20% threshold on the work intensity element seem to have been designed to produce a total that was acceptable from a political perspective. More broadly, arguments for combining a country-specific relative income measure with a deprivation standard that is common across countries, for combining these with an indicator of household joblessness, and for counting in the target group anyone who meets just 1 of the criteria rather than 2 or all 3 must be inferred rather than drawn from official EU documents or statements.

In assessing the value and adequacy of this EU target, in particular we pursue the argument we developed in Chapter 7 regarding our expectations based on a particular theoretical understanding of poverty and social exclusion, in relation to patterns of cross-national and socio-economic differentiation.

Table 11.1. Elements of EU Target by Country

	Below 60% of median income (%)	Below 60% of median or above deprivation threshold 4+ (%)	Below 60% of median or above deprivation threshold 4+ or below work intensity threshold 0.2 (%)
Austria	12.4	16.1	18.5
Belgium	14.7	17.1	20.6
Bulgaria	21.4	37.5	38.2
Cyprus	16.3	21.1	22.2
Czech Republic	9.1	13.1	15.2
Germany	15.3	17.5	20.3
Denmark	11.8	13.1	16.4
Estonia	19.5	21.2	22.0
Spain	19.6	20.8	23.1
Finland	13.6	15.4	17.4
Greece	20.1	25.0	28.1
Hungary	12.3	24.8	29.5
Ireland	15.5	18.9	23.7
Iceland	10.1	10.5	12.1
Italy	18.7	22.2	25.0
Lithuania	20.0	28.2	29.6
Luxembourg	13.4	13.6	15.4
Latvia	25.6	33.3	33.9
Netherlands	10.6	11.4	14.8
Norway	11.5	12.6	15.5
Poland	16.9	28.1	33.1
Portugal	18.5	23.8	25.9
Romania	23.4	42.2	44.3
Sweden	12.2	13.0	15.4
Slovenia	11.6	15.7	17.9
Slovakia	10.9	19.1	20.5
UK	19.0	21.3	28.3
European 27 countries (population weighted)	15.7	20.6	23.5
European Union 25 countries (population weighted)	17.0	21.7	25.2

We now proceed to investigate such variation with respect to the target population underlying the EU target and its component parts, using data from EU-SILC 2008 which has been taken as the point of reference in setting the target.[2] (France and Malta are excluded from the analysis because data were not included in the EU-SILC dataset to which researchers have been given access.) We start in Table 11.1 by presenting the percentage in each country 'at risk of poverty' in the sense of being below the 60% of median relative income threshold. This gives the familiar picture discussed in detail in Chapter 4

---

[2] While the target has been set in 2010 for 2020, the lag in availability of data means that the EU-SILC data for 2008 and 2018 are apparently to be used as the start and end-points in monitoring success.

above and elsewhere: the highest rates (of 20–5%) are seen in some of the new member states including Latvia, Romania, Bulgaria, and Estonia, the next highest levels are observed for the southern European countries, and at the other end of the spectrum the Scandinavia countries have relatively low rates of 10–12%. However, the overall extent of cross-national variation is relatively modest, and the association between the poverty indicator and the average national levels of prosperity (such as income per head) is rather weak.

The second column of Table 11.1 shows the impact on the size of the target population of adding the material deprivation element—which entails adding to column 1 those who are deprived on 4 or more items on the 9-item material deprivation scale but who are not below the 60% income threshold. We see that in the Scandinavian countries, Germany, Luxembourg, the Netherlands, and the UK this adds no more than 2% to the target population, whereas at the other extreme in Romania, Bulgaria, and Hungary the target population is approximately doubled. The combined rate for relative income poverty or material deprivation ranges from a low of 11% in the Netherlands to a high of 42% in Romania. The addition of the deprivation criterion thus produces much sharper variation across countries than seen with relative income poverty alone, but this mainly involves a much sharper contrast between a subset of new member states and the remaining countries rather than a generally more graduated pattern of differentiation. (As we shall see, this is exacerbated by the characteristics of some of the specific 9 items included in the deprivation index and by the use of a threshold of 4 rather than 3 on this index.)

In column 3 we add those living in household where the level of work intensity is less than 0.20 and who have not already been captured by the relative income and material deprivation criteria. In general, this produces only modest increases in the size of the target population, of less than 3 percentage points, with the largest increases being 7% for the UK and 5% for Hungary and Ireland. The overall variation in the size of the target population is now from 15% in the Netherlands to 44% in Romania—a smaller range than in column 2. Introducing the work intensity criterion thus produces less rather than more differentiation of countries in terms of the overall number at risk of poverty and social exclusion.

It is also helpful to look at the impact of adding each criterion on the profile of the target population in terms of social class—which is strongly associated with long-term command over resources, and which we have shown earlier to be systematically related to vulnerability to poverty and exclusion employing measures that satisfy the appropriate criteria relating to reliability and validity. Since country-by-country analysis produces a profusion of figures, we look at this in Table 11.2 for the EU as a whole which proves sufficient to illustrate the point we wish to make. Employing an aggregated version of the ESeC class schema, this shows first the social class profile of those below the 60% relative

Table 11.2. Social Class Composition of Elements of EU Poverty Target Group (Population Weighted)

	Below 60% of median income (%)	Above deprivation threshold 4+ but not below 60% of median income (%)	Work intensity < 0.20 but not above deprivation threshold 4+ or below 60% of median income (%)
HRP social class			
Higher salariat (ESeC class 1) reference category	4.6	3.8	13.5
Lower salariat (ESeC class 2)	5.8	7.0	13.9
Higher grade white & blue collar (ESeC classes 3 & 6)	12.6	13.2	20.7
Petit bourgeoisie (ESeC class 4)	15.3	5.4	6.1
Farmers (ESeC class 5)	10.5	6.8	2.4
Lower grade white & blue collar (ESeC classes 7 & 8)	25.2	33.7	24.0
Semi- & non-skilled workers (ESeC class 9)	26.1	30.1	19.4
Total	100	100	100

income threshold. We see that over 50% are drawn from the working class, while a further 26% are in the farming and petit bourgeois classes, with only 10% in the professional and managerial classes. Focusing then in column 2 on those added to the target population because they are above the deprivation threshold (though not below the income threshold), we see a somewhat different pattern. The percentage in the working class is substantially higher at 64%, while the farming/petit bourgeoisie now comprise only 12%. Thus the hierarchical dimension of class stratification is more important for this group, while property ownership is less common. This group thus appears, on this evidence, a valuable addition to the target population. By contrast, when we focus in column 3 on those added by the work intensity criterion we see a social class distribution that contrasts quite sharply with each of the other 2 groups. In this case 27% are drawn from the professional and managerial classes, almost 3 times higher than in either column 1 or 2, while only 43% are drawn from the working class. This group is substantially less differentiated in social class terms than either of the other 2: while adding the deprivation criterion sharpens the overall pattern of class differentiation in the target group, inclusion of the work intensity criterion dilutes it.

It is also helpful to look at other possible combinations of the three indicators underpinning the EU targets—that is, the size of the groups meeting 1 criterion but not the others, or each pair but not the other. We show the distribution across all 8 categories of the full cross-tabulation of the 3 indicators in Table 11.3. For convenience we now group countries into welfare regimes, using the regimes distinguished in our earlier analysis but now adding Bulgaria and Romania as comprising a 'residual regime'. We see that with

Table 11.3. Breakdown of All Persons by EU Target Indicators by Welfare Regime

	Social democratic (%)	Corporatist (%)	Liberal (%)	South European (%)	PS corporatist (%)	PS liberal (%)	Residual (%)
Not in target group	84.8	80.1	72.6	75.4	71.7	70.5	57.4
Below 60% of median income threshold only	8.5	8.2	12.2	13.6	7.2	12.8	7.4
Above 4+ deprivation threshold only	0.7	1.9	1.5	2.7	8.5	6.6	17.0
Below work intensity threshold 0.20 only	2.9	2.8	6.0	2.5	4.2	1.0	1.7
Below 60% of median income + above 4+ deprivation threshold	0.4	1.4	0.8	2.4	3.4	5.9	11.7
Below 60% of median income + below work intensity 0.20	2.0	3.5	4.3	2.2	1.7	1.4	0.8
Above 4+ deprivation + below work intensity 0.20	0.3	0.5	1.0	0.2	1.3	0.2	1.0
Below 60% of median income + above 4+ deprivation + below work intensity 0.20	0.5	1.6	1.4	0.9	2.0	1.6	2.9
Total	100.0	100.0	100.0	100.0	100.0	100.0	100.0

the exception of the post-socialist liberal and residual regimes, the 'income-poor and deprived but not low work intensity' group is below 4%; the 'income-poor and low work intensity but not deprived' group is that large only in the liberal regime; and the 'deprived and low work intensity but not income-poor' group is nowhere greater than 1%.

As well as looking at the profile of the population groups they identify, the value of including each of the EU target indicators (and of taking the overlaps between them into account) can also be assessed by looking at how much they help predict or explain outcomes that one would expect to be associated with poverty and exclusion. We illustrate this by focusing once again, as at various points in earlier chapters, on levels of self-assessed economic stress, using responses in EU-SILC to construct a variable distinguishing those in households reporting great difficulty or difficulty in making ends meet. In Table 11.4 we look at the incremental impact of the 3 EU poverty target and exclusion indicators on this economic stress measure via a stepwise regression conducted at the overall EU level. Focusing first on the net odds ratios, we see that the net coefficient for material deprivation is 13.2, much greater than the figures of only 2.5 for relative income poverty and 1.7 for low work

Table 11.4. Stepwise Logistic Regression of Economic Stress on Relative Income Poverty, Material Deprivation, and Low Work Intensity

	Odds ratio		
	Relative income poverty	Material deprivation	Low work intensity
Income poverty at 60% median	3.613	2.646	2.457
EU deprivation index 4 +		13.641	13.151
Work intensity ⟨ 0.20			1.651
Nagelkerke R^2	0.071	0.208	0.211
N	541,327		

intensity. Looking at the explanatory power of the equation in terms of the proportion of variance explained, entering the relative income poverty indicator as the first step produces a value of 0.071 for the Nagelkerke R^2, a widely used measure. The addition of the material deprivation indicator distinguishing between those with scores of 4+ and others increases this measure very substantially, to 0.208. However, adding the low work intensity indicator then produces only a modest further increase to 0.211. (Allowing for all possible 2- and 3-way interactions between relative income poverty, material deprivation, and low work intensity increases the Nagelkerke R^2 only marginally, and a similar pattern was observed when each of the welfare regimes was analysed separately.) Thus both the magnitude of the odds ratios and the levels of variance explanation indicate that the material deprivation indicator is by far the most important in accounting for levels of self-reported economic stress.

At this point, then, we can put forward two tentative but important conclusions about the way the EU target population is currently identified. The first is that one would have serious doubts about the value of including the household joblessness/low work intensity element, not merely in its present form but at all. At a conceptual level, the argument for including in the target population persons living in households that are jobless but are neither on low income (relative to their own country's median income) nor materially deprived (relative to a common EU-wide standard) is not transparent. Empirical analysis shows that the group added to the target population by the inclusion of the joblessness/low work intensity criterion has a relatively high proportion from the professional and managerial classes and a relatively low proportion from the working class, and that being in this group is not associated with high levels of economic stress. The second conclusion is that, by contrast, the addition of a material deprivation element substantially strengthens the target group identification procedure, with the social class profile of those it adds being heavily weighted towards the working class and with being above the deprivation threshold being particularly important in accounting for levels of self-reported economic stress. Furthermore, the addition of the deprivation criterion produces more variation across countries than seen with relative income poverty alone: more of the target group is then located in countries with relatively low average income, which many would regard as a move in the right direction.

11.4 The EU's 2020 Poverty Reduction Target: The Way Material Deprivation Is Measured

While the inclusion of the material deprivation element improves the identification of the target group, this is despite the fact that the specific material deprivation measure used has several weaknesses to which we have already referred. The first, as brought out in the detailed discussion in Chapter 5, relates to the inclusion in the 9-item index of several items relating to housing facilities that appear to us unsatisfactory, for reasons which we set out there and will not be repeated at this point. The second weakness arises from the fact that a threshold of 4 has been used for the purpose of identifying the target population, rather than the threshold of 3 or more used in the EU's own material deprivation indicator. Both these features contribute to limiting the variability in measured deprivation within and across countries. It is thus worth exploring whether a more suitable material deprivation indicator could do an even better job, for example the 7-item consumption deprivation variable that we have employed in much of our earlier analysis throughout this book (with a threshold of 3 or more). This can be done, for example, by adding that consumption deprivation measure to the equation predicting economic stress and including the 3 EU target indicators as explanatory variables, which we had shown in Table 11.4. This addition would increase the Nagelkerke R^2 for the estimated equation from 0.211 to 0.314, while the estimated net odds ratio for the consumption deprivation variable is close to 8 and that on the EU deprivation index falls to 2.5. So even when a measure of material deprivation is already included, adding this indicator adds considerably to the ability to predict economic stress.

This issue is explored further in Table 11.5 by distinguishing four groups and comparing their social class profiles:

1) Those neither in the EU target group nor above our consumption deprivation threshold;

2) Those identified as being in the target group by the 3 EU indicators but not above the threshold on our consumption deprivation measure;

3) Those above the threshold on our consumption deprivation index but not in the EU target group; and

Table 11.5. Social Class Composition for Groups Classified by 3 EU Target Indicators and Consumption Deprivation (Population Weighted)

HRP social class	Not in EU target group and consumption deprivation below 3+ (%)	In EU target group but consumption deprivation below 3+ (%)	Consumption deprivation 3+ but not in eu target group (%)	Both in EU target group and consumption deprivation 3+ (%)
Higher salariat (ESeC class 1) reference category	18.2	8.5	5.0	2.7
Lower salariat (ESeC class 2)	18.4	9.0	8.6	5.1
Higher grade white & blue collar (ESeC classes 3 & 6)	20.4	15.9	16.1	11.7
Petit bourgeoisie (ESeC class 4)	8.8	17.0	6.5	7.4
Farmers (ESeC class 5)	2.6	7.5	5.0	10.1
Lower grade white & blue collar (ESeC classes 7 & 8)	17.4	21.9	32.6	31.5
Semi- & non-skilled workers (ESeC class 9)	14.2	20.3	26.3	31.5
Total	100	100	100	100
% of EU-27 population	70.0	11.1	7.0	11.9
Dissimilarity index	38.3	24.5	12.3	0.0

4) Those both in the EU target group and above our consumption deprivation threshold.

The size of these groups is noteworthy: while 70% of the EU sample are neither in the EU target group nor above our consumption deprivation threshold, only 12% are both in the target group and above the consumption deprivation threshold. This leaves 2 substantial groups of particular interest: 11% of the sample who are in the EU target group but below our consumption deprivation threshold, and 7% who are above our consumption deprivation threshold but are not captured by any of the 3 EU target indicators. This means, strikingly, that about half those in the EU target population are not above our consumption deprivation threshold, while two-fifths of those above our deprivation threshold are not in the EU target population.

Looking at the social class composition of these groups, we see that there is, as one would expect, a very sharp contrast between those in groups (1) and (4)—that is, those not in the EU target group or above our deprivation threshold compared with those in the target group and above that threshold. Only 30% of the former are from the working class versus 63% of the latter, and almost 60% are from the white collar classes versus 21%. Those in group (2), in the EU target group but below our consumption deprivation threshold, have a rather mixed class composition with 41% working class, 35% white collar, and 18% farmers. In contrast group (3), who are above our consumption deprivation threshold but not in the EU target group, look very much more like group (4), who are both in the EU target group and above our deprivation threshold. These comparisons can be summarized using an index of dissimilarity, shown in the final row of Table 11.5, calculated for each of the remaining categories as the proportion of cases that would have to be moved to a different class in order to reproduce the composition of group (4). Not surprisingly this is very high for group (1), at 39. For those in the EU target group but below the consumption deprivation threshold the contrast is somewhat less sharp but the index of dissimilarity still reaches 25, whereas for those above the consumption deprivation threshold but not in the EU target group it is only 12.

This contrast between these groups is brought out by looking at how social class predicts which group a person falls into. Table 11.6 shows the results of a multinomial regression which takes group (1), those not in the EU target group or above our consumption deprivation threshold, as reference category. The estimated odds ratios then quantify the impact of social class on the relative risk of being in each of the 3 remaining groups relative to that benchmark category. A number of features may be noted. If we look in the first column at the likelihood of being both in the EU target group and above our consumption deprivation threshold rather than the reference category, we see a strong hierarchical class effect: as one moves from the higher professional managerial class to the semi- and non-skilled manual class, the relative risk rises gradually from 1 to 13 and farmers have a particularly high risk of 18. When we focus in the second column on those above our consumption deprivation threshold but not in the EU target group, we observe a weaker but still marked class hierarchy effect, with the odds ratio gradually rising to 6 for the non-skilled class. In the final column, we see a much weaker class hierarchy effect for those in the EU target group but below our consumption deprivation threshold, peaking at only 3, whereas both of the propertied classes (petit bourgeois and farmers) are particularly likely to be found in this group.

These conclusions relate to the sample as a whole, and additional analysis at welfare regime level reveals some interesting variation across regimes, consistent with the pattern of results we presented in Chapters 7 and 8. The key finding, which holds across countries and regimes, is that the consumption deprivation criterion leads to a greater emphasis on the hierarchical effects of social class while emphasizing the condition of being disadvantaged on at least 1 of the 3 indicators leads to a greater emphasis on the impact of being in the propertied classes.

Table 11.6. Multinomial Regression of EU Indicator & Consumption Typology on HRP Social Class (Reference Group Neither in EU Target Group Nor Above Threshold on Consumption Deprivation Index)

HRP social class	Odds ratio		
	In EU target group and above consumption deprivation threshold	Above consumption deprivation threshold but not in eu target group	In EU target group but below consumption deprivation threshold
Higher salariat (ESeC class 1) reference category	1,000	1.000	1.000
Lower salariat (ESeC class 2)	1.764	1.673	1.183
Higher grade white & blue collar (ESeC classes 3 & 6)	3.334	2.612	1.819
Petit bourgeoisie (ESeC class 4)	4.471	2.386	4.293
Farmers (ESeC class 5)	18.522	5.380	7.132
Lower grade white & blue collar (ESeC classes 7 & 8)	9.987	5.669	3.019
Semi- & non-skilled workers (ESeC class 9)	13.301	6.095	3.305
Nagelkerke R^2	0.116		
Reduction in log likelihood	4,672		
Degrees of freedom	18		
N	453,598		

Could a more pronounced pattern of differentiation in class terms be achieved simply by reducing the EU material deprivation threshold from 4+ to 3+? We approach this question in 2 stages. First we construct the 3-part EU indicator using a threshold of 3+ rather than 4+ for the EU material deprivation indicator. We then cross-classify this dichotomous indicator with the consumption deprivation 3+ dichotomy. In Table 11.7 we show the social class composition of the four categories of this typology. The numbers in the category fulfilling neither the EU nor consumption conditions are almost identical to those in Table 11.5 with 70% being found there. The number fulfilling both criteria rises from 11.9 to 17.7%. The number in the EU target group but not captured by the consumption measures hardly changes going from 11.1 to 11.3. Thus the total number captured by the EU measures

Table 11.7. Social Class Composition for Groups Classified by 3 EU Target Indicators with an EU Material Deprivation Threshold of 3+ and Consumption Deprivation (Population Weighted)

HRP social class	Not in EU target group and consumption deprivation below 3+ (%)	In EU target group but consumption deprivation below 3+ (%)	Consumption deprivation 3+ but not in EU target group (%)	Both in EU target group and consumption deprivation 3+ (%)
Higher salariat (ESeC class 1) reference category	18.2	8.4	3.7	3.5
Lower salariat (ESeC class 2)	18.4	9.0	6.6	6.4
Higher grade white & blue collar (ESeC classes 3 & 6)	20.5	15.8	15.0	13.2
Petit bourgeoisie (ESeC class 4)	8.8	16.8	5.2	7.2
Farmers (ESeC class 5)	2.6	7.6	6.8	8.3
Lower grade white & blue collar (ESeC classes 7 & 8)	17.4	22.1	34.1	31.7
Semi- & non-skilled workers (ESeC class 9)	14.2	20.3	28.5	29.6
Total	100	100	100	100
% of European 27 population	69.9	11.3	1.2	17.7
Dissimilarity index	35.6	19.7	3.6	0.0

goes from 23 to 29%. The number captured by the consumption deprivation measure falls from 7 to 1.2%. The revised EU measure now captures over 90% of those above the lower EU deprivation threshold. However, the number drawn in by the revised indicator additional to the consumption criterion remains unaffected at just over 11%.

Focusing on class composition, not surprisingly, the group captured by neither criterion is very similar to the comparable group identified employing the 4+ material deprivation cut-off point. The contrast with the group meeting both criteria is slightly less sharp because the class composition of the latter is marginally more heterogeneous. However, we should stress that the change is only marginal and that the results provide substantial support for incorporating the additional 5.4% drawn in by relaxing the material deprivation threshold from 4 to 3. The dissimilarity index goes from 38.3 to 35.6. The group who are incorporated by the EU target but not by the consumption measure continue to be relatively sharply differentiated from those fulfilling both criteria with a modest reduction in the dissimilarity index form 24.5 to 19.7. The 1.2% fulfilling the consumption condition but not the EU condition exhibits a class profile remarkably similar to the consistently deprived group with a dissimilarity index of 3.6.

Changing the EU material deprivation index threshold from 4+ to 3+ therefore has a number of consequences. It draws in a substantial group of individuals, who would also be captured by the consumption deprivation measure, whom the class composition analysis suggests should not have been excluded in the first place. It substantially reduces the number excluded even though they fulfil the consumption condition. However, our analysis suggests that such exclusion continues to constitute an error. It also continues to incorporate a substantial group who do not fulfil the consumption condition and who differ in important respects from those fulfilling both criteria in terms of their class composition. Thus altering the deprivation threshold does in our opinion produce a considerable improvement in the EU 3-part measure. However, problems persist with both the choice of deprivation items and the employment of the work intensity measure being contributory factors.

In order to explore this issue further, in Table 11.8 we cross-classify the dichotomous variables based on thresholds of 3+ for the EU deprivation measure and the 7-item consumption variables and then consider the class composition of each of the four clusters. With the EU deprivation threshold reduced to 3+, the number fulfilling both conditions reaches 17.1%. The number fulfilling neither condition reaches 80.9%. Those fulfilling only the

Table 11.8. Social Class Composition by EU Deprivation and Consumption Deprivation Indicator (Population Weighted)

HRP social class	Deprived on neither measure (%)	EU deprivation 3 + only (%)	Consumption deprivation 3+ only (%)	Deprived on both measures (%)
Higher salariat (ESeC class 1) reference category	16.9	3.0	2.8	3.6
Lower salariat (ESeC class 2)	17.1	4.9	5.6	6.5
Higher grade white & blue collar (ESeC classes 3 & 6)	19.9	9.5	12.8	13.4
Petit bourgeoisie (ESeC class 4)	9.9	5.1	7.1	7.0
Farmers (ESeC class 5)	3.2	28.7	8.9	8.1
Lower grade white & blue collar (ESeC classes 7 & 8)	18.0	27.4	31.6	31.9
Semi- & non-skilled workers (ESeC class 9)	15.0	21.4	31.0	29.4
Total	100	100	100	100
% of relevant population	80.9	0.3	1.7	17.1
Index of dissimilarity	33.3	20.6	2.5	0.0

EU deprivation condition but not the consumption criterion amount to only 0.3% of the population. The vast majority of those deprived on the EU material deprivation are also captured by the consumption deprivation measure. These are substantially more likely to be drawn from the farming group where 30% of them are located. The contrast in distributions produces a dissimilarity index of 20.6.

The number above the consumption deprivation threshold but not the EU material deprivation measure amounts to 1.7% of the total group. This group who are missed by the EU deprivation index but captured by the consumption measure display a social class make-up almost identical to the consistently deprived group, the value of the index of dissimilarity being 2.5%. The conclusion that emerges is that moving from a threshold of 4 to 3 in relation to the EU material deprivation index reveals a sharper pattern of differentiation only where it involves the additional inclusion of individuals who are above the consumption deprivation threshold. The limitations of the EU index relate not only to the choice of a particularly high threshold but also to its particular composition.

So the conclusion from this part of our investigation, focusing on the way material deprivation is measured in producing the EU target population, is that while the inclusion of this element is a valuable advance, the specifics of the deprivation measure by which this is done could be improved. This relates first to the (unexplained) use of a threshold of 4 or above on the material deprivation index: the indicator already included in the social inclusion process portfolio uses a threshold of 3 or more, and our analysis suggests this would also be preferable in identifying the target population. The second issue is the formulation of the index itself: our analysis also suggests that an index constructed somewhat differently, using some of the same but also some different indicators (also available in EU-SILC), would help improve the identification of the group appropriate for inclusion in the target population. This also highlights the importance of expanding and adapting the deprivation items available and employed for this purpose in the light of analysis of the broader set of items included in the special module accompanying EU-SILC in 2009, once those data and that analysis are available.

11.5 Adding a Consistent Poverty Approach

As well as the 3 component elements of relative income poverty, material deprivation, and household joblessness and the way these are framed, the other key feature of the way the EU poverty target population has been identified is that it includes all those who meet any 1 of the 3 criteria—the 3 criteria are linked by 'or' rather than 'and'. Rather than taking

Table 11.9. Percentage Meeting Poverty Target Criteria on All 3 Individual EU Indicators by Country

	% meeting all 3 EU target criteria
Austria	1.4
Belgium	2.0
Bulgaria	4.2
Cyprus	0.8
Czech Republic	1.4
Germany	1.6
Denmark	0.3
Estonia	1.1
Spain	0.5
Finland	0.7
Greece	1.1
Hungary	3.1
Ireland	1.5
Iceland	0.0
Italy	1.2
Lithuania	1.5
Luxembourg	0.2
Latvia	2.1
Netherlands	0.5
Norway	0.5
Poland	2.0
Portugal	1.1
Romania	2.4
Sweden	0.3
Slovenia	1.1
Slovakia	1.3
UK	1.4
European 27 countries (population weighted)	1.8
European Union 25 countries	1.4

the target group to be those meeting any of the 3 criteria, what would happen if we went to the other extreme and focused on those meeting all 3 criteria? Table 11.9 shows the percentage in each country below the 60% income threshold, above the material deprivation threshold, *and* in a low work intensity household, and the results suggest that this would not be a particularly fruitful approach. As we have stressed throughout this volume, where the associations between dimensions are relatively modest observed levels of multiple deprivation will be extremely low. The highest number fulfilling all 3 conditions is 4% (in Bulgaria), while in 23 of the 27 countries the figure is 2% or less and in 9 it is less than 1%. A multiple deprivation perspective involving all of these dimensions thus does not appear to have significant value in helping to understand cross-national patterns of risk of poverty and social exclusion. If one has decided to use these 3 criteria, then focusing on the union rather than the intersection between them seems more helpful.

However, we saw in the previous section that the arguments for including low work intensity/joblessness in identifying those 'at risk of poverty and social exclusion' are not strong. In addition, we have brought out in previous chapters the logic and advantages of combining the other 2 indicators—of relative income poverty and material deprivation—and focusing on the group where they overlap as 'consistently poor'. This is worth serious consideration either as an alternative way of identifying the overall target population in the EU target context or, perhaps more realistically now in the light of decisions already made at EU level, as a way of distinguishing a subset within that population which merits priority in framing anti-poverty policy.

We have explored in previous chapters the logic of combining relative income poverty and material deprivation to produce a 'consistent poverty' measure, and brought out the variety of ways in which this can be approached. As discussed in detail in Chapter 7 in particular, one can set the thresholds against which relative income poverty and deprivation are assessed at either national or EU levels before combining the 2 indicators. The indicators used in deriving the EU poverty target population frame relative income poverty against country-specific thresholds while using a common deprivation standard across the EU. Combining these 2 elements and focusing on the group who are both income-poor and deprived would provide a *mixed level consistent poverty* (MCP) indicator of the type we examined in Chapter 7. A variant of such a consistent poverty measure now worth exploring would combine being below the 60% relative income threshold with being above the 4+ threshold on the EU material deprivation index, the same 2 elements used in the construction of the EU poverty target but focusing on their intersection rather than union. This can usefully be compared first with combining relative income poverty with an alternative common deprivation measure/threshold, namely our 7-item consumption deprivation index with a threshold of 3+. It is also useful to include in the comparison what we termed in Chapter 7 a purely national consistent poverty measure (NCP), where the deprivation element is framed in country-specific relative terms by prevalence weighting and deriving the deprivation threshold so the number above it matches the number below the national 60% of median income poverty line.

In Table 11.10 we show the level of consistent poverty in each country for each of these 3 variants. The version incorporating the EU material deprivation measure with a 4+ threshold produces extremely low levels in the Scandinavian countries, the Netherlands, and Luxembourg. The only countries above 10% are Latvia, Bulgaria, and Romania, and the remaining rates are concentrated in the narrow range 1–6%. The variant incorporating

Table 11.10. Alternative Consistent Poverty Measures by Country, EU-SILC 2008

	% consistently poor		
	EU material deprivation 4+	Consumption deprivation 3+	National relative consumption deprivation
Austria	2.7	5.2	5.2
Belgium	3.3	5.9	6.5
Bulgaria	15.4	19.8	11.2
Cyprus	3.4	8.0	8.0
Czech Republic	2.7	4.9	3.4
Germany	3.0	6.3	7.1
Denmark	0.7	1.7	3.7
Estonia	3.1	7.0	8.8
Spain	1.4	4.6	9.4
Finland	1.7	4.0	5.6
Greece	6.3	10.4	9.4
Hungary	5.4	8.7	4.4
Ireland	2.1	4.9	5.3
Iceland	0.4	1.0	2.6
Italy	4.0	7.5	7.9
Lithuania	6.8	11.2	8.7
Luxembourg	0.5	2.6	6.5
Latvia	11.3	17.5	13.3
Netherlands	0.8	2.3	3.9
Norway	0.8	1.9	4.2
Poland	6.5	10.4	7.3
Portugal	4.3	9.3	7.2
Romania	14.3	18.2	9.8
Sweden	0.6	1.7	4.2
Slovenia	2.6	5.4	4.7
Slovakia	3.6	5.6	3.4
UK	2.3	5.7	8.9

our consumption deprivation index with a threshold of 3+ produces rather higher poverty rates, ranging from 1% in Iceland to 20% in Bulgaria and with a significantly greater degree of differentiation across countries. Finally, when the deprivation component of the consistent poverty measure is framed in national relative terms we observe more modest variation across countries, the range now being from 3% in Slovakia up to 13% in Latvia. Seventeen countries have rates in the narrow range between 3 and 7%: as one would expect when switching from a common deprivation standard across countries to country-specific reference points, consistent poverty levels are higher in the more prosperous countries and lower in the least prosperous than in column 2.

Table 11.11 brings out the patterns of variation across countries when they are grouped by welfare regime. With the consistent poverty measure incorporating the EU material deprivation index and a threshold of 4+, the social democratic regime has very low rates, the corporatist, liberal, and southern

Table 11.11. Consistent Poverty Indicators by Welfare Regime

	EU material deprivation 4+ (%)	Consumption deprivation +3 (%)	National relative with consumption deprivation (%)
Social democratic	0.9	2.4	4.3
Corporatist	2.6	5.4	6.5
Liberal	2.2	5.4	7.5
Southern European	3.6	7.3	8.5
Post-socialist corporatist	4.4	7.5	5.0
Post-socialist liberal	7.1	11.9	10.3
Residual	14.7	18.8	10.3

European regimes are also low at 2–3%, the post-socialist corporatist and liberal regimes are higher at over 4 and 7%, respectively, with the residual regime of Bulgaria and Romania much higher at 15%. The high threshold employed and the specific items in the index mean that deprivation rates are very low outside the post-socialist and residual regimes. Consistent poverty rates are higher when a common consumption deprivation index with a threshold of 3 is used instead, with a similar ranking of the regimes. Finally, substituting the country-specific relative deprivation measure leads to much less variation between the regimes, although it does still differentiate between them.

The consistent poverty measure based on the EU material deprivation indicator with a threshold of 4+ seems unsatisfactory if we wish to make comparisons across the full range of EU countries or welfare regimes. In Table 11.12 we restrict our attention to the 2 remaining measures in order to examine class differentiation within regimes.[3] Considering the dissimilarity indices, it is clear that there is little to choose between the other 2 measures in the extent to which they identify consistently poor groups with class profiles that are sharply differentiated from the reminder of the population. The measure incorporating nationally relative deprivation succeeds in capturing the kind of socio-economic differentiation that can be seen as its primary objective. However, the measure incorporating a common consumption deprivation index produces both this social class differentiation and substantial variation across countries and welfare regimes, thus combining the features that we have argued are desirable in a measure of poverty.

[3] As we showed in Chapter 7 an EU consistent poverty, employing EU level thresholds for both income and deprivation, will produce striking differentiation across countries and welfare regimes but is entirely unsuited to capturing socio-economic differentiation in relation to factors such as social class and economic status.

Table 11.12. Dissimilarity Rates for Social Class Composition for Consistently Poor versus Non-Poor by Types of Measure by Welfare Regime

	With common consumption deprivation, threshold 3+	With national relative consumption deprivation
Social democratic	24.9	28.3
Corporatist	38.7	34.6
Liberal	34.8	37.9
Southern European	30.6	30.7
Post-socialist corporatist	36.4	35.2
Post-socialist liberal	29.1	29.9
Residual	31.7	32.2

Table 11.13. Odds Ratios for Economic Stress for Consistently Poor versus Non-Poor by Types of Measure by Welfare Regime

	Common consumption deprivation 3+	National relative consumption deprivation
Social democratic	16.6	10.4
Corporatist	13.0	11.3
Liberal	8.9	6.8
Southern European	17.9	10.7
Post-socialist corporatist	12.1	16.7
Post-socialist liberal	13.4	11.2
Residual	6.2	14.2

Finally, as another form of validation we consider the ability of each of these consistent poverty measures to explain the variation in levels of reported economic stress within welfare regimes. Table 11.13 shows the estimated odds ratios for those who are consistently poor versus non-poor when the dependent variable is whether the household had difficulty making ends meet. With the nationally relative measure, the lowest odds ratio is observed for the liberal regime reflecting the relatively high levels of economic stress among the non-poor. At the other extreme the figure rises to 14 for the residual regime and to 17 for the post-socialist corporatist regime. For the remaining welfare regimes the odds ratios fall to between 7 and 11. The nationally relative consistent poverty measure thus succeeds well in capturing socio-economic differentiation and identifying differential risks within regimes. The mixed consistent poverty measure is more effective in capturing differential risk of economic stress in every regime but the residual cluster. Its relative advantage is greatest outside the post-socialist regimes. This is related to the fact that adopting a European (or absolute) threshold will tend to produce a higher threshold than the relative poverty measure in the more generous welfare regimes and a lower one in the less generous clusters.

11.6 Conclusions

Having set out the way the target population for the EU's central 2020 poverty reduction target is currently being identified via combining indicators of low income, deprivation, and household joblessness, this chapter arrived at a number of important conclusions with respect to that target. First, serious questions were raised about the inclusion of the household joblessness/low work intensity criterion. Secondly, it was argued that the choice of a deprivation threshold of 4+ had a somewhat arbitrary character. Thirdly, it was argued that the specificities of the way deprivation is measured for this purpose could be improved. Finally, the way low income and deprivation are combined in producing the target, and alternative approaches, were discussed. Without repeating the argumentation and analysis underpinning the first 2 of these conclusions, as we bring this book to a close it is worth drawing back from the details of the EU poverty reduction target to focus on that broader final issue, how deprivation and low income are best employed together to capture exposure to poverty and exclusion.

Non monetary indicators have been used throughout this volume to identify distinct dimensions of deprivation and explore how they relate to each other, to capture generalized deprivation and 'consistent' poverty, and to explore different ways of identifying those vulnerable to poverty and exclusion so that the causal processes at work can be traced and anti-poverty strategies designed in that light. Deprivation indicators add substantially to the ability to capture poverty and exclusion in an individual country; we have sought to bring out that this is equally true in a cross-country context, although even more complex issues and choices then have to be faced. The best approach to adopt will depend on precisely what one is most anxious to capture, but deprivation indicators are now coming to be recognized as an important element in the statistical and analytical armoury for monitoring and targeting poverty across the EU.

While offering a way to distinguish different dimensions of deprivation and explore the relationships between them, our central focus has been on the use of deprivation indicators to capture generalized deprivation and vulnerability to poverty and exclusion. We have brought out that the most straightforward approach to employing deprivation indicators for this purpose is to take a suitable common subset of key indicators across countries, look at deprivation levels in terms of these indicators, and see how those vary across countries and change over time. This is the nature of the material deprivation indicator added to the Laeken agreed set for monitoring the EU's social inclusion process in 2009. A common standard is then being applied across countries, and progress over time will be measured against a fixed standard rather than one that reflects the evolution of average levels of living. This provides very valuable information and has the great advantage of being (relatively) easily understood. It can, however, usefully be complemented by deprivation measures also based on a common set of indicators across countries, but with items weighted instead to take levels of deprivation in each country into account so as to produce what is in effect a relative deprivation indicator, in which the weights for each item also adjust over time as the extent of deprivation in the country change. In each case the choice of indicators to capture different dimensions of deprivation, and of the subset most suitable to capture generalized material deprivation, is key; expanding the available set of indicators in EU-SILC will make an important contribution to enhancing these indicators.

As well as acting as stand-alone measures, these deprivation indicators can also be usefully combined with measures of low income. Now there are 2 key choices: whether a country-specific or EU-wide standard is employed for each of the elements (i.e., low income and deprivation), and whether the combination focuses on the union or the intersection of these elements— that is, those who are either low income or deprived, or both low income and deprived. Country-specific relative income measures have been embedded in the measurement of poverty in European research and practice for many years, and in that sense represent a natural point of departure—although application of a common EU-wide income threshold also reveals important patterns. Combining such country-specific relative income measures with a common EU-wide deprivation standard then allows for two complementary approaches distinguishing:

1) Those who are both below a relative income threshold *or* above a common deprivation threshold; and

2) Those who are both below a relative income threshold *and* above a common deprivation threshold.

The EU target incorporates the first approach (and extends the indicators to include work intensity), and this does provide a way of addressing some of the limitations of relative income poverty measures on their own, in particular that some account is taken of what are now very wide gaps across member states in average living standards. However, our analysis in this chapter and throughout the book brings out that it would be valuable to also identify the subset of persons and households meeting both the income and material deprivation criteria, and that this could serve to identify a priority group as countries frame their individual contributions to meeting the overall EU target. In pursuing such an approach the choice of a deprivation threshold will need substantially more explicit justification than heretofore. It will also be necessary to pursue improved measurement of the material deprivation dimension in the context of an elaborated understanding of the underlying notion of deprivation. Finally, if it thought desirable to extend the range of dimensions, more systematic consideration will need to be given to the extent to which such dimensions can be seen to serve as manifest indicators of an underlying latent concept of generalized deprivation.

Part of the attraction of the formulation of the EU target in terms of low income or material deprivation or low work intensity may be that it suggests the possibility of focusing on a broader more vulnerable group rather than restricting attention to those currently experiencing multiple disadvantage. In turn this opens up possibilities of greater flexibility in relation to policy options and responsibilities. However, as we have sought to illustrate in Chapters 8 and 9 implementation of such perspectives requires the use of reasonably sophisticated statistical strategies. Our own exploration of these possibilities employing the 3 indicators making up the EU target suggest that issues relating to the use of the work intensity measure, the choice of the deprivation threshold, and the nature of the items making up the material deprivation are no less important in defining and measuring vulnerability than they proved to be in the analyses reported in the earlier parts of this chapter.

We have sought to bring out the value of combining country-specific relative income poverty measures with material deprivation indicators framed in more relative terms, using country-specific and time-varying weights for the individual deprivation items. We have also shown the potential of more sophisticated methodologies based on, for example, latent class analysis in identifying those vulnerable to poverty and exclusion, drawing on such relative income and deprivation indicators as well as people's own assessments of their situation. The aim of this book has been to highlight what can be learned from the application to empirical data of such approaches to capturing deprivation, hopefully serving to advance the development of this perspective in research and policy development in the future.

References

Alber, J., Fahey, T., and Saraceno, C. (2007). 'Introduction: EU Enlargement and Quality of Life: The Context and Purpose of the Book', in J. Alber, T. Fahey, and C. Saraceno (eds), *Handbook of Quality of Life in the Enlarged European Union*. Routledge, London.

Alkire, S., and Foster, J. (2007). 'Counting and Multidimensional Poverty Measurement'. Oxford Poverty and Human Development Initiative, Working Paper 7, Oxford Department of International Development, University of Oxford, Oxford.

Alkire, S., and Santos, M. E. (2010). 'Acute Multidimensional Poverty: A New Index for Developing Countries'. Human Development Research Paper 2010/11, UNDP, New York.

Atkinson, A. B. (1998). 'Social Exclusion, Poverty and Unemployment', in A. B. Atkinson and J. Hills (eds), *Exclusion, Employment and Opportunity*. Centre for Analysis of Social Exclusion Paper 4, London School of Economics, London.

Atkinson, A. B. (2003). 'Multidimensional Deprivation: Contrasting Social Welfare and Counting Approaches'. *Journal of Economic Inequality*, 1 (1): 51–65.

Atkinson, A. B., Cantillon, B., Marlier, E., and Nolan, B. (2002). *Social Indicators: The EU and Social Inclusion*. Oxford University Press, Oxford.

Atkinson, A. B., Marlier, E., Montaigne, F., and Reinstadler, A. (2010). 'Income Poverty and Income Inequality', in A. B. Atkinson and E. Marlier (eds), *Income and Living Conditions in Europe*. Publications Office of the European Union, Luxembourg.

Atkinson, A. B., Marlier, E., and Nolan, B. (2004). 'Indicators and Targets for Social Inclusion in the EU'. *Journal of Common Market Studies*, 42 (1): 47–75.

Atkinson, A. B., Rainwater, L., and Smeeding, T. (1995). *Income Distribution in OECD Countries*. OECD, Paris.

Atkinson, R., and Davoudi, S. (2000). 'The Concept of Social Exclusion in the European Union: Context, Development and Possibilities'. *Journal of Common Market Studies*, 38: 427–48.

Atkinson, W. (2007a). 'Beck, Individualization and the Death of Class'. *British Journal of Sociology*, 58: 349–66.

Atkinson, W. (2007b). 'Beyond False Oppositions: A Reply to Beck'. *British Journal of Sociology*, 58: 707–15.

Ayala, L., and Navarro, C. (2008). 'Multidimensional Indices of Housing Deprivation with Application to Spain'. *Applied Economics*, 40: 597–611.

Bane, M. J., and Ellwood, D. T. (1986). 'Slipping in and out of Poverty: The Dynamics of Poverty Spells'. *Journal of Human Resources*, 12: 1–23.

Bauman, K. (1998). 'Direct Measures of Poverty as Indicators of Economic Need: Evidence from the Survey of Income and Program Participation'. Population Division Technical Working Paper 30, US Census Bureau, Washington, DC.

Bauman, K. (1999). *Extended Measures of Well-Being: Meeting Basic Needs*. Current Population Reports P70–67, US Census Bureau, Washington, DC.

Bauman, K. (2003). *Extended Measures of Well-Being: Living Conditions in the United States*. Current Population Reports P70–87, US Census Bureau, Washington, DC.

Beck, U. (1992). 'Beyond Status and Class?', in U. Beck (ed.), *Risk Society: Towards a New Modernity*. Sage, London.

Beck, U. (2000a). *What is Globalisation?* Polity Press, Cambridge.

Beck, U. (2000b). 'The Cosmopolitan Perspective: Sociology of the Second Age of Modernity'. *British Journal of Sociology*, 5: 79–105.

Beck, U. (2002). 'The Cosmopolitan Society and its Enemies'. *British Journal of Sociology*, 51: 79–106.

Beck, U. (2007). 'Beyond Class and Nation: Reframing Social Inequalities in a Globalizing World'. *British Journal of Sociology*, 58: 679–705.

Beck, U., and Beck-Gernsheim, E. (1996). *Individualization and 'Precarious Freedoms': Perspectives and Controversies of a Subject-Orientated Sociology*. Blackwell, Cambridge.

Beckfield, J. (2006). 'European Integration and Income Inequality'. *American Sociological Review*, 71: 964–85.

Behr, A., Bellgardt, E., and Rendtel, U. (2005). 'Extent and Determinants of Panel Attrition in the European Community Household Panel'. *European Sociological Review*, 21 (5): 489–512.

Bellani, L., and D'Ambrosio, C. (2009). *Deprivation, Social Exclusion and Subjective Well-Being*, mimeo. Università di Milano-Bicocca, DIW Berlin and Econpubblica, Università Bocconi, Milan, 10 November.

Berghman, J. (1995). 'Social Exclusion in Europe: Policy Context and Analytical Framework', in G. Room (ed.), *Beyond the Threshold*. Policy Press, Bristol.

Berthoud, R., and Bryan, M. (2011). 'Income, Deprivation and Poverty: A Longitudinal Analysis', *Journal of Social Policy*, 40 (1): 135–56.

Berthoud, R., Bryan, M., and Bardasi, E. (2004). *The Dynamics of Deprivation: The Relationship between Income and Material Deprivation over Time*. Research Report 219. Department for Work and Pensions, London.

Blank, R. (2008). 'How to Improve Poverty Measurement in the United States'. *Journal of Policy Analysis and Management*, 27: 233–54.

Boarini, R., and Mira d'Ercole, M. (2006). 'Measures of Material Deprivation in OECD Countries'. OECD Social Employment and Migration Working Papers 37, OECD, Paris.

Boehnke, P. (2008). 'Feeling Left Out: Patterns of Social Integration in the Enlarged EU', in J. Alber, T. Fahey, and C. Saraceno (eds), *Handbook of Quality of Life in the Enlarged European Union*. Routledge, London.

Boehnke, P., and Delhey, J. (1999). *Poverty in a Multidimensional Perspective: Great Britain and Germany in Comparison*. FS III 99–413, Social Science Research Centre (WZB), Berlin.

References

Bossert, W., Chakravarty, S. R., and D'Ambrosio, C. (2009). *Multidimensional Poverty and National Deprivation*. ECINEQ WP 2009–129, available at http://www.ecineq.org/milano/WP/ECINEQ2009-129.pdf

Bossert, W., D'Ambrosio, C., and Peragine, V. (2007). 'Deprivation and Social Exclusion'. *Economica*, 74 (296): 777–803.

Bourguignon, F., and Chakravarty, S. (2003). 'The Measurement of Multidimensional Poverty'. *Journal of Economic Inequality*, 1 (1): 25–49.

Bovenberg, A. L. (2007). 'The Life-Course Perspective and Social Policies: An Overview of the Issues'. *Modernising Social Policy for the New Life Course*. OECD, Paris.

Bradshaw, J., and Finch, N. (2003). 'Overlaps in Dimensions of Poverty'. *Journal of Social Policy*, 32: 513–25.

Bradshaw, J., and Mayhew, E. (2011). *The Measurement of Extreme Poverty in the European Union*. European Commission, DG Employment, Social Affairs and Inclusion, Brussels.

Brandolini, A. (2007). 'Measurement of Income Distribution in Supranational Entities: The Case of the European Union', in J. Micklewright and S. Jenkins (eds), *Inequality and Poverty Re-examined*. Oxford University Press, Oxford.

Brasini, S., and Tassinar, G. (2004). 'Multiple Deprivation, Income and Poverty in Italy: An Analysis Based on European Community Household Panel'. *Statistica*, 64 (4): 673–96.

Bray, J. R. (2001). 'Hardship in Australia. An Analysis of Financial Stress Indicators in the 1998–99 Australian Bureau of Statistics Household Expenditure Survey'. Occasional Paper 4, Department of Family and Community Services, Canberra.

Breen, R., and Moisio, P. (2004). 'Overestimated Poverty Mobility: Poverty Dynamics Corrected for Measurement Error'. *Journal of Economic Inequality*, 2: 171–91.

Bukodi, E., and Robert, P. (2007). *Occupational Mobility in Europe*. European Foundation for the Improvement of Living and Working Conditions, Office for Official Publications of the European Communities, Luxembourg.

Burchardt, T., and Zaidi, A. (2003). 'Comparing Incomes When Needs Differ: Equivalisation for the Extra Costs of Disability in the UK'. CASE Paper 055, London School of Economics, London.

Burchardt, T., Le Grand, J., and Piachaud, D. (2002). 'Degrees of Exclusion: Developing a Dynamic, Multidimensional Measure', in J. Hills, J. Le Grand, and D. Piachaud (eds), *Understanding Social Exclusion*. Oxford University Press, Oxford.

Busch, C., and Peichl, A. (2010). *The Development of Multidimensional Poverty in Germany 1985–2007*. IZA DP 4922, Institute for the Study of Labor (IZA), Bonn.

Callan, T., and Keane, C. (2009). 'Non-Cash Benefits and the Distribution of Economic Welfare'. IZA Discussion Paper 3954, Institute for the Study of Labor (IZA), Berlin.

Callan, T., Nolan, B., and Whelan, C. T. (1993). 'Resources, Deprivation and the Measurement of Poverty'. *Journal of Social Policy*, 22: 141–72.

Callan, T., Smeeding, T., and Tsakloglou, P. (2008). 'Short-Run Distributional Effects of Public Education Transfers to Tertiary Education Students in Seven European Countries'. *Education Economics*, 16 (3): 275–88.

Cappellari, L., and Jenkins, S. P. (2007). 'Summarising Multiple Deprivation Indicators', in J. Micklewright and S. P. Jenkins (eds), *Poverty and Inequality: New Directions*. Oxford University Press, Oxford.

Carle, A. C., Bauman, K. J., and Short, S. (2009). 'Assessing the Measurement and Structure of Material Hardship in the United States'. *Social Indicators Research*, 92: 35–51.

Castells, M. (2000). *The Rise of Network Society*, 2nd edn. Blackwell, Oxford.

Chambers, R. (1989). 'Vulnerability: How the Poor Cope: Editorial'. *IDS Bulletin*, 20: 2.

Chan, T. W., and Goldthorpe, J. H. (2007). 'The Stratification of Cultural Consumption: Music in England'. *European Sociological Review*, 23 (1): 19.

Citro, C. F., and Michael, R. (1995). *Measuring Poverty: A New Approach*. National Academy Press, Washington, DC.

Clemenceau, A., and Museux, J.-M. (2007). 'EU-SILC (Community Statistics on Income and Living Conditions): General Presentation of the Instrument', in Eurostat, *Comparative EU Statistics on Income and Living Conditions: Issues and Challenges, Proceedings of the EU-SILC conference, Helsinki, November 6–8, 2006*. Office for Official Publications of the European Communities, Luxembourg.

Cuperus, R. (2006). 'The Vulnerability of the European Project', in A. Giddens, P. Diamond, and R. Liddle (eds), *Global Europe, Social Europe*. Polity Press, Cambridge.

D'Addio, A. C., and Whiteford, P. (2007). 'From Separated Life Phases to Interrelated Life Risks: A Life Course Approach to Social Policy'. *Modernising Social Policy for the New Life Course*. OECD, Paris.

De Haan., A. (1998). 'Social Exclusion: An Alternative Concept for the Study of Deprivation?' *IDS Bulletin*, 29 (1): 10–11.

Dekkers, G. (2003). 'Financial and Multidimensional Poverty in European Countries: Can the Former Be Used as a Proxy of the Latter?' IRISS Working paper series, No. 2003–13. CEPS/INSTEAD, Luxembourg.

Delhey, J., and Kohler, U. (2006). 'From Nationally Bounded to Pan-European Inequalities? On the Importance of Foreign Countries as Reference Groups'. *European Sociological Review*, 22: 125–40.

Delhey, J., and Kohler, U. (2007). 'Where We Stand in Europe: Citizens' Perceptions of European Country Rankings and Their Influence on Subjective Well Being', in J. Alber, T. Fahey, and C. Saraceno (eds), *Handbook of Quality of Life in the Enlarged European Union*. Routledge, London.

Department for Work and Pensions (DWP) (2003). *Measuring Child Poverty*. Department for Work and Pensions, London.

Desai, M. (1986). 'Drawing the Line: On Defining the Poverty Threshold', in P. Golding (ed.), *Excluding the Poor*. Child Poverty Action Group, London.

Dewilde, K. (2004). 'The Multidimensional Measurement of Poverty in Belgium and Britain: A Categorical Approach'. *Social Indicators Research*, 68: 331–69.

Diamond, P. (2006). 'Social Justice Reinterpreted: New Frontiers for the European Welfare State', in A. Giddens, P. Diamond, and R. Liddle (eds), *Global Europe, Social Europe*. Polity Press, Cambridge.

Dickes, P., Fusco, A., and Marlier, E. (2010). 'Structure of National Perceptions of Social Needs across EU Countries'. *Social Indicators Research*, 95: 143–67.

References

Dominy, N., and Kempson, E. (2006). *Understanding Older People's Experiences of Material Deprivation*. Research Report 363, UK Department of Work and Pensions, London.

Duncan, G., Gustaffson, B., Hauser, R., Schmaus, G., Messinger, H., Mufferls, R., Nolan, B., and Ray, J.-C. (1993). 'Poverty Dynamics in Eight Countries'. *Journal of Population Economics*, 6: 215–34.

Elder, G. (1999). *The Life Course and Aging: Some Reflections. Distinguished Scholar Lecture, Section on Aging and the Life Course*. American Sociological Association Distinguished Scholar Lecture, University of North Carolina at Chapel Hill.

Erikson, R. (1993). 'Descriptions in Inequality: The Swedish Approach to Welfare Research', in M. C. Nussbaum and A. Sen (eds), *The Quality of Life*. Clarendon Press, Oxford.

Erikson, R., and Aberg, R. (eds) (1987). *Welfare in Transition: Living Conditions in Sweden 1968–1981*. Clarendon Press, Oxford.

Esping-Andersen, G., Gallie, D., Hemerijck, A., and Myles, J. (2002). *Why We Need a New Welfare State*. Oxford University Press, Oxford.

Esping-Andersen, G., and Myles, J. (2009). 'Economic Inequality and the Welfare State', in W. Salverda, B. Nolan, and T. Smeeding (eds), *The Oxford Handbook of Economic Inequality*. Oxford University Press, Oxford.

European Economic Communities (1985). *On Specific Community Action to Combat Poverty* (Council Decision of 19 December 1984). 85/8/EEC, *Official Journal of the EEC*, 2/24.

European Commission (1997). *Modernising and Improving Social Protection in Europe: Communication from the Commission*. European Commission, Brussels.

European Commission (1999). *A Concerted Strategy for Modernising Social Protection, Communication from the Commission*. European Commission, Brussels.

European Commission (2004). *A New Partnership for Cohesion. Convergence Competitiveness Cooperation: Third Report on Economic and Social Cohesion*. Office for Official Publications of the European Communities, Luxembourg.

European Commission (2009). *Portfolio of Indicators for the Monitoring of the European Strategy for Social protection and Social Inclusion Update 2009*. DG Employment, Social Affairs and Equal Opportunities, Brussels.

European Commission (2010). *Lisbon Strategy Evaluation Document*. Commission Staff Working Document, SEC(2010) 114 final, European Commission, Brussels.

European Council (1974). *Council Resolution of 21 January 1974 Concerning a Social Action Programme*, OJ C13/1.

European Council (2010). *Council Conclusions 17 June 2010*, EUCO 13/10. European Council, Brussels.

Eurostat (1996). *The European Community Household Panel (ECHP): Survey Methodology and Implementation*. Office for Official Publications of the European Communities, Luxembourg.

Eurostat (2000). *European Social Statistics: Income Poverty and Social Exclusion (1st Report)*. Office for Official Publications of the European Communities, Luxembourg.

Eurostat (2001a). *PAN164/2001-12: Imputation of Income in the ECHP*. UDB Document, Eurostat, Luxembourg.

Eurostat (2001b). *PAN165/2001-12: Construction of Weights in the ECHP*. UDB Document, Eurostat, Luxembourg.

Eurostat (2001c). *PAN166/2001-12: ECHP UDB Description of Variables*. UDB Document, Eurostat, Luxembourg.

Eurostat (2001d). *PAN167/2001-12: ECHP UDB Construction of Variables*. UDB Document, Eurostat, Luxembourg.

Eurostat (2002). *PAN185/02: Sample Attrition between Waves 1 and 4 in the European Community Household Panel*. Working Party Document, Eurostat, Luxembourg.

Eurostat (2003). *European Social Statistics: Income Poverty and Social Exclusion (2nd Report)*. Office for Official Publications of the European Communities, Luxembourg.

Eurostat (2005). *The Continuity of Indicators during the Transition between ECHP and EU-SILC*. Office for Official Publications of the European Communities, Luxembourg.

Eurostat (2010). 2008 Comparative EU Intermediate Quality Report, Version 2. European Commission, Luxembourg.

Fahey, T. (2007). 'The Case for an EU-Wide Measure of Poverty.' *European Sociological Review*, 23: 35–47.

Fahey, T., Whelan, C. T., and Maître, B. (2005). *First European Quality of Life Survey: Income Inequalities and Deprivation*. Office for Official Publications of the European Communities, Luxembourg.

Fenger, H. J. M. (2007). 'Welfare Regimes in Central and Eastern Europe: Incorporating post-Communist Countries in a Welfare Regime Typology'. *CIISS*, August: 1–30.

Fergusson, D. M., Hong, D., Horwood, L. J., Jensen, J., and Travers, P. (2001). *Living Standards of Older New Zealanders: A Technical Account*. Ministry of Social Policy, Wellington.

Ferrera, M. (2006). 'Friends, Not Foes: European Integration and National Welfare States', in A. Giddens, P. Diamond, and R. Liddle (eds), *Global Europe, Social Europe*. Polity Press, Cambridge.

Ferrera, M. (2010). 'Mapping the Components of Social EU: A Critical Analysis of the Current Institutional Patchwork', in E. Marlier and D. Natali (eds) with Van R. Dam, *Europe 2020: Towards a More Social EU?* Work and Society, Vol. 69. Peter Lang, Brussels.

Ferrera, M., Matsaganis, M., and Sacchi, S. (2002). 'Open Co-ordination against Poverty: The New EU "Social Inclusion Process" ', *Journal of European Social Policy*, 12: 227–39.

Ferrera, M., and Rhodes, M. (2000). 'Recasting European Welfare States: An Introduction', *Western European Politics*, 23: 2–10.

Figari, F. (2009). 'Cross-national Differences in Determinants of Multiple Deprivation in Europe'. WP 2009/34, Institute for Social and Economic Research (ISER), University of Essex, Colchester.

Förster, M. F. (2005). 'The European Social Space Revisited: Comparing Poverty in the Enlarged European Union'. *Journal of Comparative Policy Analysis*, 7: 29–48.

Fouarge, D. (2002). 'Minimum Protection and Poverty in Europe: An Economic Analysis of the Subsidiary Principle in EU Social Policy'. Doctorate, Thela Amsterdam.

Fouarge, D., and Layte, R. (2005). 'Welfare Regimes and Poverty Dynamics and Recurrence of Poverty Spells in Europe'. *Journal of Social Policy*, 34 (3): 1–20.

Frazer, H., Marlier, E., and Nicaise, I. (2010). *A Social Inclusion Roadmap for Europe 2020*. Garant, Antwerp/Apeldoorn.

Frey, B. S., and Stutzer, A. (2002). *Happiness and Economics*. Princeton University Press, Princeton.

Frick, J. R., and Grabka, M. M. (2003). 'Imputed Rent and Income Inequality: A Decomposition Analysis for Great Britain, West Germany and the US'. *Review of Income and Wealth*, 49 (4): 513–37.

Frick, J. R., and Grabka, M. M. (2009). 'Accounting for Imputed and Capital Income Flows in Income Inequality Analyses'. IZA Discussion Papers 4634, Institute for the Study of Labor (IZA), Berlin.

Friedkin, N. E. (2004). 'Social Cohesion'. *Annual Review of Sociology*, 30: 409–25.

Fusco, A., Guio, A.-C., and Marlier, E. (2010). 'Characterising the Income Poor and the Materially Deprived in European Countries', in A. B. Atkinson and E. Marlier (eds), *Income and Living Conditions in Europe*. Publications Office of the European Union, Luxembourg.

Gallie, D., and Paugam, S. (2000). 'The Experience of Unemployment in Europe', in D. Gallie and S. Paugam (eds), *Welfare Regimes and the Experience of Unemployment in Europe*. Oxford University Press, Oxford.

Gallie, D., Paugam, S., and Jacobs, S. (2003). 'Unemployment, Poverty and Social Isolation'. *European Societies*, 5: 1–31.

Ger, G., and Belk, R. W. (1996). 'Cross-Cultural Differences in Materialism'. *Journal of Economic Psychology*, 17: 55–77.

Goedemé, T., and Rottiers, S. (2010). 'Poverty in the Enlarged European Union: A Discussion about Definitions and Reference Groups'. CSB Working Paper 10/06, Centre for Social Policy, University of Antwerp, Antwerp.

Goldthorpe, J. H. (2002). 'Occupational Sociology, Yes: Class Analysis, No. Comment on Grusky and Weeden's Agenda'. *Acta Sociologica*, 45: 211–25.

Goldthorpe, J. H. (2007a). 'Globalisation and Social Class', in *On Sociology*, 2nd edn, vol. 1: *Critique and Program*. Stanford University Press, Stanford, CA.

Goldthorpe, J. H. (2007b). 'Social Class and Differentiation of Employment Contracts', in *On Sociology*, 2nd edn, vol. 2: *Illustration and Retrospect*. Stanford University Press, Stanford, CA.

Goldthorpe, J. H. (2010). 'Analysing Inequality: A Critique of Two Recent Contributions from Economics and Epidemiology'. *European Sociological Review*, 26: 731–44.

Gordon, D. (2002). *Measuring Poverty and Social Exclusion in Britain: The Dynamics of Poverty*. Workshop, Central European University, Budapest, May 24–5.

Gordon, D., Adelman, L., Ashworth, K., Bradshaw, J., Levitas, R., Middleton, S., Pantazis, C., Patsios, D., Payne, S., Townsend, P., and Williams, J. (2000). *Poverty and Social Exclusion in Britain*. Joseph Rowntree Foundation, York.

Grusky, D. B., and Weeden, K. A. (2007). 'Measuring Poverty: The Case for a Sociological Approach', in N. Kakawani and J. Silber (eds), *The Many Dimensions of Poverty*. Palgrave Macmillan, Basingstoke.

Guillén, A. M., and Palier, B. (2004). 'Introduction: Does Europe Matter? Accession to EU and Social Policy Developments in Recent and New Member States'. *Journal of European Social Policy*, 14: 203–9.

Guio, A.-C. (2005). *Material Deprivation in the EU*. Statistics in Focus 21/2005, Eurostat, Office for Official Publications of the European Communities, Luxembourg.

Guio, A.-C. (2009). 'What Can Be Learned from Deprivation Indicators in Europe?' Eurostat Methdologies and Working Paper, Eurostat, Luxembourg.

Guio, A.-C., and Engsted-Maquet, I. (2007). 'Non-Income Dimension in EU-SILC: Material Deprivation and Poor Housing', in Eurostat, *Comparative EU Statistics on Income and Living Conditions: Issues and Challenges, Proceedings of the EU-SILC conference, Helsinki, November 6–8, 2006*. Office for Official Publications of the European Communities, Luxembourg.

Guio, A.-C., Fusco, A., and Marlier, M. (2009). 'A European Union Approach to Material Deprivation using EU-SILC and Eurobarometer Data'. IRISS Working Paper, CEPS/ INSTEAD, Luxembourg.

Guio, A.-C., and Marlier, E. (2004). 'The Laeken Indicators: Some Results and Methodological Issues in New EU Member States and Candidate Counties', *Emergo—Journal of the Transitional Economies and Societies*, 2: 21–48.

Guio, A.-C., and Museux, J-M.(2004). 'Comparisons between Income and Material Deprivation Approaches: What Can Be Learned from the New EU-SILC 2004 Data?'*International Association of Research on Income and Wealth 29th Annual Conference, Ottawa, Canada*.

Halleröd, B. (1995). 'The Truly Poor: Direct and Indirect Measurement of Consensual Poverty in Sweden'. *Journal of European Social Policy*, 5: 111–29.

Halleröd, B. (2006). 'Sour Grapes: Relative Deprivation, Adaptive Preferences and the Measurement of Poverty'. *Journal of Social Policy*, 35: 371–90.

Halleröd, B., and Larsson, D. (2008). 'Poverty, Welfare Problems and Social Exclusion'. *International Journal of Social Welfare*, 17: 15–25.

Halleröd, B., Larsson, D., Gordon, D., and Ritakallio, V. M. (2006). 'Relative Deprivation: A Comparative Analysis of Britain, Finland and Sweden'. *Journal of European Social Policy*, 16: 328–45.

Heath, A. (1981). *Social Mobility*. Fontana, London.

Heidenreich, M., and Wunder, C. (2008). 'Patterns of Regional Inequality in the Enlarged Europe'. *European Sociological Review*, 24: 19–36.

Iacovu, I. (2004). 'Patterns of Family Living', in I. Iacovu and R. Berthoud, *Social Europe: Living Standards and Welfare States*. Edward Elgar, Cheltenham.

Ianelli, I., and Soro-Bonmatí, A. (2003). 'Transition Pathways in Italy and Spain: Different Patterns, Similar Vulnerability?', in W. Müller and M. Gangl (eds), *Transitions from Education to Work*. Oxford University Press, Oxford.

Indicators Sub-Group of the Social Protection Committee (2005). *Indicators of Material Deprivation for Monitoring Poverty and Social Exclusion in the EU*,Document ISG/Doc/ Feb05/point 6 prepared by Eurostat for the 22/02/05 meeting of the Indicators Sub-Group, European Commission, Brussels.

Indicators Sub-Group of the Social Protection Committee (2006). *Proposal for a Portfolio of Overarching Indicators and for the Streamlined Social Inclusion, Pensions, and Health Portfolios*. European Commission, Brussels.

Inglehart, R., and Klingeman, H. (2000). 'Genes, Culture, Democracy and Happiness', in E. Diener and E. M. Suh (eds), *Subjective Well-Being across Areas*. MIT Press, Cambridge, MA.

International Monetary Fund (2003). *Vulnerability Indicators: A Factsheet*. Available at http://www.imf.org/external/np/exr/facts/vul.htm

Jarvis, S., and Jenkins, S. (1999). 'Low Income Dynamics in the 1990s in Britain'. *Fiscal Studies*, 18: 123–42.

Jasso, G. (1999). 'How Much Injustice Is There in the World? Two New Justice Indices'. *American Sociological Review*, 64: 133–68.

Jasso, G. (2000). 'Trends in the Experience of Injustice: Justice Indices about Earnings in Six Societies 1991–1996'. *Social Justice Research*, 13: 101–21.

Jensen, J., Spittal, M., Crichton, S., Sathiyandra, S., and Krishnan, V. (2002). 'Direct Measures of Living Standards: The New Zealand ELSI Scale'. Ministry of Social Development, Wellington.

Jespen, M., and Serrano Pascul, A. (2006). 'The Concept of ESM and Supra-national Legitimacy Building', in *Unwrapping the European Social Model*. Policy Press, Bristol.

Juhász, G. (2006). 'Exporting or Pulling Down? The European Social Model and Eastern Enlargement of the EU'. *European Journal of Social Quality*, 6: 82–107.

Kakwani, N., and Silber, J. (eds) (2008). *Many Dimensions of Poverty*. Palgrave Macmillan, London.

Kangas, O., and Ritakallio, V. M. (1998). 'Different Methods—Different Results? Approaches to Multidimensional Poverty', in H.-J. Andress (ed.), *Empirical Poverty Research in a Comparative Perspective*. Ashgate, Aldershot.

Kangas, O., and Ritakallio, V. M. (2007). 'Relative to What? Cross National Pictures of European Poverty Measured by Regional, National and European Standards'. *European Societies*, 9: 119–45.

Keyfitz, N. (1992). 'Development and the Elimination of Poverty'. *Economic Development and Cultural Change*, 30: 649–70.

Kogan, I., Gebel, M., and Noelke, C. (eds) (2008). *Europe Enlarged: A Handbook of Education, Labour and Welfare Regimes in Central and Eastern Europe*. Policy Press, Bristol.

Korpi, W., and Palme, J. (1998). 'The Paradox of Redistribution and Strategies of Equality'. *American Sociological Review*, 63: 661–87.

Kronauer, M. (1998). ' "Social Exclusion" and "Underclass"—New Concepts for the Analysis of Poverty', in H.-J. Andress (ed.), *Empirical Poverty Research in a Comparative Perspective*. Ashgate, Aldershot.

Layte, R., Nolan, B., and Whelan, C. T. (2000). 'Targeting Poverty: Lessons from Monitoring Ireland's National Anti-Poverty Strategy'. *Journal of Social Policy*, 29: 553–75.

Layte, R., Maître, B., Nolan, B., and Whelan, C. T. (2001). 'Explaining Deprivation in the European Union'. *Acta Sociologica*, 44: 105–22.

Layte, R., Nolan, B., and Whelan, C. T. (2001). 'Reassessing Income and Deprivation Approaches to the Measurement of Poverty in Ireland'. *Economic and Social Review*, 32 (3): 239–61.

Layte, R., and Whelan, C. T. (2002). 'Cumulative Disadvantage or Individualization: A Comparative Analysis of Poverty Risk and Incidence'. *European Societies*, 4 (2): 209–33.

Layte, R., and Whelan, C. T. (2003). 'Moving In and Out of Poverty: The Impact of Welfare Regimes on Poverty Dynamics in the EU'. *European Societies*, 5 (2): 75–99.

Leisering, L., and Liebfried, S. (1999). *Time and Poverty in Western Welfare States. United Germany in Perspective*. Cambridge University Press, Cambridge.

Levitas, R., Pantazis, F., Gordon, D., Lyod E., and Patsios, D. (2007). *The Multi-dimensional Analysis of Social Exclusion*. Social Exclusion Unit, London.

Lockwood, D. (1964). 'Social Integration and System Integration', in G. K. Zollschan and W. Hirsch (eds), *Explorations in Social Change*. Routledge, London.

Lollivier, S., and Verger, D. (1997). 'Pauvreté d'existence, monétaire ou subjective sont distinctes'. *Économie et statistique*, 308-309 310: 113–42.

McCutheon, A. (1987). *Latent Class Analysis*. Sage, London.

McGovern, P., Hill, S., Mills, C., and White, M. (2007). *Market, Class, and Employment*. Oxford University Press, Oxford.

Mack, J., and Lansley, S. (1985). *Poor Britain*. Allen and Unwin, London.

McKay, S. (2004). 'Poverty or Preference: What Do Consensual Deprivation Indicators Really Measure?' *Fiscal Studies*, 25: 201 24.

McKay, S., and Collard, S. (2003). 'Developing Deprivation Questions for the Family Resources Survey'. Working Paper 13, Corporate Document Series, Department for Work and Pensions, London.

Maître, B., Nolan, B., and Whelan, C. T. (2005). 'Welfare Regimes and House-hold Income Packaging in the European Union'. *Journal of European Social Policy*, 15: 157–71.

Marlier, E. (2003). 'Setting Targets: The Use of Indicators'. *EAPN Network News*, 98: 4–6.

Marlier, E., Atkinson, A. B., Cantillon, B., and Nolan, B. (2007). *The EU and Social Inclusion: Facing the Challenges*. Bristol: Policy Press.

Marlier, E., Cantillon, B., Nolan, B., Van den Bosch, K., and Van Rie, T. (2009). 'Developing and Learning from Measures of Social Inclusion in the European Union'. Paper presented at Joint OECD/University of Maryland International Conference on Measuring Poverty, Income Inequality, and Social Exclusion—Lessons from Europe, OECD, Paris.

Marlier, E., Cantillon, B., Nolan, B., Van den Bosch, K., and Van Rie, T. (2011). 'Developing and Learning from Measures of Social Inclusion in the European Union', in D. Besharov and K. Couch (eds), *Measuring Poverty, Income Inequality, and Social Exclusion: Lessons from Europe*. Oxford University Press, Oxford.

Mayer, K. U. (2003). 'The Sociology of the Life Course and Lifespan Psychology: Diverging and Converging Pathways?', in U. M. Staudinger and U. Linndenbauger (eds), *Understanding Human Development*. Kluwer Academic Press, Dordrecht.

Mayer, K. U. (2004). 'Whose Lives? How History, Societies and Institutions Define and Shape Life Courses'. *Research in Human Development*, 1: 161–87.

Mayer, K. U. (2006). 'Life Courses and Life Chances in a Comparative Perspective', in S. Svallfors (ed.), *Life Chances and Social Mobility in Comparative Perspective*. Stanford University Press, Stanford, CA.

Mayer, S. (1993). 'Living Conditions among the Poor in Four Rich Countries'. *Journal of Population Economics*, 6: 261–86.

Mayer, S., and Jencks, C. (1989). 'Poverty and the Distribution of Material Hardship'. *Journal of Human Resources*, 24: 88–114.

Mejer, L. (2000). *Social Exclusion in the EU Member States*. Statistics in Focus, Population and Social Conditions, Theme 3: 1/2000, Eurostat: Luxembourg.

Merton, R. M. (1957). 'Continuities in the Theory of Reference Groups and Social Structure', in *Social Theory and Social Structure*. Free Press, New York.

Merton, R. M., and Kitt, A. S. (1950). 'Contributions to the Theory Reference Group Behaviour', in R. K. Merton and P. F. Lazarfeld (eds), *Studies in the Scope and Method of 'the American Soldier'*. Free Press, Glencoe.

Moisio, P. (2004). 'A Latent Class Application to the Multidimensional Measurement of Poverty'. *Quantity and Quality*, 38: 703–17.

Muffels, R., and Dirven, H. (1998). 'Long-Term Income and Deprivation-Based Poverty among the Elderly', in H.-J. Andress (ed.), *Empirical Poverty Research in a Comparative Perspective*. Ashgate, Aldershot.

Muffels, R., and Fourage, D. (2002). 'Social Exclusion in European Welfare States: Which Road Should Policy Take?', in J. Berghman, A. Nagelkerke, K. Boos, R. Doeschot, and G. Vonk (eds), *Social Security in Transition*. Kluver International: The Hague.

Muffels, R., and Fouarge, D. (2004). 'The Role of European Welfare States in Explaining Resources Deprivation'. *Social Indicators Research*, 68: 299–330.

Muffels, R., and Luijkx, R. (2006). 'Globalisation and Male Job Mobility in European Welfare States', in H.-P. Blossfeld, M. Mills, and F. Bernardi (eds), *Globalisation, Uncertainty and Men's Careers: An International Comparison*. Edward Elgar, Cheltenham, UK/Northampton, MA.

Nolan, B., and Whelan, C. T. (1996). *Resources, Deprivation and Poverty*. Clarendon Press, Oxford.

Nolan, B., and Whelan, C. T. (2007). 'On the Multidimensionality of Poverty and Social Exclusion', in J. Micklewright and S. Jenkins (eds), *Poverty and Inequality: New Directions*. Oxford University Press, Oxford.

Nolan, B., and Whelan, C. T. (2010). 'Using Non-Monetary Deprivation Indicators to Analyse Poverty and Social Exclusion in Rich Counties: Lessons from Europe?'. *Journal of Policy Analysis and Management*, 29: 305–23.

O'Connor, J. S. (2005). 'Policy Coordination, Social Indicators and the Social Policy Agenda in the EU'. *Journal of European Social Policy*, 15 (4): 345–65.

OECD (1976). *Measuring Social Well-Being: A Progress Report on the Development of Social Indicators*. OECD, Paris.

OECD (2008). *Growing Unequal? Income Distribution and Poverty in OECD Countries*. OECD, Paris.

OECD (2009). *Society at a Glance 2009—OECD Social Indicators*. OECD, Paris.

O'Higgins, M., and Jenkins, S. P. (1990). 'Poverty in EC: Estimates for 1975, 1980 and 1985', in R. Teekens and B. M. S. van Praag (eds), *Analysing Poverty in the European Community*. Eurostat News Special Edition, Luxembourg.

Pantazis, C., Gordon, D., and Levitas, R. (eds) (2006). *Poverty and Social Exclusion in Britain: The Millennium Survey*. Policy Press, Bristol.

Paugam. S. (1996a). La consitution en paradigme, in *L'exclusion l'etat des savoirs*. Edition la découverte, Paris.

Paugam, S. (1996b). 'The Spiral of Precariousness: A Multidimensional Approach to the Process of Social Disqualification in France', in G. Room (ed.), *Beyond the Threshold*. Policy Press, Bristol.

Paugam, S., and Russell, H. (2000). 'The Effects of Employment Precarity and Unemployment on Social Isolation', in D. Gallie and S. Paugam (eds), *Welfare Regimes and Unemployment in Europe*. Oxford University Press, Oxford.

Peracchi, F. (2002). 'The European Community Household Panel: A Review'. *Empirical Economics*, 27: 63–90.

Perez-Mayo, J. (2005). 'Identifying Deprivation Profiles in Spain: A New Approach'. *Applied Economics*, 37: 943–955.

Perry, B. (2002). 'The Mismatch between Income Measures and Direct Outcome Measures of Poverty'. *Social Policy Journal of New Zealand*, 19: 101–27.

Pfoertner, T., Andress, H.-J., and Janssen, C. (2010). 'Income or Living Standard and Health in Germany: Different Ways of Measurement of Relative Poverty with Regard to Self Rated Health'. *International Journal of Public Health*, DOI: 10.1007/s00038-010-0154-3.

Piachaud, D. (1981). 'Peter Townsend and the Holy Grail'. *New Society*, 10 September: 419–21.

Piachaud, D. (1987). 'Problems in the Definition and Measurement of Poverty', *Journal of Social Policy*, 16: 147–64.

Pisati, M, Whelan, C. T., Lucchini, M., and Maître, B. (2010). 'Mapping Patterns of Multiple Deprivation Using Self Organising Maps: An Application to EU-SILC Data for Ireland'. *Social Science Research*, 39: 405–18.

Poggi, A. (2007). 'Does Persistence of Social Exclusion Exist in Spain?' *Journal of Economic Inequality*, 5: 53–72.

Politica Economica (2002). No. 1. Special Issue Devoted to 'Indicators for Social Inclusion: Making Common EU Objectives Work', 7–28.

Rendtel, U., Langeheine, R., and Bernstein, R. (1998). 'The Estimation of Poverty Dynamics Using Different Household Income Measures'. *Review of Income and Wealth*, 44: 81–98.

Ringen, S. (1987). *The Possibility of Politics*. Clarendon Press, Oxford.

Ringen, S. (1988). 'Direct and Indirect Measures of Poverty'. *Journal of Social Policy*, 17: 351–66.

Room, G. (1999). 'Social Exclusion, Solidarity and the Challenge of Globalisation'. *International Journal of Social Welfare*, 8: 166–74.

Rose, D., and Harrison, E. (2007). 'The European Socio-economic Classification: A New Social Class Schema for Comparative European Research'. *European Societies*, 9: 459–90.

Rose, D., and Harrison, E. (eds) (2009). *The European Socio-Economic Classification*. Routledge, London.

Rose, D., and Harrison, E. (2010). *Social Class in Europe: An Introduction to the European Socio-Economic Classification*. Routledge, London.

Saunders, P., and Adelman, L. (2006). 'Income Poverty, Deprivation and Exclusion: A Comparative Study of Australia and Britain'. *Journal of Social Policy*, 35: 559–84.

Saunders, P., Naidoo, Y., and Griffiths, M. (2007). *Towards New Indicators of Disadvantage: Deprivation and Social Exclusion in Australia*. Social Policy Research Centre, University of New South Wales, Sydney.

Scutella, R., Wilkins, R., and Kostenko, W. (2009). 'Poverty and Social Exclusion in Australia'. Melbourne Institute Working Paper 26/09.

Sen, A. (1983). 'Poor Relatively Speaking'. *Oxford Economic Papers*, 35 (2): 153–69.

Sen, A. (1993). 'Capability and Well-Being', in M. C. Nussbaum and A. Sen (eds), *The Quality of Life*. Clarendon Press, Oxford.

Sen, A. (2000). 'Social Exclusion: Concept, Application and Scrutiny'. Social Development Papers No. 1, Office of Environment and Social Development, Asian Development Bank, Manila.

Smeeding, T., O'Higgins, M., and Rainwater, L. (1988). *Poverty, Inequality and Income Distribution in Comparative Perspective*. Wheatsheaf Books, London.

Snijders, T., and Bosker, R. (1999). *Multilevel Analysis*. Sage, London.

Social Protection Committee (2001). *Report on Indicators in the Field of Poverty and Social Exclusion*. Brussels. Available at http://www.europa.eu.int/comm/employment_social/news/2002/jan/report_ind_en.pdf

Social Protection Committee (2003). *Common Outline for the 2003/2005 NAPs/inclusion*. Brussels. Available at http://europa.eu.int/comm/employment_social/social_inclusion/docs/commonoutline2003final_en.pdf

Social Protection Committee (2006). *Guidelines for Preparing National Reports on Strategies for Social Protection and Social Inclusion*. European Commission, Brussels.

Social Protection Committee and Economic Policy Committee (2006). *Joint Opinion of the Social Protection Committee and the Economic Policy Committee on the Commission Communication on 'Working Together, Working Better: A New Framework for the Open Coordination of Social Protection and Inclusion Policies in the European Union' (COM (2005)706 final)*. European Commission, Brussels.

Stiglitz, J. E., Sen, A., and Fitoussi, J.-P. (2009). *Report by the Commission on the Measurement of Economic Performance and Social Progress*. Available at http://www.stiglitz-sen-fitoussi.fr/documents/rapport_anglais.pdf

Taylor-Gooby, P. (2004). 'New Risks and Social Change', in P. Taylor-Gooby (ed.), *New Risks, New Welfare: The Transformation of the European Welfare State*. Oxford University Press, Oxford.

Taylor-Gooby, P. (2008). 'The New Welfare State Settlement in Europe'. *European Societies*, 10: 3–24.

Thorbecke, E. (2007). 'Multidimensional Poverty: Conceptual and Measurement Issues', in N. Kakawani and J. Silber (eds), *The Many Dimensions of Poverty*. Palgrave Macmillan, Basingstoke.

Till, M., and Giorgi, L. (2002). *Causes of Poverty and Social Exclusion: Main Report*. EUROHOME-IMPACT Project, Interdisciplinary Centre for Comparative Research in the Social Sciences, Vienna.

Tohara, L., and Malo, M. (2000). 'The Spanish Experiment: Pros and Cons of Flexibility', in G. Esping-Andersen and M. Regini (eds), *Why Regulate Labour Markets*. Oxford University Press, Oxford.

Tomaszewski, W. (2009). 'Multidimensional Poverty and Social Exclusion in Europe: A Cross-National Analysis'. PhD Thesis, European University Institute, Florence.

Tomlinson, M., Walker, A., and Williams, G. (2008). 'Measuring Poverty in Britain as a Multidimensional Concept, 1991 to 2003'. *Journal of Social Policy*, 37: 597–620.

Townsend, P. (1979). *Poverty in the United Kingdom*. Penguin, Harmondsworth.

Tsakloglou, P., and Panopoulou, G. (1998). 'Who Are the Poor in Greece? Analysing Poverty under Alternative Concepts of Resources and Equivalence Scales'. *Journal of European Social Policy*, 8: 229–52.

Tsakloglou, P., and Papadopoulos, F. (2001). 'Poverty, Material Deprivation and Multidimensional Disadvantage during Four Life Stages: Evidence from the ECHP', in C. Heady, M. Barnes, J. Millar, S. Middleton, P. Tsakloglou, and F. Papadopoulos (eds), *Poverty and Social Exclusion in Europe*. Edward Elgar, Cheltenham.

Tsakloglou, P., and Papadopoulos, F. (2002a). 'Aggregate Levels and Determining Factors of Social Exclusion in Twelve European Countries'. *Journal of European Social Policy*, 12: 211–24.

Tsakloglou, P., and Papadopoulos, F. (2002b). 'Identifying Population Groups at High Risk of Social Exclusion: Evidence from the ECHP', in R. Muffels and P. Tsakloglou (eds), *Social Exclusion in European Welfare States: An Empirical Study of Labour Market Integration and Social Exclusion in Panel Perspective*. Edward Elgar, Cheltenham

Tsui, K. (2002). 'Multidimensional Poverty Indices'. *Social Choice and Welfare*, 19, 69–93.

United Nations (2003). *Report on the World Social Situation: Social Vulnerability: Sources and Challenges*. United Nations Department of Economic and Social Affairs, New York.

Vandecasteele, L. (2010). 'Poverty Trajectories after Risky Life Events in Different European Welfare Regimes'. *European Societies*, 12 (2): 25.

Van den Bosch, K. (2001). *Identifying the Poor: Using Subjective and Consensual Measures*. Ashgate, Aldershot.

Vanhercke, B. (2010). 'Delivering the Goods for Europe 2020? The Social OMC's Adequacy and Impact Re-assessed', in E. Marlier and D. Natali (eds) with R. Van Dam, *Europe 2020: Towards a More Social EU?* Work & Society, vol. 69. Peter Lang, Brussels.

Vegeris, S., and McKay, S. (2002). *Low/Moderate-Income Families in Britain: Changes in Living Standards 1999–2000*. DWP Research Report 164. CDS, Leeds.

Vegeris, S., and Perry, J. (2003). *Families and Children Study 2001: Report on Living Standards and the Children*. DWP Research Report 190. Available at http://www.dwp.gov.uk/asd/asd5/rrep190.html

Verger, D. (2005). 'Bas revenus, consommation restreinte ou faible bien-être: les approches statistiques de la pauvreté à l'épreuve des comparaisons internationales'. *Économie et statistique*, 383–5: 7–45.

Verma, V. J., and Betti, G. (2010). 'Data Accuracy in EU-SILC', in A. B. Atkinson and E. Marlier (eds), *Income and Living Conditions in Europe*. Publications Office of the European Union, Luxembourg.

Walker, R. (2010). 'The Potential of Eurotargets: Reflecting on French Experience', in E. Marlier and D. Natali (eds) with R. Van Dam, *Europe 2020: Towards a More Social EU?* Work & Society, vol. 69. Peter Lang, Brussels.

Ward, T., Lelkes, O., Sutherland, H., and Tóth, I. G. (eds) (2009). *European Inequalities: Social Inclusion and Income Distribution in the European Union*. TÁRKI Social Research Institute, Budapest.

Watson, D. (2003). 'Sample Attrition between Waves 1 and 5 in the European Community Household Panel'. *European Sociological Review*, 19: 361–78.

Whelan, B. J., and Whelan, C. T. (1996). 'In What Sense is Poverty Multidimensional?', in G. Room (ed.), *Beyond the Threshold. The Measurement and Analysis of Social Exclusion*. Policy Press, Bristol.

Whelan, C. T., Layte, R., and Maître, B. (2002a). 'Multiple Deprivation and Persistent Poverty in the European Union'. *Journal of European Social Policy*, 12: 91–105.

Whelan, C. T., Layte, R., and Maître, B. (2002b). 'Persistent Deprivation in the European Union'. *Schmollers Jahburch: Journal of Applied Social Science Studies*, 122: 31–54.

Whelan, C. T., Layte, R., and Maître, B. (2003). 'Persistent Income Poverty and Deprivation in the European Union'. *Journal of Social Policy*, 3 (1): 1–18.

Whelan, C. T., Layte, R., and Maître, B. (2004). 'Understanding the Mismatch between Income Poverty and Deprivation: A Dynamic Comparative Analysis'. *European Sociological Review*, 20: 287–301.

Whelan, C. T., Layte, R., Maître, B., and Nolan, B. (2001). 'Income, Deprivation and Economic Strain: An Analysis of the European Community Household Panel'. *European Sociological Review*, 17: 357–72.

Whelan, C. T., and Maître, B. (2005a). 'Vulnerability and Multiple Deprivation Perspectives on Economic Exclusion in Europe: A Latent Class Analysis'. *European Societies*, 7: 423–50.

Whelan, C. T., and Maître, B. (2005b). 'Economic Vulnerability, Social Exclusion and Social Cohesion in an Enlarged European Community'. *International Journal of Comparative Sociology*, 46: 215–39.

Whelan, C. T., and Maître, B. (2006). 'Comparing Poverty and Deprivation Dynamics: Issues of Reliability and Validity'. *Journal of Economic Inequality*, 4: 303–23.

Whelan, C. T., and Maître, B. (2007a). 'Levels and Patterns of Multiple Deprivation in Ireland: after the Celtic Tiger'. *European Sociological Review*, 23: 139–56.

Whelan, C. T., and Maître B. (2007b). 'Measuring Material Poverty with EU SILC Data: Lessons from the Irish Survey'. *European Societies*, 9: 147–73.

Whelan, C. T., and Maître, B. (2007c). 'Income, Deprivation and Economic Stress in an Enlarged European Union'. *Social Indicators Research*, 83: 309–29.

Whelan, C. T., and Maître, B. (2008). 'Social Class and "Risk": A Comparative Analysis of the Dynamics of Economic Vulnerability'. *British Journal of Sociology*, 60: 637–59.

Whelan, C. T., and Maître, B. (2009a). 'The Europeanization of Reference Groups: A Reconsideration Using EU-SILC'. *European Societies*, 11: 283–309.

Whelan, C. T., and Maître, B. (2009b). 'Europeanization of Inequality and European Reference Groups'. *Journal of European Social Policy*, 19: 117–30.

Whelan, C. T., and Maître, B. (2010a). 'Welfare Regime and Social Class Variation in Poverty and Economic Vulnerability'. *Journal of European Social Policy*, 20: 316–32.

Whelan, C. T., and Maître, B. (2010b). 'Comparing Poverty Indicators in an Enlarged EU'. *European Sociological Review*, 26: 713–30.

Whelan, C. T., Nolan, B., and Maître, B. (2008). 'Measuring Material Deprivation in the Enlarged EU'. Working Paper 249, Economic and Social Research Institute, Dublin.

Wilkinson, R., and Pickett, K. (2009). *The Spirit Level*. Allen Lane, London.

Wolff, P., Montaigne, F., and Gonzalez, G. R. (2010). 'Investing in Statistics: EU-SILC', in A. B. Atkinson and E. Marlier (eds), *Income and Living Conditions in Europe*. Publications Office of the European Union, Luxembourg.

World Bank (2000). *World Development Report 2000–01: Attacking Poverty*, Oxford University Press, New York.

Yeates, N., and Irving, Z. (2005). 'Introduction: Transnational Social Policy'. *Social Policy and Society*, 4: 403–5.

Index